The Trials of Mrs. Lincoln

SAMUEL A. SCHREINER JR.

UNIVERSITY OF NEBRASKA PRESS
LINCOLN AND LONDON

First Nebraska paperback printing: 2005

Library of Congress Cataloging-in-Publication Data
Schreiner, Samuel Agnew.
The trials of Mrs. Lincoln / Samuel A. Schreiner.
p.   cm.
Includes index.
ISBN 0-8032-9325-9 (pbk.: alk. paper)
1. Lincoln, Mary Todd, 1818–1882.   2. Lincoln, Mary Todd, 1818–1882—
Mental health.   3. Lincoln, Mary Todd, 1818–1882—Trials, litigation, etc.
4. Insanity—United States—Case studies.   5. Presidents' spouses—United
States—Biography.   6. Lincoln, Abraham, 1809–1865—Family.   I. Title.
E457.25.L55S37   2005
973.7'092—dc22   2004025705

Grateful acknowledgment is made to the Illinois State Historical Library for permission to quote from its collection of the writings of the Lincoln family; the Louis A. Warren Lincoln Library and Museum for providing access to the "Mary Todd Lincoln Insanity File" collected and preserved by Robert Lincoln himself; Thomas F. Schwartz, Curator, Lincoln Collection of the Illinois State Library; Laurel G. Bowen, Curator of Manuscripts for the Illinois State Historical Library; and Mark E. Neely, Director of the Louis A. Warren Lincoln Library and Museum.

The author is also indebted to Mark E. Neely and R. Gerald McMurtry for their overview of the "Insanity File" contained in their book, *The Insanity File: The Case of Mary Todd Lincoln* (Southern Illinois University Press, 1986).

Letter from Leonard Swett to David Davis may be found in General Correspondence, David Davis and Family Papers, Illinois State Historical Library, Springfield.

This Bison Books edition follows the original in beginning chapter 1 on arabic page 13; no material has been omitted.

How sharper than a serpent's tooth
it is to have a thankless child!
        —WILLIAM SHAKESPEARE

To my wife, Doris Moon Schreiner,
who again has been a great help and inspiration
in the making of a book.

Contents

List of Illustrations

Preface

ALTHOUGH ITS ACTION took place more than a century ago and its characters were part of the most celebrated family in American history, this will be a story that really couldn't be told until very recently. True, the bare facts of Mary Todd Lincoln's so-called insanity trials were spread across the front pages of every newspaper in the country back in 1875 and 1876, but reporting then was sketchy and heavily editorialized. The court was not required to keep a verbatim transcript of such proceedings, and the Lincoln and Todd families were understandably reluctant to talk about an event so humiliating to them. It was, in fact, a general embarrassment so great that most people, including many Lincoln family biographers through the intervening years, have tried to gloss over it or ignore it entirely in an effort to preserve the aura surrounding the Great Emancipator.

The few researchers and writers who took a hard look at the case with a suspicion that the real truth never came out were stymied by a lack of fresh evidence on which to base new judgments. It was widely known that Robert Todd Lincoln, the only surviving Lincoln son, had burned some of the family papers, and it was naturally assumed that any records relating to the delicate matter of his mother's mental condition were among those consigned to the flames. Even Robert's grandson, the last person to bear the blood of Abraham and Mary Todd Lincoln in his veins, believed for most of his life that his grandfather had destroyed anything that would remind him of what had become a kind of secret shame in the family.

In 1975 when his older sister died and left the family summer homestead in Manchester, Vermont—Hildene—vacant, Robert Todd Lincoln Beckwith let an old friend, James T. Hickey, then curator of the Lincoln Collection at the Illinois State Historical Library, search through the place for anything that might be of value to scholars. Much to Beckwith's surprise, Hickey rummaged through old shirts and sweaters, golf and ski equipment, stored in a double-locked closet in what had been Robert Lincoln's bedroom and came up with a historian's treasure trove. There were some forty books containing copies of Robert Lincoln's correspondence blotted onto onion skin as they did in the days before typewriters and carbon paper—and there was one thing more. Tied up in pink ribbon was a separate bundle of papers marked in Robert's own hand "MTL Insanity File."

For a number of years, Beckwith, aging and ill himself, sat on this file, debating what to do with it. Finally, he decided to turn it over to two Lincoln scholars whom he knew and trusted— Mark E. Neely, Jr., director of the Louis A. Warren Lincoln Library and Museum in Fort Wayne, Indiana, and R. Gerald McMurtry, former editor of *Lincoln Lore* and former director of the Lincoln National Life Foundation. For the scholarly work they planned to write, Beckwith contributed a foreword in which he gave these reasons for releasing the material: "First, it is likely that this is the only definitive record of this tragic story. Second, as the last member of my family I must either take this course or destroy the file. Third, it would seem to me that although my grandfather destroyed much of his incoming correspondence and many personal family letters, this file he retained. I believe he did so knowing that in the future its contents should be made known. Fourth, and most important, I believe that because of this file history will treat my great-grandmother Mary Todd Lincoln more kindly in regard to this very disturbing period of her life and most of all recognize that my grandfather acted in the best possible way towards his mother."

Beckwith died on Christmas Eve, 1985, aged eighty-one, before he could know whether his pious hopes with regard to a final verdict would be realized. He would probably have been happy with the evenhanded treatment that Neely and McMurtry gave the material they were first privileged to examine in their book, *Insanity File.* Curiously, the authors felt compelled to confess that "we experienced fascination but not moral engagement" and, again, that "the whole event held for us the fascination of a puzzle but not the passionate engagement of a moral melodrama." But for this author who went to Fort Wayne to see the file for himself soon after he learned it was open to the public, the untold story of Mary Lincoln's trials is pure moral melodrama, a true parable of man's inhumanity to woman. Called back at last to deal with new evidence as presented by differing advocates, the jury now judging Mary Lincoln and her son, Robert—the American public—is likely to be out for a long, long time.

Over the next several years, scholars, psychiatrists, and lawyers will be weighing in with learned opinion as to what the new evidence proves. But regardless of what they conclude or of the final verdict, if one can be rendered, Mary Lincoln's trials make for a poignant and dramatic story. I have therefore chosen to use a storyteller's technique in presenting what I have learned from close study of the "MTL Insanity File," from going through the major newspapers and periodicals of the period, from reading more than fifty books dealing with the Lincoln family and the historical setting of the event. Any liberties that I have taken in such matters as turning indirect statements into direct quotations or carrying the narrative through imagined thought processes of the participants are based on a logical interpretation of the "facts" that I have found in this research. Indeed, believing that there is more verbal muscle in the actual words used by characters in the drama or by observers of the action as it was taking place than in anything I could invent, I have used raw material right from my sources wherever it can serve the story.

Fortunately for an author dealing with this subject, the telephone was only a novelty with which Alexander Graham Bell awed his friends by transmitting voice messages from one room to the next at the time of Mary Lincoln's trials. Thus, much of the thinking of the people involved was preserved in the form of letters or telegrams. A principal actor in this drama, attorney Leonard Swett, wrote long letters filled with fascinating detail. One of Swett's letters dealing with the opening scene of this book more than justifies, one hopes, an imaginative leap into Mrs. Lincoln's mind; it makes it almost imperative in telling her story. All sources agree, for example, that Mary Lincoln was very much concerned with how she looked, and my assumption that the state of her hair would cross her mind when she went to answer a surprise knock on the door is amply supported by these lines from Swett's letter: ". . . she . . . apologized for her undressed appearance, and . . . I said, 'Never mind your hair, Mrs. Lincoln . . .'"

Although, for the sake of readability, I have dispensed with footnotes, virtually every statement or assumption can be similarly tracked down to a single source or to a consensus among previous biographers. In many cases, readers will easily spot in the raw material the passage or passages that triggered reconstruction. For example, the legal thinking that went into the preparation of the case against Mrs. Lincoln and into the selection of jurors and attorneys is clearly indicated in the quoted letters from judges and lawyers. In one sentence of a letter to

Robert Lincoln, John Todd Stuart, Esq., Mary Lincoln's cousin and Mayor of Springfield, summed it up: "The presence of Messrs. Swett and Arnold (lawyers) was especially fortunate and the character of the jury not less so." Or when readers come upon Mary Lincoln's written charge that her son was playing "a game of robbery," they are likely to find the author's supposition that she bitterly attributed his actions to greed a realistic and plausible one.

If possible, letters, newspaper accounts and the like are quoted with the original spelling, punctuation and structure intact. Since much of the material was handwritten, some words were undecipherable. Deletions of such words or of irrelevant passages are indicated with dots; probable words invented in their place to carry the sense of a sentence are enclosed in brackets. Because letters were substitutes for what we would now communicate by phone, they were often written in great haste and very informally. Mary Lincoln, in particular, was a correspondent who transferred a mercurial temperament and a mind that raced so fast that thoughts tumbled over each other right onto the page. What now seem to us as irrationally misplaced commas, dashes, italics in her writing was also the style of the times and can be found to a lesser degree in the letters of her sister, Elizabeth Edwards, as well as of Mary's Harvard-educated son, and even of such an august personage as Supreme Court Justice David Davis. Significantly, Mary Lincoln's writing style was no different during her time of trials than during any other period of her life, including her carefree days as a twenty-two-year-old Springfield belle.

At the end of the narrative, major sources are cited and discussed. Even in the light of the "MTL Insanity File," mysteries do remain as they always do when human nature in its infinite variety is the subject of inquiry—and never was there a more human human being than Mary Todd Lincoln. At least, and at long last, the fresh evidence makes it possible to call for more justice in the case of this tortured woman, who was defined by a recent biographer as "the most misunderstood and slandered of President's wives." This, then, is by way of being a long overdue retrial.

—Samuel A. Schreiner, Jr.
Darien, Connecticut
December, 1986

CHAPTER I:

A Knock on the Door

T HE KNOCK ON the door of her room in Chicago's Grand Pacific Hotel on that Wednesday, May 19, 1875, startled Mary Todd Lincoln. Nobody ever came to see her but Robert, and he'd be at work unless she'd lost all track of time. She glanced at the clock: no, it couldn't be Robert, because it was only one o'clock, the middle of the day. Then she remembered that it was about the right time for the delivery boy from Allen & Mackey to bring the lace curtains she'd bought that morning. Certain it was only he, she didn't even bother to look in the mirror and tidy up her hair as she hastened across the room. Trustingly, she flung the door wide open and recoiled with surprise at what she saw.

The boy was indeed standing in the doorway with a package in his hands but behind him stood two men. One of the men was Samuel Turner, the hotel manager with whom she'd had frequent consultations in the last few weeks about the strange things going on around her. Since she hadn't sent for Turner this day, she had to guess that he was showing the other man the way to her room. That man was the surprise. Although he'd gone grey in the nearly ten years since last she'd seen him, she recognized Leonard Swett at once. People said that Swett resembled Mr. Lincoln, and she'd heard that he'd had the effrontery to pose as her martyred husband's body in a coffin for some sort of tableau. Beyond the fact that he was tall and lanky and wore chin whiskers, she couldn't see any likeness at all. Nobody would ever be like Mr. Lincoln.

Seeing her in the doorway, Swett took off his hat and bowed slightly. "Remember me, Mrs. Lincoln—Leonard Swett? May I—may we—come in?"

These last years Mary had grown suspicious of just about everybody out of the past except her son, Robert, and Judge Davis who'd handled Mr. Lincoln's estate and acted as poor Taddie's guardian. She never saw Mr. Lincoln's old circuit riding cronies like Lamon and Swett, and she seldom saw her own sisters and cousins from down in Springfield. It seemed that, once they couldn't use Mr. Lincoln, they no longer had any use for her. Her last contact with Swett, for instance, was back in '66 when she'd written him to ask for help in raising enough money to stay in her house. No help had come, but then nobody else had helped, either. Whatever the truth of that story about the coffin, Swett at least hadn't made a lucrative career out of lecturing and writing about Mr. Lincoln like Lamon and Arnold and Hay and Herndon. Herndon! Just the name of that miserable man coming to mind made her heart beat harder. As far as she knew, Swett wasn't Herndon's sort, and it was just possible that he'd heard she wasn't feeling well and was calling to be kind. She gave him a small smile and said, "Certainly, Mr. Swett—as soon as I'm finished with the boy."

Mary Lincoln wasn't about to permit a sometime caller like Swett to interfere with her dealings with real friends like this boy. Letting the men stand there in the hall, she said, "Come in, George, and put the package in the closet. You know where it goes." While the boy marched over to the closet and got a chair so that he could put the new package on top of a stack of un-opened packages already cramming the space, Mary went to the bureau for her pocketbook, rummaged through it and took out a suitably large tip. Nothing pleased her so much as the glow she could see in the faces of salesgirls and delivery boys when they realized that they were serving a grand lady. It was something Robert couldn't understand, wouldn't try to understand. Having been here before, George didn't have to look at the money she pressed into his palm to know that it was more than a day's wages, and he rewarded her with the kind of toothy grin that Willie or Tad might have worn in his place. "Oh, thank you, Mrs. Lincoln," he said, and then he ducked out between the two waiting men.

"Charming, isn't he?" Mary said. "Now, Mr. Swett . . . Mr. Turner . . . won't you come in and sit down?"

The two men edged into the room. Their large bodies seemed to shrink the already confining space around her, and Mary moved toward the window for air. Swett slid around her, barring her way, as if pacing her steps in a dance. "I'll stand if you don't mind, madam," he was saying. "I'm afraid I have bad news, and there isn't much time . . ."

Bad news? Was there any news left in the whole wide world that she, Mary Todd Lincoln, could still consider bad? Yes, something about Robert. Oh, God! Did this mean that the hunch she'd had a few months ago down there in Florida about his being hurt or sick had been right after all? She could sense the gravity of Swett's news from the way the man was behaving. His tone was tense, and he was twirling his hat nervously in his hands. This wasn't the Leonard Swett of her memory. He'd always been relaxed and jovial, too much so. She could readily believe the tales she'd heard of how he'd linger long in the barroom, swapping stories with the other men. Of course, they accused Mr. Lincoln of doing that, too, but there was a difference: Mr. Lincoln stayed sober. Swett's news might well be too much for her to take standing. She sank into the nearest chair.

"What's happened to Robert? Where's Robert?" she asked.

Even though she was jumping to the wrong conclusion, Swett felt encouraged by the opening she was handing him. It might ease a mission he'd dreaded so much that, as he wrote Judge Davis, "to have advanced on a battery instead would have been a real relief." From the way her voice rose toward the register of hysteria, he could hope that telling her Robert was all right would take some of the curse off the rest of what he had to say. He had to admit to surprise at how well Mrs. Lincoln looked considering all he'd heard about her in the last few days. True, the smile she'd given him was only a ghost of the smile that used to light up White House receptions, and none of that rosy color that once went along with the smile could be seen in her cheeks. But her most striking feature—her sky blue eyes—hadn't changed at all. They were quite clear and alert and registering an emotion most appropriate to her thought—fear.

"Robert's fine, Mrs. Lincoln," Swett said soothingly. "In fact, he's waiting for you right now—at the court."

"At the court . . .?"

Fear changed to puzzlement in those riveting eyes, and Swett hurried on, "Yes, you're expected in court at two o'clock . . ."

"Two o'clock? Today? Why, it's already past one. Whatever for? I've settled my debts long ago . . ."

"It's nothing like that, Mrs. Lincoln," Swett said. "It's a hearing on your . . . on your sanity . . ."

"My *sanity*! I've been ill, Mr. Swett, but I assure you that there is nothing wrong with my *mind*. Where's Robert? He ought to be *here*. He'd take care of this for me."

Swett was almost relieved to find anger crackling in her voice and eyes. He hadn't known quite what to expect, but he'd much rather deal with anger in females than with weeping or fainting or hysteria even though Mrs. Lincoln's anger had been well known and wisely feared when her husband was Chief Magistrate of the land. If there was anything unsettling about her anger now, it was that, like the fear before it, anger was a

perfectly appropriate and sane reaction under the circumstances, and she wasn't supposed to be sane. Perhaps her mental
derangement would reveal itself when he went on with the
worst of the news.

"Mrs. Lincoln, it's Robert who's bringing this action against
you," he said.

For a moment Swett thought that she hadn't heard him. Her
usually straight back gave way, and she sagged into the curve of
her chair. She rested her head on her hand and stared at the
floor. In the silence, he was aware of the hiss of her breathing,
of the ticking of the clock on the bureau, of the snort and jingle
of horses vying for roadway that drifted up through the open
window. He found himself holding his own breath, because he
simply couldn't imagine what she might do next. When she
lifted her eyes again, they were wet, hard and shiny as blue
marbles, but she wasn't crying. Her voice was a husky whisper:
"Robert? Robert, my son? I can't believe it . . ."

The words she was saying were meant for Swett, but the
words in her mind were winging themselves toward another
who walked always with her: *But you could, couldn't you, Mr.
Lincoln? You always said he was strange, not like the other boys. I
always laughed and said he was all Todd, but I guess it wasn't amusing.
Lord knows, we've had trouble with Todds. What should I do now, Mr.
Lincoln? Oh, I know, I know. See it through, whatever it is. Don't make
my mind up yet. Get to the bottom of it. Maybe it isn't as bad as it
sounds. But I'm Todd, too, Mr. Lincoln, as you well know. And Todds
are proud.*

"Don't blame Robert, Mrs. Lincoln," Swett was telling her.
"Judge Davis agrees with him and so does your Springfield
cousin Mayor Stuart and . . . and so do I. What we're doing is
for your own good . . ."

"For my own good?"

"Yes—to keep you from hurting yourself?"

Mary got out of her chair and drew herself up to what one
belittling reporter once called her "full five feet nothing." She

was angry again, and her chin that could dimple with a smile was squared like a bull dog's. "I'll ask you to leave now, Mr. Swett," she said. "Go back and tell Robert and the whole court if you like that I have no intention of hurting myself. If you really want to protect me, get Mr. Turner here to keep the men who are always following me out of his hotel. Every time I ask him for help, he says he can't see them. Perhaps he needs spectacles . . ."

"Mrs. Lincoln, you know I . . ." Turner started to say, but Swett silenced him with a gesture.

"If you don't believe us, your friends, or Robert, your son, Mrs. Lincoln, have a look at what the doctors think. Here are letters from half a dozen of them who say that you are in need of care," Swett said, taking a sheaf of papers from his inner coat pocket and thrusting them into her hand.

Mary just glanced quickly through the letters. "I haven't seen Danforth for a year except for a social call last week, and Dr. Isham's just been giving me something for the fever I've had since returning from Florida," she said. "I've never even laid eyes on the rest. What can *they* know about my mind? Oh, no, Mr. Swett. I know what you're all up to now. You want to get my bonds. Well, you won't get them. I have them here—right here in my clothes. And I'm *not* going to court. Please go. I've been shopping all morning, and I'm tired."

"Don't try my patience with argument, Mrs. Lincoln," Swett said. "It's ridiculous even to think that we have any interest in your money. It's only your health that we care about. Now, come along; it's almost two . . ."

"I'll *not* go with you, Mr. Swett. How can you dare to come here and tell me that I'm to be tried in an hour's time? I have no attorney to represent me. I'm not dressed to go out. If we have a republic such as my husband died to save, this is a travesty upon it. Now go. Mr. Turner, will you not show Mr. Swett out? He is annoying one of your guests, as you can plainly see."

This was fast developing into the kind of scene that Swett had fervently hoped to avoid. A glance over Mrs. Lincoln's head at that ticking clock showed him that it was already after two. Judge Wallace would be robed and fidgeting in chambers; the jury members would be cooling their heels in the courtroom, already yearning for a cigar. It never improved a case to keep a judge and jury waiting. It would totally ruin the case if he had to take the former first lady of the nation, the widow of a man who was fast becoming as close to a saint as Illinois or all of America had ever produced, into court kicking and screaming. One of the incidents that Robert Lincoln had related for the benefit of the doctors and lawyers—that is, Ben Ayer and himself—had to do with trying to take his mother off the hotel elevator by force when she'd tried to go down in dishabille to see Sam Turner. She'd screamed so loudly that everyone could hear her up and down the hall, "You're trying to murder me! Stop him, he's going to murder me!" Or so Robert told it, and it wasn't the sort of thing a son would tell about his mother if it weren't true. Swett tried to visualize some similar scene as he dragged her into court and his stomach went into a gripe.

Creating embarrassing scenes was, of course, one of the main reasons that Robert wanted to have his mother locked up. Others in the public eye whose reputations had been earned through association with Abraham Lincoln, like Judge Davis and himself, could not have agreed with Robert more. Unless it could be established that she was crazy, the public might begin to believe that Mrs. Lincoln's eccentricities were really caused, as she often charged, by neglect and misunderstanding on the part of her husband's political friends and even her own son. That could set off a dynamite charge of anger that would blow them all sky high. The Lincoln name still worked such potent political magic that anybody running for dog-catcher tried to establish some positive identification with it. So to be identified as an abuser of Lincoln's widow would have an equally negative result. If this day's action in court went according to plan, Mrs.

Lincoln would be neutralized; the public could only have pity for a crazy woman *and* the people around her. Knowing Judge Davis to be a cunning political animal, Swett had no doubt that the judge had these considerations in mind when he was advising Robert.

Swett felt that he had been accurate in telling Mrs. Lincoln that none of them, including Robert, had designs on her money. But his grounding was not as sure on that point as it was with respect to the question of embarrassment. Robert clearly wanted to get control of his mother's money, which would be logical *if* she were crazy, but Swett would have had to have been more of a mind-reader than he was to determine whether Robert's real intent was to preserve the money for himself as sole inheritor. From Swett's point of view that would be a natural, if not particularly admirable, human instinct, and no reason for not proceeding with the case. But Mrs. Lincoln, who not so unreasonably as a woman alone did have money on her mind, did not believe him and was turning dangerously stubborn.

He could have anticipated this sort of trouble. Crazy or not, Mrs. Lincoln had always been difficult in his view. He'd often wondered why Abe who could be tough as nails in court or in a cabinet meeting hadn't put his big foot down on her more often. Well, he, Leonard Swett, had no other recourse now. "Mrs. Lincoln, I don't relish this at all," he said. "I came here only to do what I see as my duty as your son's colleague at the bar and a good friend of your late husband. I could have let the two deputies waiting downstairs do the job. They have a warrant to produce you in court by force, if necessary. So right now, Mrs. Lincoln, you have two alternatives: either you go with me or with the deputies. What will it be?"

Mary Lincoln sank into her chair again. What little color there was in her face drained completely away. She didn't want to give him the satisfaction of fainting. Maybe if she got a breath of air she'd feel better. She got up and moved toward the window, but Swett adroitly headed her off again. "Please, Mrs. Lincoln, let us go," he pleaded. "We are already late . . ."

She was cornered, trapped. Her only escape was through her racing mind: *Oh, Mr. Lincoln, help me! Come get me. Take me to where you are—you and our darling boys. Save me from your friends. You know how I never trusted most of them, and you know now that I was right.* Swett raised his voice to get through to her, "Mrs. Lincoln, I'm warning you—I'll give you one more minute to make your choice. Mr. Turner, would you go down and bring the deputies up here?"

Watching Turner leave the room, Mary knew that there could be no more stalling. "Tell him it's all right—you don't need the deputies. I'll go with you," she said to Swett. "But I must change my clothes. I can't go like this; it would embarrass my son. Would you step out of the room, please, Mr. Swett? I'll only be a few minutes."

Was this a ruse, a cunning strategy of an unbalanced mind, Swett wondered. He could see no reason for a change in clothes since Mrs. Lincoln was already dressed for the street in the kind of black garments she'd worn in public throughout the whole of her widowhood. And how could she care about embarrassing Robert now? Of course, clothes were important to Mary Lincoln, so important that she'd let herself get into a lot of trouble over them when she was in the White House. Even now, according to Robert, most of those unopened boxes in her closet were full of colorful dress materials although she wore only black. Fussing about clothes was just another feminine quirk for which Swett had no tolerance, and he certainly couldn't afford to indulge it now.

"No, Mrs. Lincoln," he said. "There's *no* time; it's already half after two. Besides, I won't take the responsibility of leaving you alone in here . . ."

So that was it? That was the reason for his strange dance to keep between her and the window? Under other circumstances,

Mary Lincoln might have laughed, but she was finding anger the best emotion to hold her together now. "Mr. Swett, it's *your* reason that should be on trial if you think I would jump out that window," she said. "But I *will not* go looking like this. Can't you see what walking around the shops has done to my skirt? At least have the courtesy to turn your head while I put on a fresh overdress . . ."

"All right," Swett agreed with a sigh of exasperation. While Mrs. Lincoln stepped into a large closet to make her change, he dutifully stared out over the flat rooftops of a Chicago that seemed to be spreading in all directions at the rate of a mile or more a year. It was hard to see a trace now of the devastation caused by the great fire of '71. In a way, the fire had been a blessing, a cleansing. The new buildings were more substantial, more efficient, better looking. Swett was sure that a jury of twelve sane Chicago citizens would agree and find Mrs. Lincoln's reported feelings about the fire strange, to say the least. The rustling behind the screen stopped, and Mary Lincoln stepped out into the room, saying, "I am ready, Mr. Swett. Let us go . . ."

Swett had to concede that she did look better in a skirt that wasn't rusted at the edges by dust. She'd put on a black hat with a long veil of black crepe gracefully draped over her left shoulder. She really was a good dresser, and the mourning costume made from what was obviously the best of materials gave her a regal dignity. She did, in fact, look a lot like the pictures of Queen Victoria with whom she shared a sorrow, and Swett began to have some doubts as to how the jury might react to her presence. He hoped that Arnold wouldn't try to put her on the stand. If, looking like this, she remained as calm and made as much sense as she had in the last half hour or so despite the shock of his news, she might well convince them that the doctors were all wrong. Of course, Judge Wallace had promised to choose a jury from among a higher class of men who would understand and appreciate professional opinion, but he'd learned in thirty or more years as a trial lawyer that you could never be sure of a jury. Nobody understood this better than Abraham Lincoln, and Swett couldn't even remember all the cases he'd seen Lincoln pull out of the fire by talking a jury into his point of view. Good thing old Abe wasn't defending his wife. Swett couldn't know that the little woman in black, marching stoically and silently by his side down the corridor, into the elevator, through the lobby, was sharing his thoughts in her own fashion: *If you were only here to defend me, Mr. Lincoln, you'd make them understand. You were always so good at that—making people understand other people . . .*

Mr. Swett had two carriages waiting at the curb in front of the hotel. He handed Mary up into the first one, and she was rather pleased when Mr. Turner got in, too. She took this act of accompanying his most illustrious guest to the courthouse as a form of service, the kind of service she used to get from hotel managers in the Washington days. She was also pleased that she didn't have to ride with the deputies who got into the other carriage; they were coarse looking men who would make people in the streets wonder about her.

Turner's presence eased the strain between her and Swett a little, but not enough. A silence of embarrassment fell upon them. Ordinarily, nobody was better at making social small talk than Mary Lincoln, however trying the circumstances. An avid newspaper reader, she could usually find something in the day's events to stimulate discussion. But so little was going on in all of Chicago this day that the *Daily Tribune*'s leading story on the front page was an account of a meeting of the Council of the Reformed Episcopal Church. The adultery trial of America's most celebrated preacher, the Rev. Henry Ward Beecher of Brooklyn's Plymouth Church, that had been dominating the front pages nationwide all spring was in temporary recess. In any case, Mary always skipped over that trashy story. Whatever his personal morals, Mr. Beecher had been a staunch defender of Union and thus a great help to Mr. Lincoln. This was enough to make her hate to see his name dragged in the mud, as hers had so often been. Even the weather this Wednesday wasn't worthy of comment. Now that she was outside again, Mary realized that it wasn't just her emotions that had stiffled her up there in her room; it was warm for May, but the cloudy sky made of it a very dull day.

Perhaps because of his training as a professional host, Turner couldn't stand the silence for long. "I see by the morning's paper, Mr. Swett, that the White Stockings beat the Westerns," he said.

Swett couldn't have cared less, but he welcomed passing time with a subject that wouldn't stir up Mrs. Lincoln. "Oh, really?" he said. "So they're still in the championship race?"

"You betcha. That was their eighth win, and they're sure to win again today against the St. Louis Brown Stockings if it doesn't rain."

"Why so sure?"

"Well, Bradley, the St. Louis pitcher, has to go East to his mother's funeral, and . . ."

"Won't they put the game off for that?" Swett asked.

"No, sir. The White Stockings manager Wood has told St. Louis to play or forfeit," Turner said.

"Good for him," Swett said. "One thing I've learned in court is that you've got to be tough to win. Never give any quarter . . ."

Mary was happy to hear the men chatting about baseball, one of the few subjects in life that she knew nothing about. It meant that she didn't have to make an effort to be sociable, that she could retreat into her own thoughts. What she tried to think out as she rested her head against the side of the jolting carriage was what had possessed Robert to do this. Possibly it was just some sort of legal formality, but she doubted it from the way Mr. Swett was behaving. What had gone so wrong in the last few weeks? She was conscious of having had trouble with her nerves ever since she got back from Florida, but then she'd suffered off and on most of her life from what the doctors often called "a case of nerves" for lack of knowing what it really was. So had Mr. Lincoln. He used to call nerves the family disease, and he knew how to treat them. When she'd have one of those headaches that felt like hot wires being drawn through her brain or couldn't keep herself from crying, he'd see that everybody, including the boys, left her alone until by and by she'd be better. But most men weren't like Mr. Lincoln. Maybe her other sons Willie and Tad would have been; Robert certainly wasn't. When Willie died Mr. Lincoln went around saying that he was too good for this world, and he'd have said the same about Tad. Did people have to be cold stones like Robert and that wife of his were turning out to be in order to survive?

She could just feel the chill they gave off whenever she went into their house. It struck clear to the bone which was why she'd refused to go home with Robert when she came up from Florida. He'd said that his wife was out in Iowa with her parents, but Mary was sure that Mary Harlan Lincoln would have left that chill lingering behind her in the halls. The sad thing about it was that Robert and his Mary wouldn't have had each other today if it hadn't been for her. All the time Robert was up there at Harvard, Mary had kept a watchful eye on Senator Harlan's daughter, Mary, as she swirled through the balls and receptions of Washington. Fresh and lovely and schooled in the necessary graces from having grown up in the cosmopolitan atmosphere of the nation's capital, Mary Harlan was just perfect for Robert, and from her lofty position in the White House Mary Lincoln played puppeteer to pull the strings that would bring them together.

She'd seen to it that the Harlans were on all the right invitation lists, and she'd put in more than a good word for Senator Harlan when Mr. Lincoln needed a new Secretary of the Interior for his second term. Of course, Mr. Lincoln had known what was on her mind. He'd gone so far as to tell Senator Sumner who by then was more of a personal than a political friend to them both, "My wife is a great match-maker. She will make a match between Harlan's daughter and Bob; see if she don't." Actually, Mr. Lincoln had been as tickled as she with the prospect of Mary Harlan for a daughter-in-law. Much as they loved their sons, both Lincolns had always regretted not having a daughter. Mary had often thought in these last years when she'd had little to do but meditate on the past that knowing Robert was likely to bring such a prize girl into the family had been a contributing factor to the few brief days of happiness her husband had been granted before he was murdered.

Oh, those days, those precious days! They really began on April 6 of '65 when she took the Harlans, including Mary, with her to visit the President and the boys on the *River Queen* at City Point on the James River near Richmond. She'd been down there a little earlier in the month, and there'd been some unpleasantness over a general's wife making eyes at Mr. Lincoln. In a way she was buying insurance that this would be a better occasion by taking the Harlans, but she had another motive, too. Robert, serving as a captain on General Grant's staff there, was so good looking in his uniform and so commanding in his military ways that any girl would have to be blind or stupid to resist him. Seeing him like that almost—almost but not quite—made Mary regret that she'd used everything from tantrums to tears on both Robert and Mr. Lincoln to keep her son out of the service until he finished Harvard. She'd been hated for it by the public, but she'd been hated for just about everything she did. By the time they were all together there on the boat at City Point whatever she'd done didn't matter, because the war was nearly won.

The mood in the Presidential party was one of thankful celebration. The first day they made a trip into a still smouldering Richmond that had fallen to Union forces only the week before. The young people had fun sitting in Jeff Davis's chair, and all of them felt solemn pride in riding through the streets with a man so clearly beloved by the black people he'd freed. They would sink to their knees as he went by, crying, "Bless the Lord! Here comes our great Messiah!" Over and over again, Mr. Lincoln would stop the carriage and implore them, "Kneel only to God and give *Him* thanks for your freedom." To one of his generals who rode up and asked how he should be treating the enemy population, the President said, "Let 'em up easy, let 'em up easy." What made Mary happiest was to discover that Mr. Lincoln was letting himself up easy, too. He was still much too thin and hunched and ashen skinned, but he was laughing more often than he had for a long time and seemed eager for play. On the train ride back to City Point from Richmond, Tad spotted a turtle sunning itself beside the tracks. Mr. Lincoln ordered the train stopped, sent Tad scurrying after his new pet and spent the rest of the ride on the floor of the swaying car making the turtle execute a comic march back and forth between him and Tad. Watching them, Mary had real hope that peace would bring more times to the White House as full of innocent fun as those in Springfield when Mr. Lincoln behaved like the biggest of her boys.

Truth to tell, they didn't see a lot of Robert and Mary Harlan. By day, there were too many exciting sights, including a long range view of the men in blue closing in on what was left of General Lee's army, for an eager young captain to show off to an awed 18-year-old girl and, by night, there were too many inviting dark corners on the decks of the *River Queen* in which lovers could get lost to allow them to sit around in deck chairs with the old folks. But she and Mr. Lincoln got along so well with the senior Harlans that, back in Washington, Mr. Lincoln himself suggested inviting them for a ride on the day after Lee surrendered at Appomatox. That event had caused the little shoot of joy she'd seen breaking through Mr. Lincoln's gloomy crust to burst into full blossom. The talk on that ride was all of how bright the future looked, and she and Mrs. Harlan agreed that, from what they'd observed of the young people at City Point, they'd all be spending much of it together. The men were absorbed in discussion of what victory would require of them in the way of public policy. They were riding through the devastated countryside of northern Virginia, and Mr. Lincoln was expressing his hope to see it grow green again under the hands of rebels restored to their rights of citizenship and economically rehabilitated by a forgiving generosity on the part of the north.

There was a kind of electricity crackling through that carriage, and she wasn't alone in feeling it. Years later, James Harlan told her niece, Katherine Helm, that Mr. Lincoln that day had been "a different man. His whole appearance, poise, and bearing had marvelously changed. He was, in fact, transfigured. That indescribable sadness which had previously seemed to me an adamantine element of his very being had been suddenly changed for an equally indescribable expression of serene joy!—as if conscious that the great purpose of his life had been achieved." That was a Monday. The next night, appearing on the balcony at the White House, Mr. Lincoln shared the same happy spirit he'd shown in the carriage with what seemed like all of Washington gathered with bands and banners in the brightly lit streets. As he had at City Point, he called for the bands to play "Dixie." On Friday—*that* Friday—he shared his happiness with her alone on another ride. She could still remember telling him, "Dear husband, you almost startle me by your cheerfulness," and his responding, "Well I may feel so, Mary. I consider *this* the day that the war has come to a close. We must *both* be more cheerful in the future. Between the war and the loss of our darling Willie, we have both been very miserable." He was full of purely personal plans and promises. With what they could save in the next four years, they'd be comfortable enough to travel abroad and see California and then settle down to practice law again in Springfield or Chicago. Wasn't that about what she wanted? Oh, yes and yes . . .

"Mrs. Lincoln, we're here . . ."

The strange voice, the voice of Swett, startled her. She'd

closed her eyes against the confusion of the city streets and had followed the train of her thought until she'd been right back in that other carriage sitting beside Mr. Lincoln and hearing *his* light tenor voice. She wished she could hear it again in answer to her own inner voice that kept telling him what was happening, asking him what to do. Never had she had more need of the kind of fortitude his calm and reasoned reaction to everything could supply than right now. She was totally bewildered by this new experience that the unexpected arrival of Mr. Swett at her door had thrust upon her. Swett was waiting for her, standing outside the carriage and holding out his hand to help her down. There was nothing to do but put her hand in his and follow.

On the threshold of a menacing building that seemed about to swallow her, Mary Lincoln hesitated. Still unable to come to grips with how completely alone she was in these alien surroundings, she asked again, "Where's Robert? Wasn't he supposed to meet me here?"

"Oh, I'm sure he's here, Mrs. Lincoln—inside there, in the courtroom. You'll see him in a minute," Swett reassured her. "Now, come along. Remember: we're doing this for your own good."

Dressed always in black from the time of her husband's assassination, Mary Todd Lincoln was a sad but regal figure when she appeared for her trial in 1875. Courtesy of The Lincoln Museum, Fort Wayne IN (Ref. #97).

A rising young Chicago lawyer, Robert Todd Lincoln was the cool fashion plate his mother had groomed him to be until he broke down and wept on the witness stand. Courtesy of The Lincoln Museum, Fort Wayne IN (Ref. #112).

(*Opposite*) Not present at the trial but a powerful behind-the-scenes adviser to Robert Lincoln was Supreme Court Justice David Davis, executor of Abraham Lincoln's estate. Courtesy of The Lincoln Museum, Fort Wayne IN (Ref. #4044).

(*Above*) Attorney Leonard Swett, who rode the Illinois circuit with Lincoln and was said to resemble the martyred president physically, masterminded Mary Lincoln's prosecution. Courtesy of The Lincoln Museum, Fort Wayne IN (Ref. #1360).

First cousin to Mrs. Lincoln, first
law partner to Mr. Lincoln, mayor of
Springfield, Illinois, John Todd Stuart
urged his nephew Robert Lincoln to try
his mother. Courtesy of The Lincoln
Museum, Fort Wayne IN (Ref. #3231).

CHAPTER II:

"Good Men and Lawful"

The DOCKET OF the Cook County Court, sitting in Chicago's courts and jail building at West Hubbard and North Dearborn streets on that May Wednesday in 1875 was as dull as the weather outside. As he had the day before, Judge Marion R. M. Wallace was hearing some of the 170 unhappy people who were laying claim to bits and pieces of the Walker estate. The unusually large number of claimants, together with an attorney for each, had filled the courtroom to overflowing and had justified a paragraph in the day's morning papers, but the reporters on the court beat knew that they'd have to find something more interesting to get any space on Thursday. The prospects didn't look promising until the noon recess when Judge Wallace unexpectedly informed the Walker claimants that they'd have to come back on Friday since he had to preside over a pressing jury case that afternoon.

Knowing that jury trials tend to be juicier than hearings before a judge, the reporters looked into Judge Wallace's courtroom after lunch and got their first intimation that an interesting story might be in the making. The men who were gradually drifting in to take seats down front or in the two rows of chairs on the room's west end that were reserved for the jury were not the sort normally to be found idling in court in the middle of a busy business day. The overall effect of these weighty men in their long swallow tailed coats and black cravats was such that one reporter quipped, "Looks like a first class funeral coming up." Another said, "Or a fancy operation. Ever see so many doctors? Look, there's one taking a seat with the jury—Dr. Blake. Remember him?" The rest of the reporters who'd been around a while did remember the face, for Dr. S.C. Blake had been Chicago's city physician ten years before.

More impressive to the reporters with their experience in court were the attorneys they spotted shuffling through papers or putting their heads together for a chat. One in particular fascinated them just by being there. There'd been a time when Isaac N. Arnold's almost delicately lean figure was very familiar around the courts; because of his fast way of moving and talking, his incisive questions, he'd been called the "gadfly." But he'd been down in Washington as a Congressman during the war years, and he'd spent most of his time since in combining a personal acquaintance with Abraham Lincoln with a surprisingly strong literary skill to write and lecture about the slain president. He still looked prosperous and, with his grey beard and mustache and full curling hair, distinguished. Rare, too, in a court of this order was an appearance by B.F. Ayer of the prestigious firm of Ayer & Kales and even rarer the sight of both partners in a fairly new Chicago firm, Lincoln & Isham. Because they so seldom saw them here or in the streets, the reporters took a good look at these last two whose fortunes were said to be thriving as the legal representatives in Chicago of big eastern insurance companies and financial institutions.

This wasn't at all surprising considering that the Lincoln half of the firm was Robert Todd Lincoln, President Lincoln's only living son. Although he was just thirty-two, he had powerful friends for a lawyer. For starters, the man he himself called a "second father"—Judge Davis—sat on the Supreme Court in Washington. What eastern contacts Robert hadn't made for himself when he was being polished up at Harvard while everybody else his age was fighting would have come naturally to him through his father's associates like Seward, Weed, Welles, Sumner, Cameron—and, of course, President Grant, the great friend of the New York financiers. Young Lincoln had been on Grant's staff and had kept in touch with his former commander. Even though Robert Lincoln wasn't yet in politics himself, it was well known to the press that he was a stalwart of stalwarts, so strong a Grant supporter that he wanted to see the general given a third term next year. The never-ending scandals like that thing about the "whiskey ring," which was making almost as good copy these days at the Rev. Beecher's supposed stroll along the primrose path, didn't seem to bother Robert Lincoln. He certainly didn't take after "Honest Abe, the Rail Splitter"; didn't even look like him as the reporters first setting eyes on Robert could plainly see. A head shorter than his father, he was round cheeked with a little walrus mustache and slicked down hair and a kind of surly expression. Tell the truth, he did resemble "The Prince of Rails" which is what the papers had called him when his father's first campaign coincided with an American visit by the Prince of Wales. He dressed like a prince in that silk trimmed double-breasted frock coat and silver filigreed four-in-hand tie, and they said he lived like one in that house on Wabash Avenue.

But most of what the reporters thought that they knew about Robert Lincoln was just hearsay. He was shy and standoffish. Because his work didn't require it, he was never available to the press. He'd started ducking them back in '67 when that sad business about his mother and her clothes was in the headlines, and he'd become quite expert at that game. If necessary, his partner, Edward Swift Isham, could front for him. A roly-poly cheerful looking man with bristling burnsides, he was smiling and talking with the men around him down there in front while Mr. Lincoln kept his nose buried in papers. If there was anything that concerned the reporters about the presence of Lincoln & Isham, it was the probability that the case about to be called would involve some boring business argument—boring, that is, unless it turned out to have some of the color of the Erie Railroad war with characters like diamond-studded Jim Fisk and creepy Jay Gould. None of the men gathering here in Judge Wallace's court suggested such a possibility. They all looked as solid as steel rails, and but for the air of mystery they were creating by whispering to each other and casting rather worried glances at the press most of the reporters would have moved off when the appointed hour of two o'clock came and went with no judge taking the bench.

Robert Lincoln kept his nose buried in those papers largely to avoid conversation, because it was impossible to share his thoughts and feelings at that moment with anybody else on earth with the exception of his own Mary, who quite rightly didn't think it appropriate to join him in court. He knew the contents of the file he held in hand by heart. The only letter that required study was the one Swett had handed him just before he left for the Grand Pacific Hotel on that ticklish mission that Robert himself couldn't bear to undertake. The letter had been written this very morning by Judge Davis, who was in Indianapolis and had sent it up by special messenger on the early train. As he'd tossed it across his desk to Robert, Swett had said, "Here. I'm sure the judge would want you to see this. Don't let the part about losing the case worry you. It's airtight."

With time to burn, Robert now reread the letter carefully:

> "Indianapolis
> May 19, 1875
>
> My dear Swett—
> Your communication of May 16th in relation to Mrs.

Lincoln was received a few moments ago and I hasten to reply.

As you are aware, Robert, Mr. Stuart & I have had a protracted consultation on the subject—Your letter has in no wise changed the opinion which I entertained at the time of this consultation—On the contrary, the statement of the eminent physicians named by you "that Mrs. Lincoln is insane and ought to be confined" has confirmed it—I believe her to be a fit subject for personal restraint and fear the consequences unless action is taken soon—Indeed, my fears are greatly increased by your statement that she now talks of leaving for California or Europe—A separation from Chicago at all in her present condition would be very embarrassing and it seems to me should not be permitted— I trust that you may see your way clear to prevent it —If the physicians affirm in writing what they have verbally stated to you and Mr. Ayer, that Mrs. Lincoln is insane and ought to be confined, you would be justified in taking immediate action—If you & Mr. Ayer as lawyers are satisfied there is evidence enough to warrant you in expecting a favorable verdict from a jury, then proceedings should be commenced at once —I am aware that an unfavorable verdict would be disastrous in the extreme, but this must be risked if after maturely considering the subject your fixed opinion is that you ought to succeed—I do not see how Robert can get along at all unless he has authority to subject his mother to treatment—The appointment of a conservator without the confinement will not answer the purpose—It might do with persons of different temperament from Mrs. Lincoln but with her it would not do at all—Like you I have been satisfied for years that her unsoundness of mind affords the proper explanation for all the vagaries she has developed.

You and I were devoted friends of her husband and in this crisis it is our duty to give Robert the support which he so much needs. And I doubt not that he will receive this support from his relatives in Springfield —I know that he has the support of Mr. Stuart. I do not see the propriety of waiting until the commission of some act which wd arrest public attention—It may be that medical attention, in a Retreat for Insane Persons, would operate favorably upon her. This chance should not be lost—After all the whole case turns on the sufficiency of the evidence to procure a favorable verdict—If you are satisfied on this point, believing as I do that Mrs. Lincoln is insane and should be placed under treatment, I see no other course than judicial action. Of course this is painful to us all and especially so to Robert but like all other painful duties it must be met and discharged—Thoughtful and right minded men will approve and under the circumstances, it is to be hoped newspapers will forbear to criticise—

Robert has my deepest sympathy in this terrible ordeal—That he may have strength given him to bear it, is my earnest prayer—

Although I do not wish anything I write to be published yet I wish it distinctly understood that Robert has my support and approval—I sincerely hope that Mr. Stuart will think it advisable to be with Robert during the trial.

—Be pleased to let me know what is done.

Your friend
David Davis"

Robert slipped the letter back into the file and sat thinking. There was nobody in the world whom he trusted more than Judge Davis. Although he hadn't seen a lot of him, he could scarcely remember a time when he hadn't been *aware* of Judge Davis somewhere out there. As Circuit Judge of the Eighth Judicial Circuit in Illinois, Judge Davis was the very core of that traveling group of lawyers of which his father was a member. When his father would come home after months on the circuit, he'd regale them all with stories, many of which involved an act or decision by Judge Davis. The judge was possessed of a stature that any small boy would find impressive since he weighed nearly 300 pounds. As Robert's father once said playfully about his friend, "Davis is so big that they don't measure him for his pants—they survey him." Abraham Lincoln evidently considered Davis large in intellect as well, because he appointed him to the Supreme Court. Naturally, political enemies said that the appointment was only a payoff for the fact that Davis had engineered Lincoln's nomination in '60. This sort of thing was what kept Robert out of politics, but he paid no attention to it in personal life. On that dreadful April Saturday when Robert's world had come apart, when his father lay prostrate in death downstairs at the White House and his mother lay prostrate with grief upstairs, Robert had telegraphed Davis, then in Chicago, and asked him to come to Washington and take over the President's personal affairs, and the judge had responded at once. So it was gratifying to have the support that Judge Davis showed in this letter and, under the circumstances, comforting that Swett had already taken precisely the steps that the judge advised.

Robert hadn't thought of bringing Swett in on this case. Although Swett had ridden the circuit with his father and Judge Davis, had been Davis's lieutenant in the nominating campaign in Chicago, and been in and out of the White House during the war, Robert thought it significant that his father had never given Swett an important post. Everybody said that Swett hadn't wanted a government job, which was probably true if some of the rumors about him were also true. There was the story, for instance, that he'd cashed in by selling hay to both sides and another that he'd pocketed a hundred thousand dollars in the Alameda quicksilver mining operation in California. Mr. Welles, his father's Secretary of the Navy, whom Robert trusted as much as he did Judge Davis, was always dropping dark hints about Swett. Because of his friendship with Edgar Welles, Robert often stayed at the Welles house in Washington and even made it his headquarters during his wedding, and he overheard the kind of talk that would usually be kept within families. Secretary Welles blamed Swett's liking for high living in the matter of Mr. Lincoln's being stuck with Senator Cameron as his Secretary of War for a year or so. It seemed that Swett was sent east on some mission for Lincoln right after the nomination and, after being wined and dined at the Pennsylvania senator's estate at Lochiel, issued an invitation to Springfield against Lincoln's express wishes with the result that Lincoln was maneuvered into an appointment he didn't want to make. At that time Lincoln was greatly in Swett's debt for his efforts at Chicago, including issuing counterfeit tickets to the Wigwam in order to pack the convention with Lincoln supporters when the issue was still in doubt. Robert sometimes wondered that his father could overlook such shenanigans, but, as somebody once said, politics was the art of the possible, and his father was an artist in politics.

With respect to the present case, Robert hadn't felt in any position to argue about Swett when as respectable an attorney as Ben Ayer came up with the suggestion of consulting him. Ayer felt that Swett's known personal association with Abraham Lincoln might make the procedure look a little less distasteful to the public eye and that his acknowledged skill in the rough and tumble of criminal practice could be of help in view of the fact that the experience of Ayer & Kales was largely confined to the more gentlemanly aspects of the law. Nor was Ayer unmindful of the rumors that Swett, disillusioned by the Grant administration, was offering his still considerable political clout to the Democrats, the party of which Judge Wallace was a most loyal and outspoken adherent.

At first there'd been something a little irritating about Swett's enthusiasm for the case. Although he hadn't actually come out and said so, Swett's attitude had suggested that he'd always considered Mary Todd Lincoln crazy—a burden to her husband—and this letter from Judge Davis certainly confirmed that. Perhaps such conviction was necessary to win in court. In any event, Swett had moved with breathless speed and assurance when one of the Pinkertons Robert had hired to watch his mother reported overhearing her tell a store saleslady that she was contemplating leaving Chicago. On Saturday he had brought together some of Chicago's outstanding physicians for a locked-door session in the offices of Ayer & Kales to hear Robert and the Pinkertons relate Mary Lincoln's recent actions and sayings. They rendered a unanimous verbal verdict that Mrs. Lincoln was insane, and Swett spent the first two days of the week getting them to confirm this in writing and personally riding around in a carriage to interview other possible witnesses. By Wednesday morning he was ready to take Ayer and Robert to the court with him, make out the necessary papers and prevail upon Judge Wallace to schedule an immediate trial. To any and all who questioned giving Mrs. Lincoln so little notice of her trial, Swett responded that, with a thousand dollars in cash and $56,000 in securities always on her person, she could board a train at a moment's notice and flee the court's jurisdiction if she got wind of their intentions. You never could tell what a crazy person might do, as he, Leonard Swett, could assure them after a lifetime of successfully pleading clients insane to get them off on murder and other criminal charges.

Robert pulled out his watch. It was after two and cause for concern. Swett wasn't the kind of lawyer who would keep a judge and jury waiting if he could help it. Judge Wallace could be irascible, and attorneys who knew him were always careful not to light the fire in his eyes. Although he dreaded the moment of coming face-to-face with his mother, Robert dreaded even more the possibility of something going wrong. Not a man given to overstatement, Judge Davis hadn't done much for Robert's nerves by writing that "an unfavorable verdict would be disastrous in the extreme." Robert could see the reporters hovering at the door of the courtroom and knew that the minute they saw his mother arrive they'd pounce on every detail of what transpired here. They'd be sympathetic in their accounts only if they, along with the jury, were absolutely convinced that his mother was out of her mind and in grave danger of hurting herself. Otherwise, they'd tear him to shreds for being an unfeeling, ungrateful son, and the reputations of the doctors and lawyers supporting him would be ruined.

To try to keep from thinking about what might be transpiring between Swett and his mother in that hotel room, Robert let his lawyer's mind run over the case again looking for flaws. He really couldn't find any. Despite what Judge Davis said, he and Swett had agreed that it was probably good luck that cousin John Todd Stuart hadn't come up from Springfield for the trial in response to Robert's telegram. He could still appear, but it wasn't probable: Stuart knew the appointed time, and he was not only constitutionally prompt but respectful of the court after nearly fifty years at the bar. Based on his letter, Stuart might make a weak witness under oath, although some of his comments about his cousin Mary bore the weight of a long and close relationship and the logic of a first rate legal mind.

Robert always understood that it was John Todd Stuart who was responsible for his father's career and, indirectly at least, his marriage. Abraham Lincoln and John Stuart had first met in the brief Black Hawk war of 1832. Stuart, a blue blood from Ken-

tucky and graduate of Center College, was, at twenty-five, an
elegant major on leave from his already substantial law practice
in Springfield; Lincoln, at twenty-three, was a rawboned captain escaping the tedium of clerking in a New Salem store. They
met again three years later when Lincoln, running as a Whig,
was elected to the state legislature in which Stuart served as
leader of the Whigs. They roomed together in a boarding house
at the then capital in Vandalia, and Stuart persuaded Lincoln to
"read law," later taking him in as a junior partner. Along with
Ninian Edwards, who'd married one of Stuart's cousins from
Lexington, Kentucky, Elizabeth Todd, Stuart and Lincoln were
part of a group of legislators known as the "long nine" because
of their height, the movers and shakers in getting the capital
moved to Springfield, where it would benefit their legal business. Under the circumstances, Abraham Lincoln could hardly
have avoided meeting Mary Todd when she came up from Lexington in '39 to live with her sister, Lizzie Edwards. Although
Lincoln left Stuart's office about the time of his marriage in '42,
they worked together in politics with Lincoln following Stuart
to Washington as Springfield's representative in Congress and,
of course, were frequently involved with each other in the
courts and in Todd family affairs. Robert had grown up somewhat in awe of his handsome, starchy Cousin John, and it was
certain that any judge and jury would also find Stuart, who was
now mayor of Springfield, rather awesome.

The problem was that Cousin John, not really having seen his
mother for years, didn't fully understand the situation. That
was partly Robert's fault. Not wanting all the gossipy Springfield relatives to know more than necessary about his own personal affairs, he hadn't told Stuart any details about why he
couldn't possibly take his mother into his home. The last time
he'd tried that experiment—after Tad's death—something had
happened between his wife and mother, and Mary Harlan Lincoln had packed up and taken the children out to see her parents
in Iowa. From there, she'd written hinting that she'd never

come back as long as Mary Todd Lincoln was also in the house. That backed Robert into a very tight corner. He owed more than just his life to his mother, but he adored his wife, who'd given him so far two children—Mary, called Mamie to distinguish her from the other two Marys, and baby Abraham, called Jack. Robert himself didn't know quite why a relationship that had seemed so loving when his mother was in Europe with Tad had gone so sour. It was the kind of women's business that he tried to stay out of, and he'd been fortunate that his mother, who was nothing if not sensitive, had read the meaning of Mary Harlan's sudden departure and long absence rightly and moved out on her own. Since then, the women hadn't met or talked. Although Robert had been able to persuade his mother to drop by the house and visit the children occasionally when she was sure that Mary Harlan would be out, she refused to spend a night under his roof, a circumstance that had certainly contributed to the trying events of the last several weeks.

On Swett's advice Robert had decided not to offer John Stuart's letter to the court. In addition to being unaware of Robert's personal problems, Stuart hadn't known of the meeting of doctors when he'd written. About all that Robert could use the thing for now was to show it to his mother in the hope of convincing her that he, Robert, was doing the right thing. He reread it with that possibility in view.

> "Springfield, May 10, 1875
>
> Robt. T. Lincoln Esq
>
> My dear Cousin: I received your telegram of this day and answered that I could not meet you tomorrow. I have business engagements for the week which require me to remain at home. My wife's health has grown so much worse since Saturday that I ought not to leave her.
>
> I have carefully examined your two letters, and the

46

facts which you detail in connection with those come-
ing (sic) under my observation and related to me while
at Chicago leave no doubt of the propriety of the appointment of a conservator for your mother. I am not
so sure about the necessity of *personal restraint* but is it
not probable that if a conservator were appointed that
she would consent to remain at some private hospital?

I have no doubt but that she is insane and Cousin
Lizzie Brown expresses the same opinion. John Bunn's
information was derived through a lady boarding at
the Pacific who obtained her information through the
servants at the Hotel. The same is true of Judge Edwards.

Yourself & Mother both have my sincere sympathy
in this great affliction but I think it best for both of you
and for all friends that she should be treated as an
insane person.

You can make whatever use of this letter you think
proper.—

> Yours affectionately,
> John T. Stuart"

The proper use for this letter, Robert realized now, was to
bury it in the file if all went well with the jury. Once she was
convicted and he had the authority to put her away and take
charge of her affairs, it wouldn't really matter what anybody
else thought. For her to know that her own Springfield relatives
considered her crazy would then be a needless wounding. The
one thing in Stuart's letter that did give him pause was the
suggestion that they get her into a private hospital instead of a
state insane asylum, some of which were said to be houses of
horror. Dr. Patterson had expressed a willingness to take care
of her out at Batavia during the meeting on Saturday. Perhaps
they could propose that to Judge Wallace. Dr. Patterson's was

one of the physicians' letters addressed to Ayer & Kales that he'd copied for his file. Nothing gave him more comfort and confidence at this hour than knowing they were there and seeing several of the doctors here in court to testify.

Considering the time at their disposal, they'd been very fortunate to round up such an impressive medical panel. When his mother had complained of an effort to poison her on her way home from Florida and of a subsequent fever, Robert had asked his own family physician, Dr. Ralph N. Isham, a nephew of his law partner, to see her, and Dr. Isham had been treating her ever since. After Robert's unnerving experience with his mother in the elevator on April first, Dr. Isham had advised him to go out and have a talk with Dr. R. J. Patterson, who'd left a career of public service as superintendent of hospitals for the insane in Indiana and Iowa to set up his own private sanitarium for women, Bellevue Place, in Batavia, a short train ride west of Chicago. Dr. Patterson hadn't met Mrs. Lincoln, but, having already been apprised of some of the facts, he was a natural to include in the discussions. So were Dr. Willis Danforth, who'd treated Mrs. Lincoln for various ailments in '73 and '74 and had looked in on her again this spring at Robert's request, and Drs. Charles Gilman Smith and Hosmer Allen Johnson, whom Mrs. Lincoln herself had hired as the best in Chicago to try to save Tad's life and had called "excellent" despite their failure. Since most of these men weren't specialists in mental disorders, Swett beefed up the panel with Dr. Nathan Smith Davis, famed for papers on the nervous system and the professor of physiology and pathology at Rush Medical College, and Dr. James Stewart Jewell, editor of the *Chicago Journal of Nervous and Mental Diseases.*

Rather amazingly, none of these men hesitated to put into writing affirmative answers to two questions posed by Swett: 1) did they think that Mrs. Lincoln was insane; and 2) did they think that she should be confined to a mental institution? Some, like Dr. Jewell, let it go with scribbling "aye" and "aye" to each of the questions, but some elaborated. Dr. Davis, who'd never met Mrs. Lincoln, nevertheless felt called upon to write, "From the facts and circumstances detailed to us on the 15th inst., I am decidedly of the opinion that Mrs. Lincoln *is insane.* The character of her insanity is such that she may at times appear perfectly sane in ordinary conversation and yet she is constantly subject to such mental hallucination as to render her entirely unsafe if left to herself." Robert hoped that Swett had remembered to show these letters to his mother. He had to admit that, insane or no, she was quite competent when it came to comprehending what she read in the newspapers and books she was always poring over when she wasn't out shopping. She simply couldn't fail to understand what the doctors were saying.

If she did, it would be a great relief after all this time of trying to deal with her various vagaries and ailments. Robert could never remember when his mother's flamboyant personality had not been an embarrassment to him. She was not like other women, other mothers. She was either way, way up or way, way down. She was all fire, as hot in her hates as in her loves. She could be cuttingly cruel one minute, smotheringly tender the next. She had very strong opinions—feelings, really—about people, politics, places, religion, morals, manners, and she was outspoken to the point of rudeness in expressing them. If there was nobody within hearing when a thought came to her ever-churning mind, she would sit down and dash off one of those letters full of commas and dashes and underlinings. She was restless, impatient, driving. When she wanted something, she wanted it *now.* She never slowed down—instead, she totally collapsed with those blinding headaches or, lately, with chills and fever or something the doctors called "bloat." She was constitutionally unable to take half-way measures in *anything,* even illness. Many people, including himself, were half-afraid of her, as they might be of thunder and lightning. Even those who admired her called her idiosyncratic, one of a kind; those who feared her, like Davis and Swett, called her crazy, insane. Robert conveniently took the latter view, in light of the doctor's opinions, and it would, he felt, make things so much easier all around if his mother did, too. She might, after all, stop asserting that fierce will, which was such a bother.

By now Robert was getting used to dealing with the word "insane" in his mind. Curiously, he'd been helped in that when he and Swett had arrived at the court this morning and had discovered that the paper they had to file was printed by the state and headed APPLICATION TO TRY THE QUESTION OF INSANITY. The existence of this printed form was very tangible evidence that there must be hundreds, possibly thousands, of such cases going through Illinois courts every year. He had only to dictate information particular to this case for the clerk to fill in the blanks so that it would read that the petitioner's *"mother, Mary Lincoln widow of Abraham Lincoln, deceased, a resident of Cook County is insane, and that it would be for her* benefit and for the safety of the community that *she* should be confined to the Cook County Hospital or the Illinois State Hospital for the insane." He listed the witnesses that Swett had interviewed and went on to fill blanks to assert "that the said *Mary Lincoln* has property and effects consisting of *negotiable securities and other personal property* the value of which does not exceed the sum of *Seventy-five thousand* Dollars, and that the said *Mary Lincoln* is absolutely non compos mentis and incapable of managing her estate, wherefore your petitioner prays that a Warrant be issued for a jury of *twelve* good and lawful men, to determine the truth of the allegations in the foregoing petition contained . . ." After asking that the named witnesses be subpoenaed, the petition also prayed in the printed language "that said *Mary Lincoln* be declared an insane person after due hearing and proof and that a Conservator be appointed to manage and control her estate." Of course, Robert was only deceiving himself if he really thought that the nature of the form could make a routine matter of any proceeding having to do with a woman who'd been first lady of the land, the most glittering and controversial woman to occupy the White House since Dolly Madison.

She was not *widow of Abraham Lincoln, deceased;* she was widow of the Great Emancipator, the Noble Martyr, the Savior of the Union who was already being enshrined in a glory until then reserved for only one other American, George Washington.

Robert believed that the strain of living up to the starring roles she'd been given in one of history's most tragic dramas had "undone" his mother. When he took the stand, as unfortunately Swett insisted that he must do in defense of his own petition, Robert intended to speak over the heads of the jury to those reporters back there. He'd remind them of what his mother had been through in the hope that they would "forbear to criticise," as Judge Davis put it. He wouldn't have to put on an act to let them see his own distress. The real problem would be getting through his testimony at all with his mother's eyes on him. Much would depend on how she took it. His mother was quite capable of acting with stoic dignity when it suited her. There was a lot of iron in her. He could still remember how proud he had been of her that summer she'd suffered a head injury in a carriage accident while she was driving from the White House out to the Soldiers' Home where the family went to escape the Washington heat. By the time he got down from Boston the wound was infected, and she was in great pain. Robert was astonished by the brave front his mother put up. Instead of finding her lying in bed groaning as he'd anticipated, he'd found her sitting up and smiling. "It's better to laugh than be sighing," she'd told him. "Your father has enough on his mind without worrying about me." There was a bite to that recollection, because Robert wondered now whether that injury had had anything to do with bringing her to this sad day. The doctors wouldn't venture to say, and she had had headaches for as long as he could remember. If this were to be one of the days when it pleased her to be strong, it would certainly make things easier for him, although she might then give the jury and the press the wrong impression about her *true* condition.

Fortunately, Judge Wallace had done a good job in selecting

a jury that would be more persuaded by fact than emotion. As the judge had told Swett, he wanted no taint of political vindictiveness in a proceeding that would likely result in putting Abraham Lincoln's widow away since he personally had been a political enemy of the late President. The way to make sure of that was to empanel men so prominent that neither their motives nor their judgment would be challenged by their fellow citizens of Chicago. Looking at them now, beginning to twist a little with discomfort and impatience on their hard chairs, Robert was amazed at how many of them moved in the same circles he did. Those he didn't actually recognize by sight, he knew by reputation.

Taking the foreman's seat was Lyman Judson Gage, cashier of the Merchants Loan & Trust Company, and next to him sat none other than the Honorable Charles Benjamin Farwell, a member of the United States House of Representatives. At least one physician was required on any jury in an insanity trial, and Dr. Blake was an inspired choice because of his former city job. Two of the men had thriving State Street establishments serving the public—Thomas Cogswell, half-owner of the jewelry firm Cogswell-Weber, and William Stewart of Stewart & Aldrich, dealers in ladies' apparel. Henry C. Durant was in groceries; Silas Moore and Charles Henderson were in real estate. James A. Mason and S.B. Parkhurst were both, by coincidence, foundrymen, and J. McGregor Adams was a partner in the railway supply firm of Crerar Adams Company. Only D.R. Cameron, an unemployed bookkeeper, was anything like the kind of person you'd expect to find in a pickup jury like this.

Robert's thoughts were interrupted by a commotion at the door. He looked up to see his mother coming in with Swett on one side of her and that hotel manager, Turner, on the other. She looked very pale but otherwise in control of herself. The newspapermen were almost falling over each other to stay near her, and behind them a river of spectators flowed through the door as news of her coming travelled through the courthouse.

Nothing said or done here would go unreported to the world.

Swett seated Mrs. Lincoln at the end of one of the counsel tables just inside the railing and went over to Robert. "You'd better go to your mother," he said. "I only got her in here by promising you'd be here. But watch out: she's very angry and accuses us of hatching up a scheme to get her money."

To Robert his mother looked more fearful than angry. "What will I say?" he asked.

Swett sounded exasperated: "I don't know. Think of something. She's *your* mother. Take Arnold with you. She recognized him and seemed to like it when I told her he'd represent her."

Swett signaled to Arnold, who came over shaking his head. "Now that I see her, I don't think I can do it—too many rich old memories," he said. "I don't know how I can represent her fairly when I think she's insane, too."

This time Swett was more than exasperated; he was furious. This could be the one hitch he hadn't foreseen. "Arnold, this means that you will put into her head that she can get some mischievous lawyer to make us trouble," he said. "Go and defend her, and do your duty."

Arnold shrugged: "Well, if you all think it best . . . Let's go, Robert . . ."

Robert shook his mother's hand, saying, "Hello, mother," with enough cordiality that the reporters noted it down on their pads. Arnold just had time to sit down on his client's right, press her hand and say, "It will be all right, Mrs. Lincoln," with more conviction in his tone than in his heart when the bailiff cried out, "All rise!" Judge Wallace came in from chambers sweeping the courtroom with that fierce look that his friends attributed more to shortness of sight than shortness of temper. He did put on spectacles when he sat at the bench, glanced at a paper, then glared out over the lenses at the crowd.

"The matter before us," he said, "is a hearing into the sanity of Mary Lincoln widow of Abraham Lincoln, deceased . . ."

There was an audible intake of breath on the part of everybody in the now crowded room who wasn't a participant in the trial. This was their first inkling of what it was that had brought Mrs. Lincoln to the court. With some difficulty, the reporters refrained from whooping: this *would* be a story.

·

CHAPTER III

A *"Republican Queen"*

Wɪᴛʜ ᴛʜᴇ ᴅᴜʟʟ light from that Wednesday's overcast skies further darkened by the courtroom's smoke-grimed windows Judge Wallace had the gas lights lit, and their hissing glare bothered Mary Lincoln's eyes as she studied the faces in the crowd, looking for some that might be friendly. Having grown up with candlelight and oil lamps, she preferred their soft glow if artificial light had to be used. Squinting, she picked out Mr. Turner, who'd left her side and was sitting in the front row right behind the railing, and next to him was that nice Mrs. Harrington, the hotel housekeeper, who'd spent a couple of nights with her when she was especially nervous, and the maid Mary Gavin who sometimes stayed in her room with her, too. Why were the women here? Had Mr. Turner gone around telling everyone in the hotel what was happening? He must have, because she could see that waiter who brought meals to her room whose name she couldn't remember and Mr. Dodge, the cashier. It was good of them to come, but she was surprised that Mr. Turner had let them all leave work. She caught the eye of

Mrs. Harrington and gave her a tentative smile, but the woman looked away.

In the next row, back of the people from the hotel, were other friends, men who'd been kind to her when she was out and about her business of shopping. She couldn't remember their names, if she'd ever known them, but she knew their faces well. One of them was the salesman at the Matson & Co. jewelry store and another the nice man who sold her all those curtains at Allen & Mackey. One man she did know by name was Mr. Seaton, the agent of the United States Express Company, because he'd had to sign a receipt when he came to the hotel to pick up the trunks she'd shipped to Milwaukee for the summer. Why were they here? How would they know about this case when she herself hadn't known until an hour or so ago? It was very strange. They wouldn't respond to her smile, either.

One group of men she didn't know but hated on sight were the reporters. They were staring at her as if she were an odd animal in the zoo and scribbling into their notebooks. She'd learned to her sorrow that it was impossible to know in advance how she'd be treated by the press. Of one thing she could be sure: she *would* be treated. For the last fifteen years they'd printed just about everything about her that they could get their hands on, true or false. In her first innocent year in the White House, Mary had looked to the members of the press for friendship and understanding and had been cruelly hurt. The first wound came from the deception of Henry Wikoff when it turned out that all the time he'd been charming her with his recollections of foreign adventures and sophisticated advice on how to handle Washington society, he'd been a spy for James Gordon Bennett's New York *Herald.* The agony this had brought upon her could still make her writhe in remembering it, mostly because of her own embarrassing naiveté.

A man of inherited means, Wikoff at forty-eight had come to roost in Washington after drifting for years around the capitals of Europe where, as he told it, he'd moved in the highest social

circles. His nickname "Chevalier" reflected his style. He was
fluent in French, the international language, and very compli-
mentary when Mary Lincoln tentatively tried using again the
French in which she'd excelled as a student at Madame Mentelle's academy in Lexington. Wikoff was always full of that
gossip dearly beloved by a social person like Mary Lincoln as
well as of news of the latest book she ought to read or play she
ought to see. His almost daily visits lightened the long hours
she'd otherwise have spent alone, since Mr. Lincoln was taken
up from nearly dawn till long after dark with the increasingly
heavy affairs of state. Wikoff's became a familiar face to members of the staff, and he was allowed to wander freely about the
house. Not only liking Wikoff but trusting him completely,
Mary was shocked and upset when the *Herald* scooped every
other paper in the nation by publishing details of Mr. Lincoln's
first state of the union message to Congress before it was sent
up to the Hill, and Wikoff admitted telegraphing the material to
Bennett in New York.

Because Wikoff would not say where he'd seen a copy of the
President's message, it was rumored that Mary Lincoln herself
had let him look at it. The House Judiciary Committee launched
an inquiry with the intent, according to alarmed Republicans,
of embarrassing the President through his wife. Wikoff was
jailed for contempt of Congress for refusing to disclose his
source, and General Dan Sickles, who was a friend to both
Wikoff and Mrs. Lincoln, took on his defense. The affair was
getting so rapidly out of hand that Mr. Lincoln appeared in
secret before the committee to plead with them to spare him this
"disgrace" in a time of national peril. Sickles, a colorful charmer
of great notoriety for having shot and killed his wife's lover in
Lafayette Square within sight of the White House a few years
before, had also gone out of his way to entertain Mrs. Lincoln
and was nearly as familiar with the ins-and-outs of the White
House as Wikoff. He managed to persuade Mrs. Lincoln's gar-
dener, John Watt, to appear before the Committee and make the

unlikely confession that he'd seen a copy of the message on a table in the White House library, read it and repeated its contents to Wikoff. For reasons known only to itself, the Committee swallowed this, but Wikoff, released from jail, was banned from the White House, and Watt was "exiled" to New York. The harm didn't end there. People said that a deal had been struck, that it was Mary Lincoln who arranged with a New York businessman seeking her custom to give Watt a job. They said, too, that the *Herald,* one of the few papers to shower compliments on her, had done so only to pave the way for Wikoff's scoop.

As if that weren't enough, in that same month of February '62, while Wikoff was appearing before the Congressional committee and while she was spending every waking moment at the bedside of her dying son Willie, the press was loudly debating the propriety of her first major White House reception. Held on February 5th, it was misnamed a ball; there were too many people crushed into the public rooms to leave room for dancing a step. At that, Mary Lincoln, following what she later considered to be "evil" advice, had invited only 500 or so of the most "respectable people in private life" instead of maintaining the historic tradition of opening the White House to all comers on such an occasion. The result seemed at first a triumph. The popular *Leslie's Weekly* rushed into print with a gushing account of a "brilliant success" at which Mrs. John J. Crittendon sparkled with diamonds, General George B. McClellan's wife looked regal in a "head-dress of white illusion *a la vierge,* " Mrs. Commodore Levy was *"piquante,"* wearing a dress of white illusion and gold and earrings of Oriental pearls. But the real superlatives were used to describe the First Lady, as the article went on:

"Primarily, we must remark the exquisite taste with which the White House has been refitted under Mrs. Lincoln's directions is in no respect more remarkable than in the character of the hangings of the various rooms, which relieve and set off the figures and dresses of lady guests to the greatest advantage. First, as hostess, and second in no respect, Mrs. Lincoln. She was attired in a lustrous white satin robe, with a train of a yard in length, trimmed with one deep flounce of the richest black chantilly lace, put on in festoons and surmounted by a quilling of white satin ribbon, edged with narrow black lace. The dress was, of course, décolleté and with short sleeves, displaying the exquisitely moulded shoulders and arms of our fair 'Republican Queen,' the whiteness of which were absolutely dazzling. Her head-dress was a coronet wreath of black and white crepe myrtle, which was in perfect keeping with her regal style of beauty. Let us here add *en passant,* that Mrs. Lincoln possesses that rare beauty which has rendered the Empress of the French so celebrated as a handsome woman, and which our Transatlantic cousins call *la tête bien planté.* Her ornaments were pearls."

Such praise might have cheered her even at a time when Willie's life was ebbing, might have made her feel that at last she was doing something right, had it not been for the many strident voices being raised on the other side of the debate. One, that of the *Liberator,* accused her of being "a woman whose sympathies are with slavery and with those who are waging war" and claimed that putting on such an entertainment was unworthy of "man or woman with ears open to the wails of the bereaved throughout the country." Another called her the White House's "Delilah," and a widely reprinted poem by Eleanor G. Donelly sang of a dying soldier who could see from his bed the party in progress through the executive mansion's brightly lighted windows and lamented in rhyme:

> "What matter that I, poor private,
> Lie here on my narrow bed,
> With the fever gripping my vitals
> And dazing my hapless head!
> What matters that nurses are callous,
> And rations meagre and small,
> So long as the *beau monde* revel
> At the Lady-President's ball!

Who pities my poor old mother—
Who comforts my sweet young wife—
Alone in the distant city,
With sorrow sapping their life!
I have no money to send them,
They cannot come at my call;
No money? yet hundreds are wasting
At my Lady-President's ball!

Hundreds, ay! hundreds of thousands
In satins, jewels, and wine,
French dishes for dainty stomachs
(While the black broth sickens mine!)
And jellies, and fruits, and cold ices
And fountains that flash as they fall,
O God! for a cup of cold water
From the Lady-President's ball!"

That verse appeared four days before Willie's death, and it really finished Mary with the press. Her secretary, William Stoddard, as outraged as she, nevertheless tried to use it as ammunition in his continuing argument that she should invite reporters to go along on her hospital visits when she'd sit and hold a wounded boy's hand for an hour at a time or write a letter on his behalf to a mother or a sweetheart. If the public knew the real reason for her rides out in the White House carriage instead of putting them down as frivolous shopping trips, he claimed, verses like that would never be written or certainly not printed. And how could the poetess have known—when few of the invited guests even suspected—that she and Mr. Lincoln were alternating every half hour or so in slipping away from the "Lady-President's ball" to go upstairs and test Willie's rising fever with a fearful hand, Stoddard asked. In Stoddard's view, Mrs. Lincoln was far from heartless; she just put up too brave a front for her own good. He was more aware of this than anybody, including Mr. Lincoln, because it was his duty to stand beside her at parties such as the one in question and watch her being gracious to guests no matter what her personal problems. But Mary wouldn't listen to Stoddard. She made her hospital visits out of the prompting of her mother's heart, and she didn't want to turn them into a circus for the press. Besides, how could she be sure of their reaction? If they'd so misread her motives with respect to the "ball," which had been inspired by a patriotic desire to show the world that majesty still resided in the office of the Chief Magistrate despite the South's secession, mightn't they find a way to twist whatever they saw her say or do for the boys? She was sure, for instance, that the temperance press would raise a hue and cry about corrupting the army's morals if they discovered that she sent all the wines and liquors that arrived as gifts at the White House to the hospitals. No, she would do as Mr. Lincoln did and try to ignore the press.

The trouble was that the press would not ignore her. However harsh their treatment while she was in the White House, it was mild compared to the lashing they gave her when she tried to sell some of her ornaments and clothes in the fall of '67. Thinking about it now, it struck her as a bitter irony that the press could have compared her to the Empress of France when she was wearing those clothes at the White House but not when she put them up for sale in an effort to keep on living in her Washington Street house after Mr. Lincoln's old friends like Mr. Swett failed to help her. In France, it was considered *chic* when Empress Eugénie sold *her* old clothes; in America, it was considered a crime on the order of treason for a former First Lady to sell hers. For the life of her, Mary had never been able to understand why. She'd still stand by what she'd written to her friend Rhoda White at the time: "Never was an act committed with a more innocent intention than mine was. Having no further use for the articles proposed to be sold—and really requiring the proceeds—I deposited them with an agent & I presumed no publicity would result from it. I was not more astonished than *you* would have been to see my letters in print."

Once more, as in the Wikoff case, her undoing had been her naive trust in people who seemed to want to help her. By then she'd come to fear the press so much that she used an assumed name, Mrs. Clarke, when she met her friend, Elizabeth Keckley, the black seamstress who'd been of such help to her in Washington and in New York in September and tried to peddle her belongings. They started with small pieces of jewelry, and one of the first places they went was to W.H. Brady, a commission broker at 609 Broadway. She was heavily veiled so that nobody would recognize her, but she'd forgotten that her name was inscribed in one of the rings, and felt obliged to come out with the truth when Brady and his partner, Keyes, discovered it. The men were delighted. They promised her she'd make $100,000 if she left everything in their hands. Since such an arrangement would certainly make life easier for her, she agreed. But after she got back to her hotel and still fearing publicity, she wrote Brady some hasty notes suggesting that he try to dispose of the goods privately through Republican office holders who ought to feel an obligation to her as widow of the man who'd made them. Then, leaving Mrs. Keckley to handle things with Brady, she took off for Chicago. She was still on the train when she discovered she'd been stabbed in the back. She overheard a man reading the New York *World* make comments to his seatmate that could only have come from her letters to Brady; thank goodness she was still wearing that heavy veil.

Mary Lincoln was well-enough versed in politics to understand immediately what Brady had done. To get the maximum publicity for his firm, he'd turned her letters over to a Democratic newspaper that would gloat over her unguarded comments about how prominent Republicans like Secretary Seward and his New York henchman Thurlow Weed had let her down. When she did get hold of a copy of the paper, she was devastated to find that a letter they'd printed in full was the one referring Brady to Abram Wakeman, the surveyor of the port of New

York, who really had been a good friend to her in Washington days. Addressed to W.H. Brady, Esq., her note read:

> "My Dear Sir:
> Please call and see Hon. Abram Wakeman. He was largely indebted to me for obtaining the lucrative office which he has held for several years, and from which he has amassed a very large fortune. He will assist me in my painful and humiliating situation, scarcely removed from want. He would scarcely hesitate to return, in a small manner, the many favors my husband and myself always showered upon him. Mr. Wakeman many times excited my sympathies in his urgent appeals for office, as well for himself as others. Therefore he will only be too happy to relieve me by purchasing one or more of the articles you will please place before him."

Not content with publishing private correspondence, the paper chose to be what they doubtless considered amusing in an editorial that said, among other things: "The English language affords few things more exquisite, in its way, than this letter. Its frankness and simplicity are touching. Its directness leaves open no avenue of escape . . . Mr. Wakeman will not resist this appeal! He cannot! . . . Let Mr. Wakeman instantly take the whole lot, and send his check for the amount. The sum will be but a drop in the ocean of his reputed wealth."

In the next days Mary, cowering in the Chicago boarding house lodgings she'd taken so that she could rent out her house, absorbed shock after shock to her system as papers across the country picked up the story and exploited it for sensation or their own political purposes. One of the heaviest blows was dealt by Thurlow Weed, who exercised his privilege as editor of New York's *Commercial Advertiser* to run an unsigned article:

"If the American Congress or the American people have failed to meet the pecuniary expectations of Mr. Lincoln's widow, it is because that personage failed, during his life and since his death, to inspire either with respect or confidence. They should not, therefore, be subjected to the reproach or rest under the imputation of ingratitude. Had Mrs. Lincoln, while in power, borne herself becomingly, the suggestion of a Lincoln fund by voluntary contributions would have been promptly responded to. The national heart was warm. It gushed out in liberal endowments for Grant and Farragut. It would as cheerfully have met the appeal in favor of Mrs. Lincoln if it had not intuitively closed and chilled.

In her conversations Mrs. Lincoln is represented as bitterly denouncing Secretary Seward for which, of course, there is no warrant or excuse, for he wrongs no man, and much less is he capable of injustice, wrong, or even unkindness, to woman.

"But we happen to know—the late Caleb B. Smith, then Secretary of the Interior, being our informant— a fact which incensed Mrs. Lincoln against Mr. Seward. The President gave the Prince Napoleon a dinner, for which Mrs. Lincoln sent to the Secretary of the Interior for payment a bill of some $900. This demand, though wholly illegal, coming from the President's wife, embarrassed the Secretary, who called upon the Secretary of State for advice, where he learned that Mr. Seward had also dined the Prince, having the same number of guests and giving them a duplicate of the dinner at the White House. In fact, Mr. Seward ordered both dinners from the same restaurant and by his own bill knew the cost of each. For what Mr. Seward paid $300, Mrs. Lincoln expended $900. But whether three or nine hundred the claim was alike illegal and could not be paid. For this, however, Mrs. Lincoln quarreled with Secretaries Smith and Seward. This amount, however, was subsequently covered up in a gardener's account, but occasioned scandal which respect for Mr. Lincoln measurably suppressed.

Though Mr. Lincoln left an estate which enabled his family to live quite as comfortably as they had ever lived, Congress and the people would have promptly and cheerfully provided munificently for them if Mrs. Lincoln herself, with every advantage that high position gave her, had made friends or inspired respect. And this last exhibition proves how instinctively right the popular estimate of her character was.

The fact for which Mrs. Lincoln seeks large publicity, namely, that she received presents valued at $24,000, is a pregnant and suggestive one—suggestive, at least, of offices and contracts, unless the more charitable construction is reached through the assumption that they were expressions of regard and friendship. But it is not known that the wife of any other President, however estimable, was so loaded with shawls, laces, furs, diamonds, rings, &c.

Mrs. Lincoln's propensity to sell things was manifested early, and before any necessity was foreseen. If our information is reliable, eleven of Mr. Lincoln's new linen shirts were sold almost before the remains, which were shrouded in the twelfth, had started for that 'bourne from whence no traveler returns.'

"Individually, we are obliged to Mrs. Lincoln for an expression of her ill-will. It is pleasant to remember that we possessed the friendship and confidence of Mr. Lincoln to the last hour of his life, without paying court, as others did to Mrs. Lincoln, and in spite of her constant effort to disturb our relations.

This mortifying revelation will go abroad, and, as is natural, the Press of Europe will make the most of it, in deprecating the ingratitude of our Government and the want of liberality in the American people. This consideration alone constrains us to discharge the unpleasant duty of showing that neither the Government nor the people are justly obnoxious to these accusations."

Later, Mary would realize that Weed's anger had blinded him to the fact that he virtually admitted to the justice of the case she was trying to make for a pension or some other token of gratitude from a ruling Republican party that Mr. Lincoln had brought to power. If personal animosity toward *her* was the only reason they withheld financial help, what about Mr. Lincoln's innocent sons? At the time she was too upset to reach this point of reasoning as other papers, like baying hounds in a pack, followed Weed's lead and attacked her personally. She'd had no one around her with whom she could discuss her feelings. Taddie was too young, and she couldn't get through to Robert, who as she wrote to a friend, reacted "like a maniac" to what he considered the humiliation she'd brought upon *him*. So she'd spent much of her time confiding by letter in the one person who really understood the whole matter and who was still working on her behalf in New York—Elizabeth Keckley. Like the proverbial farmer who tries to lock the barn after the horse is stolen, she first wrote Mrs. Keckley soon after she reached Chicago:

"You know yourself how innocently I have acted, and from the best and purest of motives. They will *howl on* to prevent my disposing of my things. What a *vile, vile* set they are! The *Tribune* here, Mr. (Horace) White's paper, wrote a very beautiful editorial yesterday in my behalf; yet knowing that I have been deprived of my rights by the party, I suppose I would be *mobbed* if I ventured out. What a world of anguish this is—and how I have been made to suffer! . . . You would not recognize me now. The glass shows me a pale, wretched, haggard face, and my dresses are like bags on me. And all because I am doing what I felt to be my duty. Our minister, Mr. Swazey [Arthur Swazey, pastor of the Third Presbyterian Church of Chicago] called on me yesterday and said I had done perfectly right. Mrs. F [Mrs. Fowler, a housekeeper at Clifton House, where she'd been living just before going to New York] says every one speaks in the same way. The politicians, knowing they have deprived me of my just rights, would prefer to see me starve, rather than dispose of my things. They will prevent the sale of anything, so I have telegraphed for them. I hope you have received from B [Brady] the letters I have consigned to his care. See to this. Show none of them. Write me every day."

She'd been too optimistic in supposing that there might be a rising tide of sympathy for her out there, and by October 9 she was writing:

"My dear Lizzie:

It appears as if the fiends had let loose, for the Republican papers are tearing me to pieces in this border ruffian West. If I had committed murder in every city in this *blessed Union,* I could not be more traduced. And you know how innocent I have been of the intention of doing wrong. A piece in the morning *Tribune,* signed 'B,' pretending to be a lady, says there is no doubt Mrs. L—*is* deranged—has been for years past, and will end her life in a lunatic asylum. They would doubtless like me to begin it *now.* Mr. Swazey, a very kind, sympathizing minister, has been with me this morning, and has now gone to see Mr. Joseph Medill, of the *Tribune*, to know if *he* sanctioned his paper publishing such an article . . . Pray for me, dear Lizzie, for I am very miserable and broken hearted . . ."

By October 13, the situation was growing still worse, as she wrote:

"My dear Lizzie:

Was there ever such cruel newspaper abuse lavished upon an unoffending woman as has been showered upon my devoted head? The people of this ungrateful country are like 'dogs in the manger': will neither do anything themselves, nor allow me to improve my own condition. What a Government we have! All their abuse lavished upon me only lowers themselves in the estimation of all true-hearted people. The Springfield *Journal* had an editorial a few days since, with the important information that Mrs. Lincoln had been known to be *deranged* for years and should be *pitied* for all her *strange acts*. I should have been *all right* if I had allowed *them* to take possession of the White House. In the comfortable stealings by contracts from the Government, these low creatures are allowed to hurl their malicious wrath at me, with no one to defend me or protect me, if I should starve. These people injure themselves far more than they could do me, by their lies and villany. Their aim is to prevent my goods being sold, or anything done for me. *In this*, I very much fear they have succeeded.

Write me, my dear friend, your candid opinion about everything. I wished to be made better off, quite as much to improve your condition as well as for myself. Two weeks ago, dear Lizzie, we were in that *den* of discomfort and dirt. *Now* we are far asunder. Every other day, for the past week, I have had a chill, brought on by excitement and suffering of mind. In the midst of it I have moved into my winter quarters, and am now very comfortably situated. My parlor and bedroom are very sweetly furnished. I am lodged in a handsome house, a very kind, good, *quiet* family, and their meals are excellent. I consider myself fortunate in all this. I feel assured that the Republicans, who, to cover up their own perfidy and neglect, have used every villainous falsehood in their power to injure me—I fear they have *more* than succeeded, but if their day of reckoning does not come in this world, it *will surely* in the next . . ."

Mary's fears were well founded, and the press—or those using it—succeeded in injuring her. Although the widespread publicity did crowd Brady's Broadway showroom with the curious who studied and fondled the merchandise, the tone of most of the stories apparently made people feel that they would be performing a shameful act if they bought anything. One lady, after pawing through every shawl in the place, told Brady that she'd come only to reclaim an ashes-of-roses shawl that she'd sent as a gift to Mrs. Lincoln at the time of the Emancipation Proclamation and didn't want profaned by the public. Fortunately, that shawl wasn't there, but in the end Mary had to take back most of the clothes and pay Brady an $800 fee for what she thought was a gross mishandling of them.

Worse was yet to come. Two enterprising New York newspapermen learned of Mrs. Keckley's role in the affair, tracked her down to the garret room on Carroll Place, where she was taking in sewing, and prevailed upon her to dictate to them intimate reminiscences of her relationship with Mrs. Lincoln. They quickly published a book with Keckley's byline entitled *Behind the Scenes: Thirty Years a Slave and Four Years in the White House* in the spring of '68 to take advantage of the lingering interest aroused by the clothes episode. Mrs. Keckley claimed that her motive in publishing was to clear Mrs. Lincoln's name, and Mary had no reason to doubt her, since the book itself was honest—too honest, like having a sister divulge your pillow talk. Keckley had, for instance, let them use verbatim the letters Mary had written from Chicago about the clothes, had reconstructed with chilling accuracy private White House conversations and scenes between Mary and Mr. Lincoln, had ripped away the veil with which she'd tried to conceal the prostrating sorrow of that awful Easter weekend. Mary felt as exposed by the book as if she stood naked in the streets, and she used the excuse of finding special schooling in Europe for Taddie to escape what she took to be the knowing leers and snide whispers of people around her.

And now the press had her at their mercy again. The eager look on the faces of the reporters as they waited for the start of the trial was unmistakable. Would it please them if she were branded insane? This time they'd quite possibly wallow in pity instead of censure, but that could be worse. Remembering how nearly insane *Robert* had become over the publicity about the clothes, she was more puzzled than ever at how he could do this to them all. She looked at him. He was sitting only a few feet from her, on her left, but he'd hitched around as if to pay attention to the judge, and she could see only his neatly dressed hair, a handsome curve of ear and cheek. Even in this terrible moment, she took a certain pride in the well-groomed appearance of Robert, her son, much of it due to her teaching. Growing up, Robert couldn't have missed her efforts to see that Mr. Lincoln looked appropriate. Many were the times, in fact, that the boy had been miffed when she'd had to postpone some request of his in order to get the ruffles sewed on Mr. Lincoln's shirt in time for him to start off on the circuit. Another misconception she could lay to the press was that Mr. Lincoln didn't dress well. They usually pictured him in caricature or, at best, in the solemn black he wore for state occasions or to pose for photographs. She liked to remember him in the white linen suit she prevailed upon him to wear when he was debating Douglas, or the deerstalker's cap he'd pull down over his tousled head when he'd walk over to the War Department in the cold, or that combination of a blue chinchilla coat and buff-colored gloves she'd picked up for him on one of her New York shopping trips. It was *her* contribution. It was this colorful Mr. Lincoln, a figure who belonged to her instead of the nation, that she often held in mind and to whom she often talked, as now: *Let me rise above those ink-stained wretches as you did, Mr. Lincoln. Give me a measure of your strength . . .*

She'd been letting her mind wander freely because the proceedings in court were routine, without interest. A Mr. Ayer whom she didn't know arose and announced that he, with the assistance of Mr. Swett, would represent the petitioner, Robert T. Lincoln. Then Mr. Arnold popped up and introduced himself as *her* representative, asking at the same time for a postponement to prepare a case. Judge Wallace denied the request brusquely and instructed the jury members to rise and identify themselves, presumably to impress the press. While this was going on, Arnold whispered in Mary's ear that the judge's choices were probably as good as he could have made himself. It mattered little to Mary, since she recognized none of them although she had been in some of their stores. But Mary did trust Arnold and finding him here to help her had been the only good thing that had happened to her in the recent hours.

Her acquaintance with Arnold went far back to what she looked upon now as sort of golden days when she really was a sort of queen in her little house on Eighth Street in Springfield, a house she couldn't bear to return to because of all the happiness it had contained. She'd read and much appreciated Arnold's *true* picture of his visits there: "Mrs. Lincoln often entertained small numbers of friends at dinner, and somewhat larger numbers at evening parties. In his (Mr. Lincoln's) modest and

71

simple home, everything was orderly and refined, and there was always on the part of both Mr. and Mrs. Lincoln, a cordial, hearty, western welcome, which put every guest perfectly at ease. Her table was famed for the excellence of its rare Kentucky dishes, and in season was loaded with venison, wild turkeys, prairie chickens, quails, and other game, which in those early days was abundant. Yet it was the genial manner and ever kind welcome of the hostess, and the wit and humor, anecdote and unrivaled conversation of the host, which formed the chief attraction, and made a dinner at Lincoln's cottage an event to be remembered." How different from that dirty drunken dog Herndon's description of the Lincoln home as a "domestic hell!" But then she'd never invited Herndon into her home as a social guest for what any sensitive person must now realize was good reason.

Mr. Arnold certainly was sensitive. Evidently he could tell where her mind was, because he nudged her and whispered again, "Mrs. Lincoln, better pay attention," when Judge Wallace called for the first witness. Incredibly, she was actually on trial—she, Mary Lincoln, branded the "Republican Queen."

CHAPTER IV:

". . . and nothing but the truth . . ."

As he'd tried to tell Swett at the last minute, Isaac Arnold had no stomach for the job that had been thrust upon him, and he wished mightily that he were anywhere else in the world than Judge Wallace's courtroom in the Cook County Court house when Dr. Willis Danforth, brass buttons on his flowered vest winking in the gas lights, marched up to take the oath as the first witness against Mary Todd Lincoln. Arnold had little more notion of what Dr. Danforth and the other witnesses would say than did his client. But as an educated admirer of Leonard Swett's courtroom acumen, he could anticipate that it would be devastating. Swett was not in the habit of losing cases, and, although he hadn't seen Judge Davis's warning, Arnold was quite aware from his own knowledge of the high stakes involved in this one. Once accused, Mrs. Lincoln *had* to be convicted and confined or there would be no knowing how she might retaliate. It was as much—or more—in his, Arnold's, interest as in that of anyone else in the courtroom to have this case go "right," because he was making a living by keeping the

Lincoln image bright through speeches and books. Swett had cleverly, diabolically, used Arnold's vulnerability to maneuver him into this most uncomfortable spot.

When he'd been summoned rather mysteriously to the courthouse by Judge Wallace around noon, Arnold had had no idea in the world that Mrs. Lincoln was in this kind of trouble. He'd heard that she was back in Chicago, but she'd become such a recluse by her own choice after Tad's death that he hadn't tried to see her. He'd been content to quit visiting her because his presence always seemed to trigger her into going over again the painful details of that terrible Good Friday. It was understandable. He'd gone to the White House early that evening hoping to conduct some Congressional business and had run into the Lincolns getting into their carriage. "Excuse me, Arnold," the President said, "I am going to the theater. Come and see me in the morning." Mrs. Lincoln had been quite gay: "Oh, yes, do come back in the morning, Mr. Arnold; you'll find Mr. Lincoln as cheerful as ever he was in Springfield." Ever since, their visits had ended with her saying, "Oh, that he'd stayed to talk to you!" The image of the Lincolns smiling together as they'd climbed hand-in-hand into the carriage remained indelible and made the news that greeted him when he arrived at the courthouse all the more incredible.

It was explained to Arnold that Judge Wallace, determined not to give cause for criticism in his conduct of this particular case, wanted an attorney for Mrs. Lincoln who, like the jurors, would command public respect and who would also be perceived as an old and true friend of the defendant. Had he not already been on the other side, Swett might have qualified, but there was now literally no other lawyer in all of Chicago but Arnold who could meet the judge's requirements. Knowing the law as well as he did, Arnold had to appreciate the difficult spot they were all in. Some said it was the glory and others the shame of Illinois that no citizen of that state could be committed to a mental institution and/or forced to surrender his or her holdings to the control of a conservator without a public jury trial. In most other states, Robert could have taken care of all this quietly with nobody the wiser. But, given the law and in view of the testimony they would produce, they were sure that Arnold would see that the best defense any true friend of Mrs. Lincoln could give her would be the least defense in order to minimize the damage from public exposure. An open quarrel in court between mother and son, for instance, would just be playing into the hands of scandalmongers. They realized that they were asking him to assume a ticklish task, to be more of a diplomat than a defense counsel, but who else could they turn to? It wouldn't do to have Judge Wallace appoint one of the ambulance chasers hanging around the courthouse, would it?

Almost immediately after Arnold had given his reluctant assent, Swett had taken off to get Mrs. Lincoln. There'd been no time for preparation. The best he'd been able to do was to read the doctors' letters and to get a quick briefing from Robert on what he considered his mother's crazy shopping sprees and hallucinations. Arnold had noted that there were seventeen hostile witnesses on the court filing, and he'd been visited with the sickening feeling that the Mary Lincoln he'd meet in court wouldn't be the Mary Lincoln he'd known, that she *would* be insane. Not that he could blame her after what she'd been through. He could only thank the Lord that he hadn't added to her trials by falling for Herndon's romantic nonsense about Lincoln and some girl named Anne Rutledge. Becoming convinced that Mrs. Lincoln might have gone insane and had to be taken in hand for her own good had made it easier for Arnold to accept the role he was about to play in the abstract. But in the concrete—when he'd been confronted with Mary Lincoln in the flesh, when he'd seen that but for being pale and anxious she looked very like the woman he'd always liked—he'd choked on the prospect of posing as her protector. He would be lending himself to what could only be called a conspiracy, however well-intentioned, and he had to pray that Swett's case would be so strong that none of the sophisticated, cynical reporters out there would get it into their heads that there might have been a defense.

From this point of view Dr. Danforth made a compelling first witness. He looked prosperous and confident, and his firm voice carried to the back of the room as he swore to tell "the truth, the whole truth and nothing but the truth." He spoke warmly of Mrs. Lincoln as an old friend and patient. He said that he first visited her while she was living on Wabash Avenue in 1873. She was suffering from "nervous derangement and fever in the head," and he found her talk rather alarming. She told him that she thought that somebody or something was working on her head. This presence was taking wires out of her eyes, bones out of her cheeks and face, steel springs out of her jaw. She thought that it might be an Indian spirit . . .

Arnold heard Mary Lincoln snort and then whisper in his ear: "Stop the old fool. I was just telling him what it *felt* like. Haven't you ever had such a headache, Mr. Arnold? If that doctor had a sense of humor, he'd laugh. I used to tell Mr. Lincoln my head felt like one of those rails he was supposed to have split, and he would always laugh . . ." Judge Wallace was giving them one of his fiercest glares, and Arnold squeezed Mrs. Lincoln's hand and put a warning finger to his lips. Fortunately, she subsided.

Dr. Danforth said that he attributed these hallucinations about Indians to her physical condition at the time, since Mrs. Lincoln seemed to recover her sense with her health. But in March, 1874, he was called in again when she was suffering from general debility and complaining once more of wires being hauled from her head. He saw her almost daily for six months, and at times her condition was so grave that it was reported in the papers. Aside from her account of what was going on in her head, he found nothing unusual in her behavior until she told him that she knew the day of her death—September 6, 1874. This information was conveyed to her, she told the doctor, by means of taps on a table from her late husband, the President, who was in the spiritual world. Although Dr. Danforth knew that there were spiritualist seances in some of the best social circles of Chicago, he, as a man of science, did not believe in such nonsense and so expressed himself to Mrs. Lincoln. She thereupon consulted a goblet on the table as to whether she was right about her impending death. Nothing seemed to happen, but she picked it up, turned it in the light and then handed it to Dr. Danforth, saying, "I *am* right. See there—see how it's cracked."

Out in the courtroom audience somebody said in a tone loud enough to carry, "That's not all that was cracked," and there was a general titter. Judge Wallace rapped furiously. "Silence— or I'll clear this court," he said. Arnold stole a quick glance at Mary Lincoln. She seemed quite composed. Either she hadn't heard the disturbance or didn't care, nor did she seem disposed to challenge the doctor's story at this point.

In answer to a question by Ayer, Dr. Danforth said that he couldn't account for Mrs. Lincoln's belief that she was communicating with the spirit world on the grounds of physical ailments. In fact, she'd been so well that he'd stopped seeing her until a few weeks ago when he'd called on her at the Grand Pacific Hotel at her request. He'd thought it merely a social call because she'd talked quite sensibly and pleasantly about how much she enjoyed getting away from the Chicago cold and into all that sunshine in Florida. He'd been delighted to see her so well, and then suddenly she'd started telling him how some "rebels" had tried to poison her on her way home. She was thirsty, and she got off the train at a little station outside of Jacksonville and had a cup of coffee. It tasted bitter and didn't sit well, but she tried a second cup to make sure: it made her vomit. Dr. Danforth, however, couldn't detect any physical evidence of poisoning . . .

Mary Lincoln gripped Arnold's arm. "That was months ago, back in March, and I'd vomited it right up. Nobody knows up here, but there are people in the South who still hate my husband, and don't you remember, Mr. Arnold, how they tried to poison him in the White House through the coffee? Two servants got deathly ill . . ." Arnold pointed to the judge who was looking their way and said, "Ssssh." He didn't remember hearing of any incident of poisoning at the White House, but it was credible. In retrospect, the assassination itself shouldn't have been as much of a surprise as the fact that it hadn't happened earlier. They'd had to smuggle President-elect Lincoln through Baltimore in the dark of night to get him safely to Washington; they'd had to station sharpshooters on every cornice of the capitol during the inauguration to look out for members of the "rifle clubs" that Southern hotheads were organizing in Washington to train assassins; they'd had to supply a troop of cavalry to accompany his carriage after somebody put a bullet hole through Lincoln's stovepipe hat in that first summer when he'd been riding alone from the White House to the Soldier's Home. Yes, a little poison in the coffee was credible, and it could easily lead Mary Lincoln to believe that the murderous hatred that had brought down her husband had included her.

Dr. Danforth, winding up, said solemnly, "From my own experience and from what I've heard of her activities from others, I conclude that Mrs. Mary Lincoln is insane and is a fit subject for an asylum."

Here Arnold had to make his first hard decision, take his first risk of having Mary Lincoln see through him. He was going to let Dr. Danforth step down without cross-examination. He could rationalize that he was serving his client well because he'd found that tangling with the authority of a physician in front of a jury was a tricky business; people wanted to believe in their doctors. Besides, Dr. Danforth had not testified to anything too alarming—he had even called the things Mrs. Lincoln did "vagaries" at one point—and it might be best to leave it at that. The law required something much stronger—proof that a person was a threat to herself or others—to warrant a verdict of insanity. Arnold was marshalling these arguments for Mrs. Lincoln in case she objected to his silence, but he didn't need them.

Apparently shocked into her own silence by hearing herself publicly branded insane, she had no time to recover before she was shocked again by seeing Mr. Turner, whom she'd thought of as a friend or at least a respectful host, walk to the stand.

At first Mr. Turner talked as if he were her friend, as if the prosecution had called the wrong witness. He testified that Mrs. Lincoln looked perfectly well when she checked into his hotel on March 15. He hadn't seen much of her after that because she'd asked for her meals to be served in her room. Considering her age and station in life, he hadn't found it too strange when she also requested that a hotel employee sleep in her rooms because worry over her son's health made her nervous and wakeful. Rather impatiently, Ayer interrupted the flow of testimony to ask, "What about April first, Mr. Turner?"

Before he answered, Turner glanced briefly at Mary Lincoln, whose bright eyes were fixed on his face, and then looked quickly away as if embarrassed by what he had to tell. Early that morning Mrs. Lincoln's bell rang like an alarm in the office, and he sent a colored boy up on the run to investigate. Before the boy could have reached the room, he reappeared with Mrs. Lincoln, wearing a shawl over her undressed hair and carelessly attired, on his heels. She drew Mr. Turner aside into a reception room and told him that the whole south side of Chicago was ablaze. When he expressed doubts, she prevailed upon him to come to her room with her and look out the window. There was a pall of black smoke rolling from the stacks of a factory firing up, but he managed to convince her that it was harmless and thus quieted her down. When he started to leave, Mrs. Lincoln asked him to sit with her and leaned forward and told him confidentially that she'd heard a voice speaking through the wall and telling her that a Mr. Shoemaker wanted to meet her in Room 137, and she wanted a witness to go with her for the meeting. Mr. Turner told her that there was no Room 137 in the house but decided to humor her when she insisted that she could have been mistaken, that it could have been Room 127 or 107 or

27. After he took her around to these rooms and demonstrated that there was no Mr. Shoemaker, she expressed a fear of being alone, and he tried to leave her with Mrs. General Dodge, the only other female guest of comparable standing, but Mrs. Dodge was out, and he assigned a female servant to stay with Mrs. Lincoln in her own room. A few minutes later he was summoned again by her bell. When he arrived at the room she complained that there was a strange man in the hall seeking to do her harm, but he was able to show her that the hall was empty. There were no more calls that day, and the next day she was well enough to go out shopping which she did nearly every day, but since that April first it was "the prevailing opinion in the house that it was not safe for her to remain there alone."

This was very strong stuff, indeed, and Arnold kept expecting an outburst from his client. Instead, she listened quietly, intently, and leaned to him. "That was the day of my fever, Mr. Arnold," she said in a very low voice. "That was the day when I'm afraid I gave Robert a scare, too. I must have been quite out of my head."

This aroused Arnold's legal instincts. She'd raised a point on which he ought to challenge the witness just to get it into the record. It would look a little better to the press, too, if he made some show of defense. When Ayer turned the witness over to him, Arnold asked, "Did Mrs. Lincoln look as though she had any fever that day? Was she flushed?"

"No," Turner said. "Her face was as white as it is today. There was more an expression of fear than anything else about her—a fear of personal violence."

Arnold thought that he'd better let it go at that. He was beginning to admire in a professional way the selection and order of witnesses by Ayer and Swett as they next called Mrs. Harrington, the hotel housekeeper, to the stand. She would evidently nail down that "prevailing opinion" of the house. She didn't have anything very damning to say except that she considered Mrs. Lincoln "strange." She'd consented to sleep a few nights not only in the room but in the bed with Mrs. Lincoln when they couldn't get a maid. Mrs. Lincoln had complained of the little window in the water closet—"as if a body could ever climb through *that* from the outside"—and she'd mixed all the medicines Dr. Isham had left with her together and taken them in one dose. Although she didn't know what was in them, Mrs. Harrington had seen all those unopened packages from the stores that were piled up in Mrs. Lincoln's closet. Mrs. Lincoln didn't act like other ladies, according to Mrs. Harrington, and in her opinion was insane and ought to be put away somewhere for treatment.

At last Mary Lincoln had had more than she could bear in silence. She said aloud to the whole courtroom: "Is a person like *that* to be allowed to express an opinion as to *my* mental condition?"

"Mr. Arnold, please instruct the defendant as to the courtesies of the court," Judge Wallace said. "For the sake of the record and the instruction of the jury, I'll rule here and now, however, that such testimony is admissible as long as it is expressed as personal opinion."

Ayer proceeded to pour more of this personal opinion into the jury's mind through a quick succession of supporting witnesses from the hotel. The maid Mary Gavin, who often stayed in the room with Mrs. Lincoln, testified that her companion talked of hearing voices through the walls and floors, that she expressed fear that somebody was out to kill her, that she predicted the city would burn down again, that she worried about her son's health and walked the floor at night, that she went shopping once and sometimes twice a day—that she was, in short, insane. A waiter, John Fitzhenry, had the same feeling after he found Mrs. Lincoln out in the hall saying, "I'm afraid! I'm afraid!" when he came up to deliver her meal one day. Although she was scarcely dressed, she wanted him to take her down to "the tallest man in the dining room" who turned out to be Charles Dodge, the cashier. Called to the stand, Dodge corroborated Fitzhenry's story, adding that he had to accompany Mrs. Lincoln to her room, where she thought there was a strange man seeking to molest her.

Mrs. Lincoln listened to this parade of witnesses impassively. Sitting straight in her chair, she seemed to take some satisfaction out of staring them down; all of them looked everywhere but at her as they testified. She didn't suggest to Arnold that he challenge them, and he went gratefully along with her. By now he knew for sure that the most he could do for his client was to get this thing over quickly. It might still be possible to raise some doubts in the jury's mind that Mrs. Lincoln's eccentricities were harmful to herself or anybody else, but Arnold knew from Robert's briefing that they'd drive that point home through Robert's own testimony. They'd been clever to hold him until Mrs. Lincoln's odd behavior was established by supposedly impartial witnesses. Robert, as her son, would appear to the jury more victim than accuser when he took the stand.

Arnold couldn't quite figure out why they followed up the hotel testimony by calling a Mr. Stratton from the United States Express Company. He said that Mrs. Lincoln came to his office in a carriage on the 28th of April. She appeared very normal when she discussed arrangements for having some trunks sent to Milwaukee and stored there for her arrival in the summer. When he agreed that this could be done, she asked him to go back to the hotel with her and get the trunks. Stratton remembered that there were a lot of packages in the carriage, and it seemed to him that Mrs. Lincoln's manner changed as they approached the hotel, that she became quite excited. He was certain that something strange was going on when he discovered that there were *eleven* trunks. But she had the money to pay for what she wanted, and he went ahead and delivered them to storage in Milwaukee where he believed they were still resting.

Mary Lincoln's side comment to Arnold on this testimony was only: "Well, that's a comfort to know they're there. You know, I often go to Wisconsin in the summer—the air's much better . . ."

With that seemingly irrelevant bit of business out of the way, Ayer moved toward the heart of his case through Edward Isham, Robert Lincoln's law partner. Isham brought some papers with him to the stand. They were, he said, telegrams to him from Mrs. Lincoln in Florida, the first of which was dated March 12. Fishing glasses out of a breast pocket and putting them on, Isham read:

> "To Edward Isham, 554 Wabash Avenue: I am persuaded that my son is ill. Telegraph me without delay. I leave for Chicago as soon as I receive your telegram."

Isham testified that he went with this telegram to Robert's house at once and that, together, they went to a telegraph office and sent a message to reassure her that Robert was perfectly well and that there was no need for her to come to Chicago. Nevertheless, several similar messages from Mrs. Lincoln arrived and then there came one that made them worry about her mental state. Although addressed to Isham, it was intended for Robert. Isham put his spectacles back on and read again:

> "My dearly beloved son: Rouse yourself and live for my sake. From this moment all I have is yours. Live for your mother. Deliver without fail."

Mr. Lincoln was very upset when he saw that, according to Isham, and they enlisted the aid of the manager of the telegraph office in Chicago to get reports on Mrs. Lincoln's whereabouts and condition from the telegraph office managers in Jacksonville and points enroute to Chicago. Meanwhile, Isham received a last message from Mrs. Lincoln herself: "I start for Chicago tonight. You shall have money as soon as I arrive."

There was obviously no point in questioning testimony based on quotation from sheets torn from telegraph pads. Arnold just sat back to study the faces of mother and son as Robert Lincoln took his seat in the witness chair. Robert had a handkerchief in his hand with which he dabbed at the corners of his eyes; they were ashine with tears as he looked up briefly at his mother and down again. Mary Lincoln's clear eyes were dry. Her expression was hard to read, but Arnold thought that her whole attitude at this point suggested astonishment at what was happening to her rather than anger or sadness. Her eyes seemed to be asking Robert, "How can you *do* this to your mother?"

In a husky voice so low that the judge had to ask him to speak up, Robert started out by verifying what his partner had said. He couldn't imagine why his mother had thought he was ill since he hadn't been sick for ten years. The only rational explanation might be that she'd seen an erroneous paragraph in the paper. As he said this, Robert raised his voice and seemed to direct himself to the reporters as if to serve notice of the damage that they could do to a woman like Mrs. Lincoln with false reports. As for her concern about money, Robert said that his mother knew very well that he wasn't in need of money, that, in fact, he held money in trust for her. Just before she'd started telegraphing he'd sent her $375 for her expenses in Florida. His mother had been very generous with him, he told the jury, which made the duty he now felt obliged to perform doubly unpleasant. At this, Robert had to use his handkerchief again to blow his nose, and Arnold detected a slight shiny film on Mrs. Lincoln's eyes.

Robert then launched into an account of his mother's behavior in the last two months. He tried to make it as factual and unemotional as he could. From time to time, however, he'd pause in an apparent effort to regain control over himself, keep his voice steady. Arnold couldn't help thinking rather cynically that it was a good act, the kind he'd always hoped for from a witness in a jury case. More to give Mrs. Lincoln confidence that he was looking after her interests than for any practical use, Arnold made notes as Robert Lincoln talked:

—Says that, thinking him ill, mother surprised when he meets her on the cars. She's tired, having ridden 72 hours, and he wants to take her to his home. She won't go, says she's made arrangements to stay at Grand Pacific. He collects her baggage and goes with her to the hotel where she asks him to stay to supper and then stay the night as her guest in an adjoining room. Reason is that she's very nervous and afraid. Although she'd seemed normal when he met her on the train, she tells him at supper that somebody tried to poison her coffee at the first breakfast she took after leaving Jacksonville. Wife being out of town, he agrees to stay at hotel.

—Mother sleeps well that night. But the next night and several nights after she comes to his room in her nightdress and knocks on the door. He tries to get her to calm down and sleep in her own room but one night he has to admit her twice, letting her use his bed while he lies down on the couch. After that, he asks Dr. Isham, his own doctor and partner's nephew, to attend her, and gets his mother to stay in her own room by threatening to leave the hotel if she doesn't. In about a week, having made arrangements for hotel servants to stay with his mother, he feels confident in going home.

—Wants to emphasize that concern about mother never leaves him. Stops in to see her on way to work the morning of April first. Finds her half-dressed and trying to go down the elevator to see Mr. Turner. Stops the elevator and she accuses him of being impertinent. He steps in and puts his arms around her gently to force her out and back to her room. She screams, "You

are going to murder me." With help of Mary Gavin
finally does get her back to her room, where she talks
about her purse being stolen and hearing voices
through the walls, but he thinks she's calmed down
when he has to leave her. The jury has already heard
about the rest of that day.

—Goes into the shopping business referred to in previous testimony about packages in mother's closet. Not
sure what all is in them but does know she bought $600
worth of lace curtains; three watches at a total cost of
$450; $700 worth of other jewelry; $200 worth of soaps
and perfumes; a whole piece of silk. Mother has no
need for any of this. Hasn't worn anything but black
since his father's death, never wears jewelry, has no
home in which to hang curtains, already has trunks—
at least eleven, as they've heard—full of dresses she
never wears. Says he's managed to get storekeepers to
take some of this back behind mother's back but worries she'll spend all her money.

—Comes now to the crucial point: fear of fire. Says that
although mother missed fire in '71 by being out of city
she put all of her trunks and securities in Fidelity Safe
Deposit Company's building to protect them. One
morning toward end of April mother comes rushing
into his office all excited about fire. She says all Chicago
is going to burn again except his house. She tells him
she's shipped her trunks to Milwaukee. Thinking to
persuade her into bringing them back, he argues that
Milwaukee is too close to Oshkosh which has just
burned down so why not put them in his house if it's
to be saved? She won't agree. A few days later, on a
Sunday when he visits, she shows him a pocket sewed
to her petticoat and says all of her securities—$57,000
worth—are in there if she has to run from fire. Feels
now that his mother is truly insane and talks to doctors

who say fear of fire can cause a person to jump out of window. Talks to Judge Davis of the Supreme Court and cousin John Stuart, mayor of Springfield, who advise this course. In his opinion mother's mind never right since tragic death of father and increasingly deranged since brother's death four years ago . . .

At this point, Arnold stopped taking notes to put a comforting hand on Mary Lincoln who was finally overcome. She drew her veil across her face for some protection from the roomful of eyes focused on her, put her head in her hands and wept. Robert was busy with his handkerchief, too, and a few of the members of the jury and quite a few of the spectators, particularly the women, were blowing noses and wiping eyes. Ayer could probably have let it end there, but he wanted to drive home the necessary legal point the way a good carpenter sets a nail.

"Do you regard it safe, Mr. Lincoln," he asked, "to allow your mother to remain as she is, unrestrained?"

"She has long been a source of much anxiety to me," Robert started to say and then had to pause to wipe away tears. "I do not think it would be safe or proper. In fact, I have had a man from the Pinkerton agency watching her for the last three weeks, whose sole duty was to watch after her when she went on the street. She knew nothing about it . . ."

Although moved himself by the anguish that both mother and son were now displaying, the part of Arnold's mind trained to stay alert in court kept functioning. He scribbled a note on this, as the witness continued.

". . . She has no home, and she does not visit at my house because of a misunderstanding with my wife. Although she has always been exceeding kind to me, my mother has really been irresponsible for the last ten years. She has been eccentric and unmanageable and never heeds my advice . . ."

Robert started to break down again, and Ayer said, "Thank you, Mr. Lincoln; that will be all."

Although Mrs. Lincoln was also still sniffling, Arnold took another look at his last note and leaned close to her. "Did you know you had Pinkertons watching you, Mrs. Lincoln?" he asked. She shook her head but then whispered back, "I did know there were men following me, but I didn't know who they were. Robert and Mr. Turner said I was imagining things . . ."

Arnold sat back and wondered what he should do with that. He hadn't made any sign that he wanted to cross-examine, and Robert Lincoln was leaving the stand. Surely, the jury had heard what he'd heard, but in any other case he'd have been sure to emphasize it by asking the witness to repeat it. That's how you raised what they called "reasonable doubts." Much of the damning testimony had to do with Mrs. Lincoln's seeing and hearing things that supposedly weren't there. If, as it now developed, there had actually been men spying on her, might there not be some rational basis for her other delusions, such as the coffee poisoning at the White House? Now that he was thinking along those lines, Arnold recalled that there'd been a very traumatic incident when the White House stables burned down. Mrs. Lincoln had watched the engulfing flames from her window, had heard the horses, among them her sons' ponies, screaming in their last agony. There'd been rumors then that her mind had been adversely affected because she'd had to go away for a while to recover from the shock. The thought of Robert's putting spies on his mother was chilling to Arnold, and he had a great urge to start asking questions just to make the young man squirm. But wasn't this the very point of decision where everybody *but* his client was counting on his good judgment? He had to acknowledge that the case in general was every bit as overwhelming as he'd expected it to be and that challenging Robert Lincoln now, with both mother and son in touchy emotional states, could result in the sort of explosion that would do nobody any lasting good. Although Arnold was beginning to think that Robert might have had a hand in driving his mother insane, he, for one, was now convinced by the testimony that she *was* insane, and he didn't want the responsibility on his shoulders of persuading the jury to decide otherwise. It was a comforting conclusion. So, silently, he watched Robert Lincoln come back and take that seat on the other side of Mrs. Lincoln—so near and yet so far away from his mother.

What little fight Mrs. Lincoln might have had in her seemed drained away by the experience of hearing her son reveal to the world the awful thoughts he'd had about her. Her own weeping subsided, and she sat like a stone while a number of store clerks stepped up to support Robert's testimony about her purchases, and four more doctors—Isham, Davis, Johnson and Smith— testified in a kind of repetitious litany that they considered her insane and in need of confinement for her own protection. Listening to the doctors, Arnold decided that there was, after all, something that he might do for his client's lasting good. In order to have the testimony he hoped to get linger more in the minds of the press than the jury, he waited until the last of them, Dr. Smith, was about to step down and then asked, "To what do you attribute the fact that, as you say, Mrs. Lincoln is not of sound mind?"

"To the events of her recent past," Dr. Smith said. "I was with her at the time of Tad's death, you know, and I was afraid then that, coming on top of all the other deaths in her family, it might be more than a mortal could bear. So it has proved to be."

"Thank you, Dr. Smith," Arnold said.

Surprisingly Robert Lincoln was recalled, but it was only to allow his attorneys to insert some necessary information into the record that Arnold would have been glad to stipulate on Mrs. Lincoln's behalf. Robert stated that there was no hereditary insanity in his mother's family and that she was fifty-six years old. When he sat down again Ayer joined him, and Leonard Swett arose. He told the jury that he wanted to express on behalf of the petitioner and of himself as a representative of the many friends and admirers of the martyred president the almost unutterable sadness with which this action had been undertaken. It was done because it was the only way under the statutes of the state of Illinois that the life and property of the tragically widowed Mrs. Lincoln could be protected. Although he was supposedly addressing the jury, Swett turned away from them and faced the press when he went on to say that he was happy that Mr. Arnold had elicited medical opinion in support of what all who were intimate with the Lincoln family knew— that Mrs. Lincoln, never a strong woman, was the innocent victim of the terrible accidents of her life. "As it has been the very disagreeable duty of Mr. Ayer and myself and especially of Mr. Robert Lincoln to bring this action before you," he concluded, "it is your duty as members of the jury to find Mrs. Mary Lincoln insane."

Taking another long risk of having his client volubly complain, Arnold signalled that he had nothing to say to the jury; in a way, Swett had said it all. When the jury filed out of the room, Robert turned to his mother and held out his hand. She took it, but as she did, she said quite loudly, "Robert, I did not think you would do this." Out of the corner of his eye Arnold saw that the reporters, hanging over the rail to catch whatever they could, were noting down those words, and he took some satisfaction in knowing that they'd go around the world. In the last three hours, Arnold had come to the conclusion that he finally could agree with Billy Herndon about one thing: he didn't much like Robert Lincoln, a young man who'd always appeared to have his nose in the air. Tears or no, it was very hard to decide how sincere Robert was in his concern for his mother's safety, but it was all too easy to tell that she'd become an embarrassment and a burden to him and that he was most eager to dump her on the state. There was a whine in his complaint that his mother wouldn't heed his advice and a weakness in what amounted to an admission that he couldn't control his wife any more than he could control his mother. Well, Herndon would say that Mary Lincoln was getting exactly what she deserved for making spoiled brats out of her boys, and Arnold would have to concede that there might be some truth in that, too. At the moment, though, Robert did seem to be struggling with some genuine guilt, choking up too much to respond to his mother. Swett took over smoothly and said, "As I've told you, Mrs. Lincoln, it was for your own good." She shook her head and said again with enough emphasis to carry to the ears of the press, "What do you know of *my* good? It's only for your good. But I shall try to bear my persecutions."

Within the few minutes that this conversation took place, the jury concluded its deliberations and tramped back into the room. From a paper he held in a slightly trembling hand, Foreman Gage read aloud a verdict that had obviously been prepared in advance:

"We, the undersigned, jurors in the case of Mary Lincoln alleged to be insane, having heard the evidence in the case, are satisfied that the said Mary Lincoln is insane, and is a fit person to be sent to a State Hospital for the Insane; that she is a resident of the State of Illinois, and County of Cook; that her age is fifty-six years; that the disease is of unknown duration; that the cause is unknown; that the disease is not with her hereditary; that she is not subject to epilepsy; that she does not manifest homicidal or suicidal tendencies, and that she is not a pauper."

Arnold thought that Mary Lincoln exhibited considerable sanity in the stoical way she accepted this verdict. In fact, she didn't even listen while Gage raced through the formal wording. Instead, she whispered to Arnold with a strange emphasis on one word, "Thank you for *appearing* for me, Mr. Arnold. I'm sensible that there was little you could do against Robert's plot . . ." In that, too, she was so right—so sane. For the sake of his own reputation, Arnold hoped that those reporters who were already running for the door would see it that way, too. He was ashamed of the relief he felt in knowing that the trial was over for him, because he was certain that it was only beginning for Mary Lincoln.

CHAPTER V:

"A noble & devoted son . . ."

NEVER, IT IS safe to say, in all of the testings to which she had been subjected by life, had Mary Lincoln felt so desolate, or desperate, as she did in the gathering dark of that May afternoon when she found herself pinned between Leonard Swett and Isaac Arnold in a carriage headed for the Grand Pacific Hotel. In the four hours since she had left the hotel in that same carriage she had been shorn of all dignity in the glare of a crowded Cook County courtroom. By morning, through the columns of the newspapers, the whole world would be told that the once "Republican queen" was an aging, ailing lunatic. Worst of all, nobody would really care. The one person in all the world who should care, who should share her shame—her son, Robert— was, in fact, the one person responsible for this afternoon's dreadful work. She had had to come to grips with this bleak reality while she listened to him relate from the witness stand the most shocking and private details of their relationship. Now, the very presence of these men, sitting in silent embarrassment beside her, must have been forcing her to reach the only conclusion that made any sense about Robert's reason for his action: greed.

Thank God, she had been left with enough wits about her after the trial to keep *him* from getting her securities. After Robert and Swett had gone up and conferred with that hawk-eyed Democrat of a judge who probably enjoyed getting even with Mr. Lincoln, Swett had come over to her purring like a satisfied cat and said, "I have good news for you, Mrs. Lincoln. Judge Wallace has agreed that you can go to Dr. Patterson's private asylum in Batavia instead of a state institution. Robert will make the arrangements and take you there in the morning. Now, the judge suggests that you give your securities to Robert . . ."

She had had the gumption to say, "Never. You've heard that he could have had all I own, but not now. I won't give them to *him*—"

"The court insists, Mrs. Lincoln. He can order them taken from you by force," Swett said.

"Right here?"

"Yes. Why don't you give them to your counsel, Mr. Arnold?"

"Here? Will you—will you and my son—leave me without a shred of self respect, Mr. Swett? They are in a pocket sewed to my undergarments. At least grant me the favor of removing them in the privacy of my room."

Swett had shrugged, gone to the bench to confer with Robert and the judge, come back to ask, "Will you give them to Robert there at the hotel?"

"No, I don't want him with me."

"All right," Swett had said. "I'll go with you. You, too, Arnold. I want you there as witness."

She had thought that Mr. Arnold looked sad when, just as he was saying goodbye, he had been pressed into this new duty. Maybe he was one person who did care although he had made no real effort to defend her. Not that it would have done any good. The cards had been stacked against her, as a gambler would say, by her greedy and treacherous son, and the only thing that truly worried her about her mental condition was that she had not been canny enough to catch him at it. Like those garish lights in that courtroom, today's events washed out all the soft shadows of wishful thinking with which she had surrounded Robert's image, and she now had to put up with the hurt of seeing him clearly, of looking steadily at past words and actions that were chillingly revealing in this new light.

Money was the root of the evil here. She had heard that Robert for years went around saying behind her back that she was sane on every subject but money. He had even written that to Mary Harlan before they were married, and the girl had been so tactless as to quote Robert's letter when they were having a little tiff about the clothes she had sent over from Europe for Mamie. But was it not Robert who was strange about money? He wanted all he could get of it, took everything she gave him, but dirtying his hands to make it or hold on to it was, it seemed, beneath him. It was probably her fault—hers and Mr. Lincoln's—for spoiling him. Robert hadn't known the hard times. He'd been much too small to remember the cramped quarters in the Globe Tavern where they'd been living when he was born because the four dollars a week board there was all that they could afford while Mr. Lincoln was paying off his New Salem debts. She doubted that Robert would even remember the Eighth Avenue place before they raised the roof and put a second story on it. By the time money mattered to Robert, Mr. Lincoln was making good fees from the railroads and there was nothing that they had to deny him. Mr. Lincoln always took the position that he didn't want to put his sons through what he'd had to go through in grubbing for money, but he'd said an odd thing when Robert proposed going to Harvard Law School: "If you do, you should learn more than I ever did, but you will never have so good a time."

Trying to get to the bottom of this money business through sorting memories, Mary suddenly caught for the first time the real meaning of that remark. Mr. Lincoln always said that he'd learned the law by the variety of practice he got on the circuit, and on the circuit he did have a very good time by all accounts. Back then when she was left at home with a houseful of boys and spending her time scrubbing, mending, feeding, nursing, often without a competent hired girl to help, she hadn't always appreciated the accounts of high-jinks on the circuit. One that was told to her by Hill Lamon she surely found particularly galling since she was sitting there at the time sewing patches on Robert's jeans for lack of money to buy new ones.

Mary couldn't recall all the details of the incident but it had to do with a time when Mr. Lincoln and Lamon had a partnership to practice in Vermillion County. A client had paid Lamon $250 for winning a case before Judge Davis. Since the court appearance had taken only twenty minutes, Lincoln considered the fee excessive and argued Lamon into returning half of it, even though the client was satisfied. Overhearing the argument between Lincoln and Lamon, the other lawyers and the judge sided with Lamon. Lincoln was summoned to the bench, where Judge Davis told him, "Lincoln, you are impoverishing this bar by your picayune charges of fees. You are now almost as poor as Lazarus and if you don't make people pay you more for your services you will die as poor as Job's turkey." That night in his room at the tavern in Danville, Judge Davis set up what he dubbed an "Orgmathorial Court" and held a mock trial in which Lincoln was found guilty of ruining his profession and was ordered to pay a fine.

Lamon no doubt thought that he was doing Mr. Lincoln a favor by telling a story that would make Mary proud of her husband's generous nature. But Lamon didn't have to live with that generosity, and it was almost more than Mary could bear when Mr. Lincoln insisted on splitting every fee right down the middle with his Springfield partner, Billy Herndon. All Herndon did, at least as far as she could tell, was hang about the office and look up law and keep the books while Mr. Lincoln went out on the circuit and brought in the business. But Mr. Lincoln could be stubborn, and there was no arguing with him about how he handled his money. If he wasn't very interested in earning money he also wasn't very interested in spending it. Surprisingly for one who had been so poor, money really meant little to him. As Lamon said of him, "Mr. Lincoln did not think money for its own sake a fit object of any man's ambition." When you had the kind of appreciation of nice things she had acquired growing up in the household of a wealthy Lexington banker, a nature so noble with respect to money could be hard to take at times. It would, in fact, have been impossible had Mr. Lincoln not been as generous with her as he was with others. He gave her as much as he could spare and went around quietly paying up the bills she had sometimes run up when there wasn't anything to spare. Although she had never felt really deprived, she had never been sure of how much money would be coming in, or how much she would get of it, and money per se became meaningless to her, too. She turned what money she did get into her hands into tangible assets that she could appreciate and enjoy and tuck away against a day when Mr. Lincoln might finally overdo his "generosity" and leave them destitute.

Although that possibility seemed to have been wiped out by Mr. Lincoln's elevation to the presidency, her feelings about the uses of money did not change. It was to be spent for things of real value. A salary of $25,000 was probably five times more than Mr. Lincoln had ever made in any year, and she could not imagine that there would be need to think about money itself. The need, instead, was to demonstrate through what she could buy and display on their persons and in their dwelling the fact that she and Mr. Lincoln had the taste and discrimination to belong among the leaders of the world. In the wake of the assassination, people conveniently forgot how the rail-splitting image that was exploited to get the country votes had been turned against them in the cities of the East, and particularly in Washington. Even Stanton who would later become his Secretary of War was widely quoted as calling Mr. Lincoln an "ape." Whatever else could be said of her, she changed that image. If she sometimes came back from her New York shopping trips with more gloves and shoes and scarves than it would seem that one woman could ever use, it had to be remembered that she often changed clothes several times a day for different functions and that the big merchants like A.T. Stewart were always pressing things upon her to have it said that they supplied the White House. What the public did not know, what even her family did not appreciate, was that she put a lot of care into her shopping. Just because it was there, she didn't throw money around. Even in the smallest things, she insisted on getting her money's worth, and there were letters to prove that, like the ones from the White House that she wrote to Ruth Harris who made her bonnets.

"Dec 11th, 1864

My Dear Madame,
    Your last note has been received—I sent the velvet—which you will doubtless receive today—I did not wish *any lace* on the outside—therefore the bonnet must cost but $25.00 which is more than I had expected to pay for a bonnet—furnishing the velvet myself—the feather must be long & beautiful—lace trimmings *very* rich & full; the outside you can arrange to your taste—
    You can certainly procure black velvet ribbon—of the shade of the velvet of the bonnet—for strings—a finger length wide—very rich. I saw some in New York when there—I do not think the edge *inserted* on the ribbon would look well. Q'en pensez-vous? It is a bonnet for *grand occasions* & I want it to be particularly stylish & rich. Very especially, blk velvet is so *expensive,* do not fail to turn in the sides of the front, more than an inch of course, it will some day, have to undergo, a

new foundation—I am sure, you will not fail me in this. Another favor, I have to request. Can you have my bonnet, sent me Express, on Monday next, leaving N.Y. on that day, and will you, send down to Tiffany & Co—for a blk velvet headdress, which he has as a measure, & enclose with the bonnet. Some of the narrow blk velvet ribbon, which you sent as a sample, with white edge, would look well, on one side of the front trimming. My strings must be one yard long each—*Do* have my bonnet got up in exquisite taste.

Very sincerely your friend
Mary Lincoln"

"Washington, Dec 28th, 1864

Madame Harris—

I can neither wear, or settle with you, for my bonnet without different inside flowers—As to inside flowers of black & white, I saw some beautifully fine ones, in two or three different establishments, in N.Y.—By going out, for them, you can procure them—I need to wear my blk velvet bonnet on Wednesday next. Do send me the flowers—By a little search you can procure them—I cannot retain or wear the bonnet, as it is—I am certainly taught a lesson, by your acting thus

I remain &
Mrs Lincoln"

Of course, such was the sort of female business she would never talk to Mr. Lincoln or the boys about, and possibly it was too much to expect Robert to have any understanding of the care and concern she devoted to what he thought of as useless geegaws. She could well remember the first time that Robert displayed his uncomprehending, unfeeling attitude about what mattered to her, because it happened at a time when she most needed support. She and Keckley were packing her things in boxes to leave the White House and Robert wandered into the room, picked up a garment and asked, "What are you going to do with that old dress, mother?"

"Never mind, Robert," she told him. "I will find a use for it. You do not understand this business."

"And what is more, I hope I never may understand it. I wish to heaven the car would take fire in which you place these boxes for transportation to Chicago, and burn all of your old plunder up."

Robert was as unkind as the press. In all, she took some sixty boxes with her to Chicago, and they wrote that she had stolen White House furniture and fixtures that had been bought with public funds. What they did not know was that the servants had been vandalizing the place during the month that President Johnson had let her stay in the house while she was too sick with grief to function, and she would have to thank Keckley for setting *that* straight in her book. What nobody in the world but Keckley and some store owners knew was that she *had* to hang on to those personal belongings since many of them weren't paid for. Even then, she'd had the thought that she might return some or sell some to settle her debts. Keckley thought that she owed $70,000, but, what with some charges "forgiven" and some others taken care of by the few true friends, it had not come to more than a third of that. Still, that debt she had counted on being absorbed through Mr. Lincoln's generosity during the second term loomed larger than all of the compensation granted by Congress to their fallen Commander-in-Chief—namely, the balance of his 1865 salary less income tax, or about $22,000.

As soon as she could bring herself to realize that Mr. Lincoln had really left her, worry about money made black her days and white her nights. Death revealed Mr. Lincoln's true disregard for money. Not only had he died intestate, as so many lawyers did, but there were uncashed pay vouchers crammed into the drawers of his White House desk. Nevertheless, after going through Mr. Lincoln's papers and accounts, Judge Davis assured her that her husband had been surprisingly thrifty and had bought enough solid 1881 bonds to provide an income for her and the boys. It was inconvenient in that the estate would have to be divided three ways, but if they stuck together and pooled their resources they could survive. What was immediately clear to her from the preliminary figures that the judge revealed was that her third of the estate would not cover her debts, and that if she did expend it for that purpose she would be left destitute. As she'd kept them secret from her husband, she was determined to keep her debts secret from his surrogate, Judge Davis, who might talk carelessly in Washington, and from her boys, who had enough to deal with in losing their father. She would pay them off herself, but to do so she simply had to become "insane," in Robert's terms, on the subject of money.

With far from insane logic, she felt that the only lasting solution to her financial problems was to get more money from somewhere. Because Robert at twenty-two was just getting started in the law and Tad at twelve was just getting started on an education largely neglected in view of his speech impediment and the more pressing problems of a wartime presidency, she could not look to them for help. Although well educated and well read for a woman of her time, she had had no employment other than as wife and mother, a function she still had to perform for Tad. Since she was sure that there would have been enough money to justify her spending had Mr. Lincoln lived, she felt entitled to go after the money lost through what she saw as his death in the line of duty. So once she was settled in Chicago she spent most of her days writing letters to anyone and everyone she had known who might persuade Congress to act on her behalf, meanwhile employing Alexander Williamson, who had been tutor to her boys in the White House, as a kind of secret agent to try to minimize or defer her outstanding obligations. It was hard work involving a great deal of emotional expenditure, and she dirtied her hands at it by staining them with spilled ink.

That December of '65, when families that were still whole were celebrating Christmas, was particularly difficult for· her, and she tried to cope with her worries and sorrows by sticking to her desk. One typical letter was to Elihu B. Washburne, a Congressman who was one of Mr. Lincoln's closest political friends. She showed him that she had done her homework by alluding to what had happened in the case of William Henry Harrison, whose family was given only the remainder of one year's salary when he died in office.

"Chicago—Dec 15, 1865

My dear Sir:

I see by the papers, that your Committee, in reference, to our affairs meets next Monday—May I urge you, in view, of the necessities of your case *insist* upon the *four years salary* & have the tax removed from it— The $10,000—off—the 4 years salary, would be a great deal to us, who have a home to obtain, furniture & need the interest to live on—It will be small enough & I shall have to exercise much economy with *that*—If a *grateful* American people—only give us the $25,000—our portion, is a boarding house forever—a *fitting* place, for the wife & sons, of the man—who served his country so well & lost his life in consequence—Those false friends—who urge—the Harrison *precedent*—*he*—Pres —for *one month*, will perhaps place it on the ground, that it would be an improper example—Perhaps, never in history, will such a case, again occur as ours—therefore there is *no* parallel—to our case. Every day, as you see, *is* strengthening the opposition, will you not relieve my mind, at least, of this small portion of its burden—by settling it in both houses of Congress—

before next Wednesday morning—*after that,* believe me, most truly, there will be, no chance, for us—In the excitement of dispersing, before the holidays—It would undoubtedly pass & prevent *further* opposition to us—which *it is well known,* is going on, *from those,* who should be *our* friends. I will rely on yourself and Mr. Wentworth, to have this carried before Christmas, also the tax removed—which will be, a great consideration. I see that an app- bill—was passed for W. (White) H. (House) of $50,000—Why cannot *ours,* be then urged, before others come up—to kill ours off—Please see to this—dear Mr Washburne

> I remain very truly
> Mary Lincoln"

After a bleak Christmas with no action as a result of her Washburne letter, she moved ahead on the other half of her plan by writing to Alexander Williamson in Washington:

> "Chicago—Dec 26th, 1865

My dear Sir:

Will you go, PRIVATELY & kindly to Mr Galt—and ask him, if there *is,* any thing on my bill, he would allow me to return. *He* has always treated me, as a gentleman—I would willingly return—the gold ear rings & breast pin—with grecian pattern—the two gilt clocks—many little things—if *he* says *so*—if you choose, show him this note—I would not inconvenience, Mr Galt, for he has been very patient—but, in my great trouble—he will not be unmindful—It is most singular—Lizzie K. (Keckley) does not send, the articles she has of mine—plenty of opportunities occur—Without any delay, fail not, to send me the bills when Con- gives me the money, which of course will be very soon, I will settle—Say this to Mr G- & *all* parties. Judge D- (Davis) has nothing, to do, in the matter—Your silence, is very remarkable, at this time.

Your friend Sincerely—
Mrs A.L."

A few days later she revealed all of her feelings—except her anxiety about her secret debts—to one of her best Washington friends, Mary Jane Welles, possibly with the hope that some of it would reach the administration through her husband, Secretary of the Navy Welles, who had stayed in the cabinet. She had never entertained a thought of approaching President Johnson directly. Because of his being drunk at Mr. Lincoln's inaugural, she considered him an inebriate, and the fact that he had not called upon her or even sent her a letter of condolence since the assassination suggested his insensitivity. Johnson's neglect had to be compared in her mind unfavorably with the concern of Queen Victoria of England who had written a personal letter freighted with the kind of sympathy that only another widow of a much beloved husband could have. One reason that she could open herself up to Mary Jane Welles was that her own loss of a son had made her especially supportive when Willie died.

"Chicago Dec 29th, 1865

My dear Mrs Welles—
Your last very kind sympathizing letter is received: How well assured, I am, from your past appreciation, of our overwhelming griefs, that you were pained, with the recent decision of Congress—which leaves us, forever without a home—In reality, we are only given $20,000, one month's salary, had been paid, my darling

husband, and the tax of $2500—will be deducted, from
the remainder. The $20,000—will not be sufficient
here, to procure us a home—besides we would require,
to have it furnished, and means to keep it up—What a
future before us—The wife & sons, of the Martyr President, *compelled* to be inmates of boarding houses, all
their lives. I am bowed with humiliation at the thought
—how much *such* a thought would have pained my
beloved husband, who, last March, expressly told me,
that he did not intend using a cent, of his next four
years salary, as we had every thing handsome we required—he intended living on what we had and re-
serve, his means, for a handsome home. One block from
the warehouse, where our goods are stored—was burnt
to the ground, a week since—and we are in daily fear,
that what little, we have, may share the same fate. The
precious relics, belonging to my husband, are a contin-
ual source of anxiety to me—Yet I *had anticipated* we
would soon, have *had,* a place, to put them—but alas!
my hopes, like everything else, that is pleasant, has
vanished—each morning as I awaken from my troubled sleep, I wonder—if it can be true—that after my
noble husband's services to his Country & dying in its
cause—all this great sacrifice, is ignored. We, without
him, our all, are forever to dwell, as we *now* are doing,
Living Monuments of a Nation's ingratitude! Without
a home to shelter us, we, of course, are bound, to no
particular spot, to keep together the few of us, who are
left, was, one, of my cherished wishes—A visit to
Springfield & the Cemetery—where my beloved ones
rest, last week—convinced me, that the further
removed, I am, the better, it will be, for *my reason,* from
that spot. I am now sitting up, the first day since my
return, I am almost too miserable to live—Three days

of each week, almost, I am incapable of any exertion, on account of my severe headaches—Our physician says, I must go, out more, in the open air—As I have become known here, and my deep mourning, is very conspicuous, as the interest, of $20,000, is only $1500- All I can do with it is to procure a carriage—and *this* interest will keep it up. Besides—the sum, so generously bestowed upon us, by a *grateful* nation, we each, have $1800- to live upon. In what way, could I convert *that* sum—into a house—This is certainly, not an age of miracles, I consider that so far, as our poor afflicted family is concerned, the close of the year 1865 with the *indignity,* to say the least, thrust upon us by this *great nation,* is very well worthy, of the dark deeds, that have been committed—Sir Morton Peto—in return for the *polite civilities* of his American friends gave them a dinner in N.Y. costing $25,000. The councils of our Nation—deny, the family of the man, who lost his life in their cause—a home. I was pained to learn that Senator Morgan, quoted the 'Harrison-precedent,' he a president, for a month—his family with an elegant place, on the Ohio—my husband—gave up, everything connected with himself—gave his all—to his Country—I bow my head in deep sorrow that, broken hearted, as I am, we are thus left, without shelter, to return to— in our grief.

Please burn this, for I have written in the bitterness of my sad heart."

In the new light, she could see so clearly how little help Robert had been during these early trials. She had excused him then because of his youth, because of his own loss. On the very day that they had moved into their lodgings at Hyde Park because she had found the downtown hotel they had come to from the White House too expensive, Robert had let his feelings be known in no uncertain terms. After he had finished unpacking his books with Lizzie Keckley's help he had asked her, "Well, Mrs. Keckley, how do you like our new quarters?"

Always the diplomat, Lizzie had said, "This is a delightful place, and I think you will pass your time pleasantly."

But Robert had thought otherwise: "You call it a delightful place! Well, perhaps it is. Since you do not have to stay here, you can safely say as much about the charming situation as you please. I presume that I must put up with it, as mother's pleasure must be consulted before my own. But candidly, I would almost as soon be dead as be compelled to remain three months in this dreary house."

Mary had overheard that exchange and had wept with frustration at being so powerless to make her son happy. Not long after that Robert, presumably with the connivance of Judge Davis, moved out to apartments of his own on the grounds that he had to learn to be independent. What that did was force more economies on Mary and Tad since he took with him a third of the available income. In a vain effort to get him back by providing quarters he would consider suitable to his station she further postponed and juggled the debts that kept her writhing with anxiety when she should have been sleeping and put most of the $20,000 in salary that Congress did give her into the purchase of a house on fashionable Washington Street. It didn't work. Robert didn't come back and, with only her and Tad's income, Mary couldn't afford enough coal to heat the house, as she had written to this double-crossing Swett, who was now riding beside her to make sure that Robert finally got it all. So she had rented the house and tried to sell her clothes to let Robert go on living as he liked—and what thanks did she get? An insanity trial, branding *her* overly concerned about money.

At the time she had been so depressed, so shattered by the way she was being attacked in the press, so hurt by Robert's reaction that she had not really seen the cold-blooded calculation behind what he and Judge Davis did to her. In the midst of the publicity about the clothes sales they announced in the press the final distribution of Mr. Lincoln's estate. As it appeared in the Springfield *Journal* in that fall of '67 and was reprinted in the New York *Times*, the announcement read:

> "Hon. David Davis, administrator of the estate of the late President Lincoln, made a final settlement of the estate with Hon. William Prescott, Judge of the County Court of Sangamon County, on Wednesday last. After paying all debts and expenses, there remains to be divided among the heirs the sum of $110,295.90. Of this amount Mrs. Lincoln receives $36,765.30, Robert T. Lincoln and Thomas Lincoln each the same amount. It is a remarkable fact that the total amount of Mr. Lincoln's indebtedness, at the time of his death, as per schedule filed in the County Clerk's office, was only $10.81.
>
> Since the death of the President, Mrs. Lincoln has received from the estate $4,085.51, Robert Lincoln $7,300.15, and Thomas Lincoln $1,096.54.
>
> We learn that Judge Davis, who was a warm personal friend of the lamented President, made no charges for his services in the settlement of the estate."

It had given Mary some little pride to realize that keeping her debts to herself had allowed for another nice touch of color on Mr. Lincoln's image of frugal honesty. It had startled her a bit, even though she had known that Robert was forever after Judge Davis for money, to find that he had taken nearly twice what she had out of the estate. She had been put off by Judge Davis' using that announcement for a pat on his own back, but she could understand it better now that he had come out from behind his black robes and showed his true colors as a politician in trying

to get the Liberal Republican nomination for president in '72.
What she could not understand to this day was why her nephew,
Edward Baker, Lizzie Edwards' son-in-law, who was editor of
the *Journal,* chose approximately the same time to publish every
detail of the estate as it had been probated the year before. It was
meant to be an answer to the Democratic New York *World,*
which, still making political hay out of the clothes sale, charged
that Lincoln had left his descendants penniless, making worse
than it really was the Republican reluctance to do anything for
them. Mary thought that Baker was probably using the whole
thing as an excuse for the Springfield relatives' neglect of her.
Whatever his motive, the effect when his editorial, too, was
reprinted in New York was to ruin her sale, and no wonder:

> "We were not at first disposed ourselves to make any
> comments upon this strange and mortifying publica-
> tion, though we felt sure, from what we knew of the
> pecuniary circumstances of Mr. Lincoln at the time of
> his death that the statements put forth in the *World*
> were not true, and that they should be received by the
> public with very considerable allowance. A Republi-
> can contemporary, however, insists, now that the sub-
> ject has been brought thus prominently before the pub-
> lic, that 'it should not be permitted to sleep without a
> statement of facts from some authenticated source, or
> a thorough investigation,' urging that 'this is de-
> manded not only by the honor of the Republican party,
> which is assailed in the article of the *World,* but of the
> whole Nation.' In this view, we have deemed that the
> publication of the inventory of the estate of Mr. Lin-
> coln, as filed by Judge Davis, the administrator, in the
> office of the Clerk of the County Court of Sangamon
> County, would not only not be out of place but would
> be the easiest and surest way of placing the facts before

the public. We therefore give it below. It was filed on the 29th of November, 1866, by 'N. W. Matheny, clerk,' and recorded in Book 4 on Inventories, page 70:—

Inventory of the estate of Abraham Lincoln, late President of the United States, so far as the same has come to my knowledge. DAVID DAVIS, Administrator

In registered bonds bearing 6 per cen. payable in coin
.... $57,000.00
In temporary loan bearing six per cen. in currency
.... 2,781.04
In Treasury warrants, issued to him for salary and not paid, as follows:
No. 554 .... 1,981.67
" 826 .... 1,981.67
" 900..................................... 1,976.22
" 1217.................................... 1,981.67
Draft of National Bank of Springfield........... 133.00
Balance of salary received from Treasurer of the United States....................................... 847.83
Claims *vs* Robert Irwin of Springfield, which Mr. Condell paid...................................... 9,044.41
Balance in hands of Riggs, banker, at Washington
.... 1,373.53
Balance in hands of First National Bank, Washington
.... 881.66
$79,482.70

This sum is all invested in United States securities bearing interest.

Also the following:

N.B. Judd's note, dated Sept. 1, 1859, bearing 10 per cent. interest for................................ $3,000.00
Thomas J. Turner, (Freeport), July 1, 1858, due November 1, 1858; interest 10 per ct....................... 400.00
A. & J. Haines, (Peking), two notes for $200 each, one due

October 15th, 1858, the other January 1st, 1859 .... 400.00
With the following credits:
February 16, '59, $50; May 2, '59, $50; July 14, '59, $100;
September 12, '59, $50; August 13, '60, $50.
N.B. Church, (Springfield), November 5th, 1864, at five
    months, given at Washington................. 260.00
Jas. H. & J.S. McDaniel, (Sangamon co.), April 23, 1863, 1 day,
    10 per cent. int 250.00
Golden Patterson, (Vermilion co.), April 25, '59, due one year
    after date 60.00
Milton Davis, (Vermilion co.), November 7, '57, due Decem-
    ber 25, '57, 10 per cent. with credit of $30, March 28th, '59
    .... 80.00
John P. Mercer, (Shelbyville), May 25, 1852 .... 7.59

REAL ESTATE IN ILLINOIS

Mr. Lincoln's homestead in Springfield, Ill., on lot 5 and
part of lot 7, in block 10 E. Iles' addition to Springfield.
Lot 3, in block 19, town of Lincoln, Logan county, Ill.

REAL ESTATE IN IOWA

Crawford county, Iowa.—120 acres east half, north-east
and north-west, north-east, section 18, town 84, range 39.
Tama county.—40 acres, description not recollected. Certificate of entry in hand of C.H. Moore, of Clinton, DeWitt
county, Ill.

DAVID DAVIS, Adm'r, etc.

The following is a transcript of the oath filed by Judge
Davis, upon taking out letters of administration:

State of Illinois
Sangamon Count.

David Davis being duly sworn deposes and says that
Abraham Lincoln, late of the county of Sangamon and

State of Illinois, is dead, and that he died on or about the 14th day of April, A.D., 1865, intestate, as it is said, and that his estate will probably amount to the sum of $85,000; that said Abraham Lincoln left at the time of his decease, Mary Lincoln, his widow, and Robert T. Lincoln and Thomas Lincoln, his children.

(Signed)   DAVID DAVIS

Subscribed and sworn to before me this 14th day of June, A.D., 1865.

(Signed)   N.W. MATHENY, Clerk.

The above figures speak for themselves. To be added to them, however, is the $25,000 which was appropriated by the last Congress on account of Mr. Lincoln's salary, making altogether the total value of the personal estate to be about *one hundred and ten thousand dollars,* to say nothing of the real estate described in the schedule above. So that the statement made in the *World* that Mr. Lincoln saved nothing and left nothing from his salary and that Mrs. Lincoln has no resources but what remains from the appropriation of Congress, $22,000, and rents of the homestead, returning altogether but $1,700 per year, can not possibly be true. That Mr. Lincoln did not leave his family wealthy is very evident, but no one in view of the above inventory will say that they are in the deplorable condition of 'want' and 'destitution' in regard to which the public has with so much astonishment, just been informed.

We say this much, not for the purpose of preventing 'personal contributions' from being made to Mrs. Lincoln, if she desires them, much less to deter Congress from making a further appropriation for her support, which we should be glad to have it do; but simply in order that the people of the nation may not suppose that Mrs. Lincoln is in anything like destitute circumstances. Her income may not be sufficient to meet all her wants and necessities, but it is certainly enough to maintain her at least as comfortable as she lived before going to Washington."

Having anticipated something like this, Mary had tried to head it off by writing to Mrs. Keckley in New York: "Robert goes with Judge Davis on Tuesday, November 12, to settle the estate, which will give us each about $25,000, with the income I told you of $1,700 a year for each of us. You made a mistake about my house costing $27,000—it was $17,000. The $22,000 Congress gave me I spent for house and furniture, which, oweing to the smallness of my income, I was obliged to leave. I mention about the division of the estate to you, dear Lizzie, because when it is done the *papers* will harp upon it. You can explain everything in New York; please do so to everyone. There must not be an hour's delay in this. Robert is very spiteful at present, and I think hurries up the division to *cross* my purposes. He mentioned yesterday that he was going to the Rocky Mountains so soon as Edgar Welles joined him. He is very *deep* . . ."

Devious, she now realized, might have been a better word for Robert than deep, but her mother's feeling for him, her need for him as a possible protector, were then still too strong to let herself believe anything worse about him than that he might have a case of spoiled immaturity. After all, the fix they were in was no fault of his, and he wouldn't be a true Todd if he weren't unhappy and humiliated by what she felt forced to do to save their assets and protect Mr. Lincoln's reputation. His need for money was real because, as she had more reason than most to know, the law business was slow in generating income, and the marriage that she herself had engineered for him was coming up. In that marriage lay much of her hope for a future with some segments of happiness. It would mature Robert and provide her with grandchildren to take the place of Taddie who would soon no longer need her, judging from the way his voice was breaking and the interest he was showing in girls that year before they left for Europe. So even while she went on scrimping to pay off her own debts, she gave in to Robert's requests, and for a while it appeared to be a good investment.

In September of '68, just before her ship was to sail, Robert and Mary Harlan were married in the Harlan home in Washington. The ceremony was a very simple one with few guests, and Mary was never sure whether this was done out of embarrassment over her recent notoriety or Senator Harlan's. The press was then questioning how the Harlans could afford such an expensive Washington establishment unless the stories that he'd personally profited from the sale of Indian lands during the brief time he was Secretary of the Interior under Johnson were true. Knowing the senator for a temperance Methodist who had lifted himself up by hard work from a log cabin every bit as humble as Mr. Lincoln's youthful home, Mary paid little attention to such charges, but she began to take a different view of Harlan later when he absented himself from the debates over her pension resolution that her good friend Charles Sumner introduced into the Senate. If Harlan thought that he was displaying principle in taking no stand on a bill that might enrich a relative by marriage, the effect of it was lost when he was defeated for the Senate in '73 after the press linked him with the Crédit Mobilier scandal through a $10,000 gift to his campaign fund by a Union Pacific Railroad executive. Instead of making Robert and his wife more sympathetic with her, instead of convincing them that misunderstanding of motives and exposure of eccentricities was the going price of fame, Senator Harlan's problems with the press made them all the more skittish about anything *she* might do. She could only speculate on why this was so since their relationship had deteriorated to the point where they didn't discuss such matters.

It sometimes took an eye-opener like she had had this day in court to sharpen hindsight. With an ocean between her and the young Lincolns, she had gone blissfully along thinking that her love for them and the intense interest she had in their doings was reciprocated. True, Mary Harlan had written very seldom and Robert's notes had been rather stiff, but she had put that down to the natural involvement with each other of the newly married, to the busyness of a young man just making his way and a young woman preparing for her first baby. Now, however, with her new hunch about money focusing her memory, she could plainly see how and when their feelings for her began to chill. It had started when for the first time she refused Robert's request for money, and it had started only months after his marriage. It had so pained her to do it—or perhaps she had been so instinctively fearful that it might finally bring them to this—that she could still recall the letter she had written Judge Davis:

> "Hotel D'Angleterre
> Frankfort-on-the-Main
> Germany Dec 15th 68

> My dear Sir
> I wrote you quite a long letter, on my arrival in Germany, which I presume you have received. Taddie is settled in his school & I hope he will make up for lost time. When you see Robert, may I request you—to speak to him about forwarding the money to Dr Hohagen for Taddie's first quarter. Owing to a false impression which has gone abroad that I receive a liberal pension from our government, I am charged very high for my living &c. and of course I have no means of my own to advance, as it is, the school where Taddie is placed, is very moderate in terms. On the subject of Robert, I wish to write you. Please consider all I say, as perfectly private. About three weeks since I received

a letter from Robert, in which he requests the loan of
my 1881 bonds, to be converted into money—and to be
used—in connection with John Forsythe of C [Chicago] in building 28 houses on the North Side—thereby
of course increasing his money & he offering me 10
percent on the money, for four years. (R. has been a
noble & devoted son to me & I love his sweet little wife
very dearly, & their advancement is my first desire—
With the thought of this before me—soon after I received the letter, without much reflection, I wrote him
that I would consent. But the thought since of parting
with *those* bonds—which were *so* placed by my dear
husband, has made me unhappy—so, on yesterday
after consultation with Consul Murphy & a banker,
who could be relied on—they, greatly disapproving of
my giving them up—I sent R. a telegram, saying that
I could not part with them. The telegram cost me *fifty-
six florins*, & of *course*, I made it, as short as possible. I
was compelled to send the telegram, for fear—poor
fellow, he would receive my letter & make arrangements which might involve him in difficulty. With my
great love for my good son, the necessity for refusing
his request, has made me quite ill. My health continues
poor, & the physicians here urge me to go immediately
to Italy. The trip & living there will involve such an
amount of money, that thus far, I have had to remain
in this damp climate—and I cannot explain to these
strange physicians, why I do not obey their commands.
I cannot but believe if Congress knew the circumstances of this case, they would allow me a pension of
say $3,000- a year—to help me out of my difficulties.
With my certain knowledge of your great goodness of
heart, dear Judge—I am sure if *it is*, brought up before
Congress, *you* will rather aid, than oppose it. Owing to
my station, which of course is greatly regarded in

Europe, I am charged—the highest prices & I am living in one room, in the most economical manner—And to go to Italy, where I am daily urged, by my physicians to go & where prices have become so exorbitant—I shall have *myself* to dispose of a few bonds—which it appears a sacrilege to do—without Con- will grant me the pension. *Thad Stevens is gone* & they speak of increasing Grant's salary to $100,000- a year. My husband, was Commander in Chief & directed every move Grant ever made—Surely, surely with ill health upon me & physicians bills, that often *Appall* me—*I will be remembered. You can do much,* dear Judge, in influencing public opinion, will you not use, that great influence? I am sure you will. I wish you would write me your opinion, regarding the 1881 bonds. Did I do right? All you say, will be sacredly regarded, and never mentioned.

If Mrs Davis and your daughter are with you, please present, my kindest regards—

Hoping to hear from you, very soon, I remain, always, with great respect

Yours truly,
Mary Lincoln

I did not mention to you that I should be required to take a maid or companion with me to Italy as I could not travel alone. As it is with such prices as we have to pay in Italy—I could barely with great economy, go there alone—Will not Congress, while ill health is upon me, grant me a pension?

M.L."

Were it not for the fact that it would further confirm her companions' belief in her "madness," Mary Lincoln might have laughed aloud at the bitter humor in her situation. She was supposed to be insane about money, and yet it was those same bonds she wouldn't let Robert have seven years ago that they were expecting her to hand them from the pocket in her petticoat. Insane about money? Robert had been forced to accept that decision, and it had kept him out of real estate speculation that would doubtless have left him bankrupt in the panic of '73—a panic that still wasn't over, which was one reason that she felt better about having her securities on her person than in a bank that might close its doors against her. Insane about money? Only in thinking that any amount of it would buy her love from Robert and that chilly wife of his. That was why she would have to agree that the fever must have temporarily affected her mind there in Florida when she had written those telegrams with the notion that getting more money would cure whatever ailed Robert. Thanks largely to the persistence of her true friend Charles Sumner—a man who knew her mind so well he would have come from Massachusetts to defend her sanity were he still alive—Congress did grant her a $3000 yearly pension in '70, and she wrote another letter she could not now forget to Judge Davis, Tad's guardian, when the boy died the next year:

"Nov 9th 1871

My dear Sir:

I feel that I would be carrying out the wishes, of my dearly beloved son Taddie, when I suggest that an equal division be made of the bonds in your possession. Dividing them equally between Bob & myself—I understand that by the law, I am entitled to two-thirds of them, but I should prefer only the half. In making the division however, some other matters will be settled between us, so that of the bonds you have, I will receive the 19-thousand 1881-bonds, and also the 37 hundred & 50-lot 5/20—if it has not been broken by the sale just made for Bob. Otherwise $4000—of the twelve thousand lot—Bob had read over his letter to me & what he says in it, meets my approval.

Dear Judge, I well know, how deeply you sympathise with us, in our great sorrow—My beloved boy, was the idol of my heart & had become my inseparable companion—My heart is entirely broken, for without his presence, the world is complete darkness—I am sure under the circumstances, you will kindly excuse this scrawl. I remain your deeply afflicted friend

Mary Lincoln"

Apparently greed was a monster that grew more hollow, more empty of human sensibility. Perhaps she should not blame Robert, who, having lost the model of his father, was shaping himself into one of the examples of greed to be seen on all sides these days. Whether or not Robert's father-in-law was actually involved with the Crédit Mobilier, which milked the Union Pacific with inflated contracts, many of his Republican associates in the Senate, including Vice-President Colfax, admittedly were, and Senator Harlan had gone out of his way to defend on the floor the policies of President Grant, whom she had always thought of as a stupid butcher and who now tolerated and associated with these people. It saddened her that Robert would idolize Grant and, like his father-in-law, see no wrong in the use of government to promote private gain. If there was anything that might reconcile her to Mr. Lincoln's untimely death, it was knowing that he did not have to see how his dream of a shining Republic was being tarnished by such greed. He had favored funding the Union Pacific, for example, as a steel ribbon to bind together the union he loved and not as a source of personal plunder, and one of his last wishes had been to ride it to California when it was finished. He had helped to forge the Republican Party to serve the causes of union and freedom rather than the uses of money grubbers. The only way Mr. Lincoln could have tolerated present conditions would have been to laugh at them as Mark Twain and Mr. Warner had in that novel *The Gilded Age* she had read down in Florida. But Robert had no sense of humor and would go along with the prevailing wisdom of the times that getting money by any means was, it seemed, the essence of sanity, whereas spending it for things of beauty or giving it away was somehow a mark of insanity.

Unfortunately, like his father-in-law, Robert's "second father," Judge Davis, was a man of his time with respect to money. He had only been half joshing Mr. Lincoln in that mock trial so many years before, and he had taken great pleasure in demonstrating to them what a man with money sense could do by increasing the estate a third or more in two years by cashing the paychecks and collecting the debts that Mr. Lincoln let ride. Judge Davis had probably put in the paper about taking no money as administrator to take the onus off the sort of public reputation that prompted paragraphs like the one she had read recently in *Harper's Weekly:* "Davis is not only a heavy man in person but 'warm' in purse. He is the largest landowner in central Illinois, and pays $27,000 yearly in taxes. He commenced life with a fortune represented by three small figures, and is now alluded to as a two-millionaire. His residence near Bloomington is one of the finest in the state. He is an early riser and hard worker." A man with a mind like that would not appreciate wealth in trunks—land, yes, trunks no. He'd never trusted her with money, was always complaining about what was spent on Taddie in Europe even though Robert himself admitted that Taddie showed an astonishing development in speech, despite a little German accent, when they returned. Now the judge had poisoned Robert's mind into taking control of all her money to make sure it would grow and grow and grow instead of giving her any pleasure. With her money in their hands they wouldn't need bars to make a prisoner of her . . .

The carriage was stopping in front of the hotel, and she went into a kind of panic. She wanted to escape with the money still under her skirts, and looked around for some way of doing so. There was none. The men sat stolidly beside her until another carriage pulled up behind and two guards and a sturdy looking woman got out. Only when this trio came up to escort them inside did Swett say, "All right, Mrs. Lincoln, let's go."

They hardly gave her breathing room; Swett took her arm on one side, Arnold on the other. They rushed her through the lobby, but at the elevator she said, "If you gentlemen will just wait here I'll bring the securities down to you."

Swett shook his head. "Oh, no, Mrs. Lincoln, we're going with you, and so are these folks," he said nodding to the guards who stepped inside the elevator car with them. "They've been sent by the court. The lady will be your companion in your room, and the man will watch the halls to see that those men who have been threatening you won't bother you."

"Robert's Pinkertons, you mean."

Arnold cleared his throat, and she thought she saw a slight smile play across his lips, but Swett was deadpan in look and tone when he said, "Robert has dismissed his guards; that's why we need these men."

When both lawyers started to follow her into her room, she said, "Can't you at least wait at the door and let this woman help me? As I've said, what you want is in my undergarments."

"The matter is of too much importance for such delicacy, Mrs. Lincoln," Swett said.

Their crowding in on her increased her panic. Even though this man had become loathsome in her sight, she went to her knees, took his hand, wept over it. "I beg of you, Mr. Swett. I'll go with Robert tomorrow without a fuss, anything you ask of me, but leave me . . ."

"Please, Mrs. Lincoln, don't make this any more difficult than it already is," Swett said. "Get up, please." He lifted her to her feet, bent over so that he could look her in the face. "Once more I have to warn you that I could have these guards take the money from you by force. I don't want to do that. We've acceded to your wishes in not wanting to give it to Robert or even to me. If you give it to Mr. Arnold, he'll hold it until the court appoints a conservator—"

"But why? Why must it be taken? I've guarded it for ten long years—"

"It's because of the verdict this afternoon. You've been judged incompetent. It's the law. None of us can do anything about it."

Suddenly she simply wanted nothing more than to have these men out of her room. She turned and went half behind the curtain, pulled up her skirts, tugged at the pocket on her petticoat. She couldn't see for the blur of her tears, couldn't make her shaking fingers behave. She called for Mr. Arnold to help her. She was beyond shame. He had to get down on his knees. He couldn't open the pocket either and she said, "Rip it away. Rip it away." She could hear the tearing as he did, could hear his mumbled, "Mrs. Lincoln, I'm so sorry, so sorry . . ."

Now utterly defeated, she sat on her bed and let herself cry as she had not cried since Taddie died. No wonder she had cried so hard then . . . she must have had a premonition that with him gone she had lost her last son, that she was left all alone.

The White House in Washington as it
looked during the years 1861–1865 when
it was home to the Lincoln family and
command post for the Union forces in
the Civil War. Courtesy of The Lincoln
Museum, Fort Wayne IN (Ref. #578).

Before the death of her son Willie put her into mourning, Mary Lincoln was criticized for wearing expensive ball gowns and jewelry at White House functions. Courtesy of The Lincoln Museum, Fort Wayne IN (Ref. #104).

The enduring image of a gentle
Abraham Lincoln was, in part,
created by the many photographic
studies of him and son Tad in
the last years of his presidency.
Courtesy of The Lincoln
Museum, Fort Wayne IN
(Ref. #0-93 and #0-114b).

Although he finally ended up in uniform, Robert Lincoln was the handsome Harvard student pictured here during most of the war—at his mother's beseeching. Courtesy of The Lincoln Museum, Fort Wayne IN (Ref. #110).

CHAPTER VI:

"The Poor Lady a Victim . . ."

O<small>N THE MORNING</small> of May 21, 1875, too early for the papers to have come down from Chicago, Attorney John Todd Stuart sat at his desk in the offices of Stuart, Edwards & Brown above J. Bunn's Bank in the heart of Springfield and wrote a letter to:

"Robert T. Lincoln, Esq

My dear Cousin: I received your Telegram of Tuesday advising me that the inquisition would be held the next day and requesting my presence. I answered that I could not come. The condition of my wife was one reason and another reason was that the State House and Penitentiary Boards were holding on that day a joint meeting in relation to some stone cut for the new State House which was alleged to be improper to be used. My reputation was too much involved in the question for me to leave. Moreover I did not think I could be of any service.

I am very glad that it is over and so far as I am able to judge from the newspapers everything was done that the melancholy occasion required of you. The presence of Messrs Swett and Arnold was especially fortunate and the character of the jury not less so.

In my consultations with you from the beginning I had no doubt of the insanity of your mother and the necessity of legal proceedings but counselled delay that when you did institute proceedings that it should be done under such circumstances that your friends and the public should sustain and justify you. In this you have been fully successful. You have the sympathy of all in the sad affair.

Yours Affectionately,
John T. Stuart"

The news reaching Springfield was a day behind the events in Mary Lincoln's life, and the smug satisfaction that Stuart took in the way that the lawyers had handled his difficult cousin Mary was understandable. It may have seemed heartless for him to put the matter of the quality of stone for the State House ahead of the pitiful human drama taking place in Chicago, but he was obviously confident that Robert, a fellow lawyer and man of affairs who put a high enough value on his own reputation to lock his mother away so that she wouldn't embarrass him, would accept this excuse as valid. From the papers on the morning of the 20th it was very evident that he hadn't been needed. If the nervous Judge Davis himself had composed them, the newspaper accounts could not have been more sympathetic with respect to the course Robert Lincoln had taken on their advice. A reader just scanning the bank of headlines in the Chicago *Times* would have been left with the desired impression:

A SAD REVELATION

MRS. MARY LINCOLN, THE WIDOW OF

THE LATE PRESIDENT,

ADJUDGED INSANE.

AT LAST THE STRANGE FREAKS OF THE

PAST TEN YEARS ARE

UNDERSTOOD

AND THE UNFRIENDLY CRITICISM WILL CHANGE TO

HEARTFELT COMMISERATION

THE POOR LADY A VICTIM TO

MANY STRANGE AND STARTLING

HALLUCINATIONS

WALLS HAD VOICES, INDIANS TROU-

BLED HER SCALP, AND SHE HAD A

MANIA FOR SHOPPING.

A SORROWFUL SPECTACLE IN COURT.

A mania for shopping! Under these headlines, the *Times* story began: "The conduct of the widow of the lamented Abraham Lincoln has been criticized by many people since the death of her husband. Some have accused her of serious indiscretion, while others have pitied her and pronounced her actions the result of mental weakness." After reminding readers of the attempted clothes sale, the reporter continued:

"This action on her part years ago, and soon after the death of Mr. Lincoln, will be viewed in an entirely different light by the people who read in THE TIMES this morning an account of the terrible misfortune which has overtaken her and her family. All her former actions are now explained, with the motive which prompted them, and the public will pity the poor woman who had lived alone, almost entirely apart from her near relatives and friends, for so long a time. Universal sympathy will take the place of censure, for her actions will be understood now.

Mrs. Lincoln has never been considered a woman of strong nature, and being so closely connected with a man of noble purposes and sound judgment, the contrast was the more striking. It has been mistrusted by her near friends and relatives that she has been the victim of mental aberration, and they have studiously avoided making the discovery public, but have striven to conceal the fact in the hope that she would eventually recover. In this, however, they have been sadly disappointed, and yesterday disclosed the secret to the people of the nation, who will this morning again mourn the cowardly assassination of the beloved president . . ."

After thus spelling out for its readers the significance of what it was about to report, the *Times* got around to covering the proceedings, noting editorially that "the testimony was of the most startling nature, and served to show a great degree of forbearance and patience on the part of her son and her friends." No comment was made on the fact that there was *no* testimony on behalf of Mrs. Lincoln. The Chicago *Daily Tribune's* opening paragraphs were only slightly more restrained. "The death of President Lincoln was one of the nation's saddest misfortunes—a misfortune that it has not yet outlived," the *Tribune* asserted in its lead and went on to link the burden under which Mrs. Lincoln's mind had been "tottering" to this event. But throughout its version of the case, the *Tribune* emphasized the burden that *Robert Lincoln* was bearing by noting, for instance, that when he took the witness stand "his face indicated the unpleasantness of the duty he was about to perform, and his eyes were expressive of the grief he felt." Even more likely to turn

Robert rather than his mother into the victim of the occasion was the Chicago *Inter-Ocean's* contrast of their behavior during his testimony: "His face was pale; his eyes bore evidence that he had been weeping, and his whole manner was such as to affect all present. His mother looked upon him benignly, and never betrayed the emotion which must have filled her breast during the recital of the unfortunate and regretful scenes they were parties to."

The complacency that Attorney Stuart felt over the fact that no observer had raised the slightest question about the justice of the coup that Stuart, Davis, Swett, Ayer, Lincoln & Co. had pulled off couldn't have lasted longer than it took for the papers to reach him that morning of the 21st. Since nobody else had raised the question, Mary Lincoln raised it herself in the most dramatic fashion possible. She tried to kill herself. In view of the fact that she had been found insane by due process of law, this effort of Mary Lincoln's was reported generally as another sign of that insanity. Nothing was made of the fact that this same process of the law had found that "she does not manifest homicidal or suicidal tendencies." Stuart's eye had picked that phrase out of the verdict because it seemed to confirm his judgment when he had told Robert that his mother was not in need of confinement. With this news, he had to admit to being wrong in that instance or face the fact that what had been done to Mary with his support had made her suicidal. It was not a nice thought to live with when he was surrounded here in Springfield by Mary's sisters and in-laws and cousins to whom this whole affair had come as a ghastly surprise when they opened their newspapers on May 20. Now this . . . well, he could argue that it was the fear of confinement that he had warned against that made her do it. The devil of it was that he found it hard to believe that an insane person could have done what Mary reportedly did.

According to the accounts she had been left Wednesday evening after the court case in her hotel room under guard—a woman inside with her, two men in the corridor—awaiting transportation the next morning to Batavia. Somehow she had talked both the woman with her and the guards watching her into letting her go downstairs to Squair & Co., the drugstore off the lobby of the hotel, to get a preparation of laudanum and camphor that she said she needed to rub on her shoulder to ease the pain of neuralgia. With so many hotel employees partici- pating in the trial, the news of what had happened to the Grand Pacific's most distinguished guest had buzzed its way through the entire establishment. The clerk at Squair's was, therefore, surprised and a little frightened to see Mrs. Lincoln walk in alone. He had watched her come and go from the hotel for months now without giving it a thought, but this time was different: she was a lunatic. Lunatics weren't supposed to be loose, were they? How does one handle one?

Although she did seem rather nervous, Mrs. Lincoln made good sense when she explained how the opium in the laudanum took away the pain and the camphor drew the heat from the neuralgia. The clerk kept smiling at her and nodding and pre- tending to take notes on the dosage she wanted until he could catch the eye of Mr. Squair, who was across the room with another customer. When Mr. Squair came over and sized up the situation he had a hunch that Mrs. Lincoln wanted the drugs for other purposes; in the same situation he might do the same thing himself. He told her that he would be pleased to serve her but it would take thirty minutes. Mrs. Lincoln thanked him, said she would be back and left the store.

As soon as she had gone, Squair scribbled a note and sent it by his clerk to Robert Lincoln's home on Wabash Avenue. Then he went out into the lobby to keep an eye on Mrs. Lincoln. She was just going through the front doors. Squair followed. He saw Mrs. Lincoln climb into one of the for-hire carriages that were always waiting at the door. He jumped into another one behind. Mrs. Lincoln's carriage stopped at the corner of Clark and Adams streets, where she got out and went into the Rogers & Smith drugstore. Standing at the counter and waiting for her order from the clerk who had already gone back among the bottles to fill it, Mrs. Lincoln did not see Squair slip in behind her. He knew the layout of the store so well that he was able to work his way around out of sight and get to the clerk to warn him. Although he seemed miffed to lose a sale, the young man recognized Squair as one of the city's leading druggists and thought it best to take his advice. He went out and explained to Mrs. Lincoln that they had run out of laudanum. Taking the rejection with good grace, Mrs. Lincoln got back into her carriage and headed down Clark Street. Squair anticipated her destination—William Dole's drugstore two blocks away—outran the carriage and arranged to have her request refused there, too.

Squair was back behind his own counter when, as he had guessed, Mrs. Lincoln returned. There was no sign of either his clerk or Robert Lincoln. To gain more time, he poured a mixture of burnt sugar and water into an authoritative looking vial and handed it to Mrs. Lincoln. Although her back was turned to him, Squair could tell by her gestures that Mrs. Lincoln had paused half way across the lobby to drink off the contents of the vial and drop it into a spittoon. Distasteful as it was, Squair recovered the vial to make sure of what he thought he had seen as soon as she disappeared into the elevator. He wondered how long it would be before she realized that she wouldn't die. Pray it would be long enough for her son to arrive. It wasn't. Within fifteen minutes Squair saw Mrs. Lincoln coming into his store again. Knowing what she was going through, he could detect her nervous anxiety in the way her eyes kept darting about and her fingers kept clasping and unclasping, but he thought her admirably self-controlled. She thanked him for what he had given her but explained that it was too weak for relief. Perhaps it was the camphor. Could he give her just an ounce of plain laudanum? She demonstrated at once that her mind was clear enough to suspect what he had been doing; she stepped around the counter to watch him mix her order. He had to think quickly. "Mrs. Lincoln," he said, "I keep the laudanum in the cellar so that it won't get into the wrong hands. Wait right here." Downstairs he mixed another batch of burnt sugar and water but this time put an ounce of it into a vial conspicuously labeled "Laudanum—Poison," returned with it and handed it to her. She smiled, thanked him, left the store, drank it off as soon as she was out of his door, and marched to the elevator.

Minutes after Mrs. Lincoln disappeared from his sight, Squair saw Robert Lincoln coming his way with a man he recognized from pictures in the paper as the famous attorney Leonard Swett. They paused only for the few seconds it took him to blurt out the gist of his story and then they left at a run for the elevator. When they had gone, Squair, tired and a little shaken, turned off the gas jets, locked the door of his store and headed home. Robert Lincoln had thanked him profusely for what he had done, but he wondered if Mrs. Lincoln would share that gratitude. No matter what that jury had decided, she had nearly outwitted him, and he was as sane a citizen as you could find in Chicago. In Squair's opinion Mrs. Lincoln knew very well what she was doing and why she was doing it, and he, for one, was not at all sure she was crazy.

Neither was the person who probably knew Mary Todd Lincoln better than anybody else, including her own son. Sitting in her Springfield home on the hill and reading about the trial and then about Mary's attempt to kill herself, Elizabeth Todd Edwards found herself doubting the picture that the newspaper writers were trying to paint of her younger sister. She could well believe that Mary overdramatized her ailments with wild words, and she knew all about Mary's shopping. From the time she had been a small girl Mary had done and said quite outrageous things—things that sobersided people were always misinterpreting. It had made living with Mary—and especially being responsible for her as she had considered herself to be after their mother died—both an excitement and a trial. But unless she had completely changed in the last few years when they had not seen much of each other the description of Mary Lincoln as a pitiful person with a weak nature had to be very far off the mark. Mary was a willful person, and Lizzie Edwards saw in that suicide attempt a sign of her sister's strong will at work. How could Mary's mind be as far adrift as they claimed if she comprehended what had happened at the trial so well that she would try to kill herself to thwart the will of the court, the will of her son?

It was not hard for Lizzie to put herself in Mary's place and understand how she had felt at the trial. For the Mary Todd who had been sure from birth that a glittering destiny awaited her, it could only have been sheer hell to sit there in her widow's weeds and hear her only remaining son, the last bit of flesh of her flesh, describe her as an unmanageable lunatic, a "source of anxiety," an embarrassment unwelcome in his home. It was in Mary's nature to take fiercer joy over triumphs and indulge in deeper sorrow over tragedies than most other people, and her dramatic reaction to the trial was in character. Lizzie couldn't help but wonder whether Mary's failure to carry out her plan might not be in itself a tragedy ... she simply could not imagine the spirit she cherished as Mary caught in any cage.

Five years older than Mary, Lizzie had been thirteen, the oldest girl in the family when her mother, Eliza Parker Todd, died just after the birth of her seventh child, George. For a year, before her father married Betsy Humphreys, Lizzie was a mother to the rest of the brood, and she had gone on helping with the first family when Betsy started having baby after baby of her own. Whether it was because she was a middle child in need of shining to get attention or whether it was something born into her, Mary was the most spirited of them all—the liveliest and sunniest and, yes, most unmanageable. Whether or not the rest of them recognized at the time how exceptional Mary's life would be, *she* did. Mary loved to ride, and Lizzie carried in her mind a picture of her sister, hair streaming out from under a plumed hat, long skirts whipping in the breeze as she sat her sidesaddle and galloped off to some adventure. One of these that shocked the whole proper Todd family happened when Mary was about twelve and took it into her head to ride over to Ashland, Henry Clay's estate, push her way past the house slaves and tell the famous statesman in the presence of his guests, "My father says you will be the next president of the United States. I wish I could go to Washington and live in the White House. My father is a very peculiar man, Mr. Clay. I don't think he really wants to be president. So if you were not already married I would wait for you." Amused by the incident, Mr. Clay enjoyed telling it and adding his own opinion: "You know, I think that young lady *might* one day live in the White House—with somebody else, of course."

Lizzie found it very interesting—and a bit strange—in the light of the testimony at the trial that Mary's willful escapades that stuck in the mind so often had to do with clothes. Come to think of that, Mary was the only one of the nine girls among the seventeen children in both families who became expert with the needle. Mary couldn't have been more than ten when she first used her ability to sew for a typical escapade. A niece of their stepmother's about Mary's age—Elizabeth Humphreys—was living with them then, sharing Mary's room. Mary decided one Saturday as the girls were inspecting the plain white muslin frocks they were supposed to wear to church the next day that the time had come for them to look more grown up. What they needed were hoops to make their skirts swing and sway as they walked like those they admired on older "belles." Since there was no chance that a stern and practical minded woman like Betsy Humphreys would let them have hoop skirts at such a tender age, Mary argued that they should make their own. That afternoon she persuaded a neighbor to let her cut branches from a weeping willow tree, sneaked them into the house and hid them in her bedroom closet. When the house quieted for the night, the girls lit a candle, settled on the floor and stitched the willow branches into the muslin skirts. The branches became hoops of sorts although the ends they brought together were awkwardly different sizes. The work took them most of the night, and they chattered the rest of it away in excitement over the sensation they were sure to create in church. Immediately after breakfast they put on their creations. The effect was not exactly what they had wanted—hoops that bulged grotesquely front and back and fell flat at the sides. Nevertheless, Mary wasn't one to waste so much effort, and she made it as far as the street enroute to church before her stepmother caught a slower Elizabeth just going out the door and, after having a good laugh, ordered the girls to change into proper clothes for church. Mary was mortified by the laughter and wept in anger over the injustice meted out by stepmothers.

Another time that Mary wept in anger had to do with clothes, too, and it was an occasion that nobody in the Todd household would ever forget. Lizzie was sure that Mary was fourteen then, since it was the year that Lizzie married Ninian Edwards, a student at Transylvania College, and went back with him to Illinois. It was also the year that Mary started to go to boarding school and she evidently considered herself quite mature. She asked permission to attend the Derby Day races where all of Lexington gathered, and this time it was their father who decreed that she was too young to mingle with that hard drinking crowd. Mary threatened to go anyway and was locked into her room. Instead of sulking as they all supposed she was doing, she slipped into clothes she'd appropriated from her stepmother's closet. She had picked the most expensive garments—a deep rose silk dress with a skirt gathered six inches above the ground, a Byronic collar and puffed sleeves; for a crowning glory, a wide-brimmed hat with a foot long plume in matching rose. At considerable risk to this finery, Mary climbed out the window and down a clematis vine on the side of the house. Her timing was bad. Ducking behind hedges she reached the street but ran smack into her father making his own way to the races. Within minutes Mary was again locked into her room with one of the slaves posted outside to watch the window. In a crying rage, Mary tore off the clothes, stuffed them into the grate and set them afire. Then she yelled, "Fire! Fire!" When everybody else in the house came running and crowded into her room, Mary went down on her knees in front of her stepmother and, tears streaming down her cheeks, handed over all her money that she had been saving from her allowance for more than four years and pleaded, "Whip me. The devil got into me." But, seeing Mary's repentant anguish, nobody had the heart to punish her more.

Actually Mary was mostly a good child—not only in Lizzie's memory but in that of others. When Mary did become famous as First Lady, Elizabeth Humphreys told Lizzie that she wasn't surprised. "My first recollection of your sister Mary runs back to the time when your father lived on Short Street," Elizabeth said. "Mary was then about ten years old. She was a pupil of the celebrated Mr. Ward. He was a splendid educator; his requirements and rules were very strict; and woe to her who did not conform to the letter. Mary accepted the condition of things and never came under his censure. Mary was bright, talkative and warm-hearted. She was far advanced over other girls of her age in education. We occupied the same room, and I can see her now as she sat on the side of a table, poring over her books, and I on the other side, with a candle between. She was very studious, with a retentive memory and a mind that enabled her to grasp and thoroughly understand the lessons she was required to learn . . ."

Lizzie had gone off to Springfield by the time Mary was established at Mentelle's, where she boarded during the week although it was only down the street from home. It was a good school, as Lizzie knew from going there a few years herself. Run by Madame Victorie Charlotte LeClere Mentelle and her husband, Augustus Waldemare Mentelle, who had been "historiographer" to King Louis before the revolution, the school taught young ladies the cultural subjects and the social graces. Very good reports about Mary filtered through to Lizzie in Springfield, one classmate claiming: "Mary's one of the brightest girls in Mentelle's; always has the highest marks and takes the biggest prizes. She's a merry, companionable girl, with a smile for everybody. She's really the life of the school, always ready for a good time, and to contribute even more than her own share in promoting it." She was so good in French that a homesick French gentleman studying English at Transylvania sought her out just for the pleasure of hearing his native tongue. But with tomboy enjoyment of exercises like riding, Mary was equally good at Madame Mentelle's specialty—the dance—and she learned, as advertised, "the latest and most fashionable Cotillions, Round & Hop Waltzes, Hornpipes, Galopades, Mohawks, Spanish, Scottish, Polish, Tyrolienne dances and the Beautiful Circassian Circle."

By the time she came up to Springfield to live with them in '39, Mary was a very polished gem for her proud sister Lizzie to dangle before the eyes of society. Just as glass cannot be faceted into a diamond, no amount of polish would have availed if Mary had not been made of good material. She was stunning to look at, but people often had a hard time putting a finger on why. "She had clear blue eyes, long lashes, light brown hair with a glint of bronze, and a lovely complexion. Her figure was beautiful and no Old Master ever modeled a more perfect arm and hand," Elizabeth Humphreys said. Another admirer claimed: "Mary, although not strictly beautiful, was more than pretty. She had a broad white forehead, eyebrows sharply but delicately marked, a straight nose, short upper lip and expressive mouth curling into an adorable slow coming smile that brought dimples into her cheeks and glinted in her long-lashed, blue eyes. Those eyes, shaded by the long, silky fringe, gave an impression of dewy violet shyness contradicted fascinatingly by the spirited carriage of her head." But it was Lizzie's husband, Ninian—not one to be bowled over by people—who paid her sister the most memorable compliment. "Mary," he said, "could make a bishop forget his prayers."

Ninian was alluding to more than his sister-in-law's good looks. With her mercurial temperament, she was incapable of being a bore. One person described her as being like the weather of an April day; Elizabeth Humphreys used a different image to say much the same thing: "Like the varying patterns made by each slight turn of a kaleidoscope, her face expressed her varying moods, with eyes half-closed and looking through her long lashes she had the demure shyness of a little Quakeress, but presto, they now gleamed with mischief, and before one could be quite sure of that, her dimple was gone and eyes were brimful of tears." One could never be sure of what she would do. One spring day when she walked down the Edwards' hill to town she found herself sinking over her boot tops into the soft mud of the street. Quite sensibly as she thought, Mary talked a drayman into letting her climb up among the barrels in his wagon and ride home, but the sight of a belle in such a situation inspired a poem in the paper that was embarrassing to people in the Edwards' social position. Another embarrassment fell upon the suitor that Lizzie and Ninian had always thought most promising for Mary. Although he was small of stature, Stephen Douglas more than compensated with an acquired dignity—ramrod posture, deep voice, fine grooming. Considering what it must have cost him in masculine self-esteem, it was quite a tribute to Mary's persuasive power that she persuaded Douglas to wear a wreath of flowers she had plaited on his head when they walked down to town for an ice cream.

As charming as it could be much of the time, Mary's impulsiveness could also lead to trouble. The same skill that enabled her to pick up French so readily also allowed her to mimic the speech and manners of just about anybody she met. Like a cartoon or caricature, her performance could be wounding. The cleverness that made her entertaining also served to sharpen her

tongue to a cutting edge, and the blood it drew left her with
enemies even within the family. A very unfortunate case in
point in Lizzie's view was Billy Herndon. Lizzie thought that
much of Mary's present difficulty was caused by the mean
things that Herndon was saying in his lectures about her relationship to Mr. Lincoln, and she also thought that Herndon was
in part taking revenge for the tactless way that Mary had
slighted him nearly forty years before. It was a mishap that they
had met at all since, even though he was going over to Illinois
College at Jacksonville, Billy, the son of the owner of the Indian
Queen Tavern, was one of the town's rough boys who didn't
mix in their circles. But the occasion was one of those big,
all-inclusive balls at Colonel Allen's, the first Springfield event
that Mary had ever attended, and she had granted Herndon a
dance when he was brash enough to ask. Herndon could recognize polish when he saw it but didn't know how to compliment
it. When the dance was over he said, "Miss Todd, you glide
through the waltz with the ease of a serpent." Mary snapped
back, "Mr. Herndon, comparison to a serpent is rather severe
irony, especially to a newcomer," and she turned and walked
away, leaving Herndon permanently scarred.

Mary had come very close to making the same sort of social
shambles out of her first meeting with Abe Lincoln. It was at
a party at their house, and Lizzie could remember being surprised to see Lincoln break away from swapping stories with his
male cronies to go over and ask Mary for a dance. Since it was
the first time she had ever seen this tall, awkward partner of her
cousin John Stuart on the dance floor and since she had no great
esteem for his social graces, Lizzie laughed heartily at Mary's
version of the incident: "Mr. Lincoln said that he wanted to
dance with me in the worst kind of way—and he did." It was
a comment too clever by half not to get around through the
crowd, but Lincoln was made of different stuff than Herndon
and laughed his own head off when he heard it. Lincoln loved
the outrageous in Mary even when it brought upon him serious

consequences as in the case of the duel he nearly fought with James Shields. Lincoln was attacking Democratic Shields' performance as state auditor through anonymous humorous letters in his friend Francis' *Sangamo Journal.* Joining in what they considered good fun, Mary and her friend Julia Jayne composed some letters of their own about Shields. As unbridled in print as in speech, Mary's imputations about the auditor's manhood provoked Shields into seeking "satisfaction" when Lincoln stepped forward to claim authorship in order to protect the girls. The time, place and Lincoln's choice of weapons—broadswords—had been decided upon before friends were able to arrange an acceptable "out" for both men. Lincoln found the episode so embarrassing that he refused ever afterward to speak of it, but he didn't hold it against Mary . . .

Lizzie was sitting there in her favorite rocker in the same parlor where Mary and her Mr. Lincoln had been married and nodding over the memories stirred by the dreadful news in the papers on her lap when Ninian came in from his daily walk to town. He was a little out of breath because he'd hoped to get up to the house before Lizzie would have a chance to look at the paper. Lizzie was as thin as her sister Mary was chubby, and lately she had not been feeling at all well. Because he was afraid of how it might affect her, he'd wanted to break the news of Mary's attempted suicide in his own time and in his own way. But when he saw that he was too late he was glad that he had at least come bearing fresher news that might be of some comfort.

"Well, I see you know," he said, "but you'll be glad to hear that things aren't as bad as they look in the paper. I just stopped by John Stuart's office and he's had a telegram from Robert. He got his mother over to Batavia all right, and she seems to be feeling fine. Robert says she even enjoyed the trip because the president of the railroad, a friend of his, laid on his private car for them even though the ride takes only ninety minutes. Mary *would* like that, wouldn't she?"

"I don't know. I don't think so unless she *is* insane," Lizzie said. "How could a woman of Mary's spirit enjoy anything about being locked away? Remember when you once said that Mary could make a bishop forget his prayers, Ninian? How could *that* Mary have come to this?"

Ninian doubtless smiled a little at the picture of a young Mary brought to mind by his words of praise, but then realized that a smile was not appropriate this day. "I'm sorry about all this, Lizzie," he said, "but there's nothing to be done about it now. She's safe for the moment and that's the important thing. It might make you feel better to know that Cousin John did *not* advise confining her. I don't think we've seen the end of this yet, and we've always got room for her in this big barn of a house."

"Do you mean that, Ninian?"

"Of course, she's my little sister, too. Let's just wait and see."

CHAPTER VII

"A Gross Outrage"

T HE ADVERTISEMENTS THAT Dr. Richard J. Patterson ran for Bellevue Place in Batavia, Illinois, in the Chicago Journal of Nervous and Mental Diseases made this facility with the capacity to house some thirty female mental patients sound like a high class resort. Dr. Patterson quaintly called it a "Hospital for the Insane of the Private Class" in which he promised "modern management of mental disease by rest, diet, baths, fresh air, occupation, diversion, change of scene" with no more medicine than necessary and the least restraint possible for "only a select class of lady patients of quiet unexceptionable habits." Even to Robert Lincoln with his taste for luxury the handsome, solid three-story brick building fronted by an imposing columned porte cochère looked inviting. Set amid green acreage in the Fox River Valley, it had, according to Robert, "nothing to indicate an asylum except only that outside there is a wire netting such as you may see to keep children from falling out." He felt comfortable in leaving there a mother whose own taste and style had once caused Washington's most experienced journalist, Ben

Perley Poore, to glow: "I am sure that since the time that Mrs. Madison presided at the White House, it has not been graced by a lady as well fitted by nature and by education to dispense its hospitalities as is Mrs. Lincoln. Her hospitality is only equaled by her charity, and her graceful deportment by her goodness of heart."

What his mother thought of it all, Robert could not really know because she had hardly spoken to him since he and Leonard Swett had arrived in her rooms at Chicago's Grand Pacific Hotel the night before to take over from the guards and see that she made no more suicide attempts. Matter of fact, she had been so docile, so *quiet*, in the intervening hours that he could scarcely credit the reports of what she had tried to do to herself. At the Chicago station she had surprised them both by bidding goodbye to Swett very graciously and insisting that he come to visit her; on the train, she had given every appearance of enjoying the splendid appointments of the private car they occupied. Such was her behavior that Robert might have considered the events of the day before when he had persuaded a jury to declare her insane, when she had tried to kill herself drinking what she thought was laudanum and camphor, all a bad dream except for one incident that he later described in a letter to a friend: "There was in her room a considerable number of carpet covered footstools, such as are made in furniture stores to use up remnants of carpets. She had a large number of these, and when she was getting ready to go to Batavia, she took a number of carpet bags with her; and I had the curiosity, when her back was turned to look into some of them; and I found that each of the bags which I opened contained nothing but one of these footstools. I said nothing but let them go with the rest of her baggage, to Dr. Patterson's at Batavia." In Robert's view, sane people didn't lug worthless footstools around, and his mother's penchant for acquiring and hanging onto things for which she had no apparent need had nearly driven *him* crazy.

Robert's conviction that he had found a suitable retreat for his difficult mother grew through the next several weeks. From what he learned reading Dr. Patterson's notes on the case or discussing it with him during his duty visits to his mother, her mood of sweet resignation persisted. True, she sulked a bit in June and would not go out in the carriage, and she had a crying fit in early July, but on the whole she presented no problems. He felt fully justified in writing to Mrs. J.H. Orne, one of his mother's oldest and best friends who had been alarmed at what she had read in the papers while summering at Saratoga, New York: "My mother is, I think, under as good care and as happily situated as possible under the circumstances. She is in the private part of the house of Dr. Patterson, and her associates are the members of his family only. With them she walks and drives whenever she likes and takes her meals with them or in her own room as she chooses, and she tells me she likes them all very much. The expression of surprise at my action which was telegraphed East, and which you doubtless saw, was the first and last expression of the kind she has uttered and we are on the best of terms. Indeed my consolation in this sad affair is in thinking that she herself is happier in every way, than she has been in ten years. So far as I can see she does not realize her situation at all. I can tell you nothing as to the probability of her restoration. It must be the work of some time if it occurs."

Of one thing Robert could be fairly certain: Dr. Patterson and his associates—his wife acted as matron, his son as assistant physician and they hired a dozen nurses and attendants—would not maltreat his mother. They were proponents of what was known in the medical literature of the day as "moral treatment." Spelled out by an early practitioner, Dr. T. Romeyn Beck of New York, "this consists in removing patients from their residence to some proper asylum; and for this purpose a calm retreat in the country is to be preferred; for it is found that continuance at home aggravates the disease, as the improper association of ideas cannot be destroyed. A system of human vigilance is adopted. Coercion by blows, stripes, and chains is now justly

laid aside. The rules most proper to be observed are the following: Convince the lunatics that the power of the physician and
keeper is absolute; have humane attendants, who shall act as
servants to them; never threaten but execute; offer no indigni-
ties to them, as they have a high sense of honour; punish
disobedience peremptorily, in the presence of other maniacs; if
unruly, forbid them the company of others, use the strait waist-
coat, confine them in a dark and quiet room, order spare diet;
tolerate noisy ejaculations; strictly exclude visitors; let their
fears and resentments be soothed without unnecessary opposition; adopt a system of regularity; make them rise, take exercise
and food at stated times. The diet ought to be light, and easy of
digestion, but never too low. When convalescing, allow limited
liberty; introduce entertaining books and conversation, ex-
hilarating music, employment of body in agricultural pursuits;
and admit friends under proper restrictions. It will also be
proper to forbid their returning home too soon. By thus acting,
the patient will 'minister to himself.' "

This relatively benign philosophy was stretched to its limits
for Mrs. Lincoln, who had, after all, been First Lady of the land.
Every effort, for instance, was made to keep her from confront-
ing her more obviously maniacal fellow inmates such as the
woman who was shaved bald to keep her from pulling out her
hair or the woman who spent her days picking at her sores, all
of whom were housed in an ell off the main house. About the
only restraints put upon Mrs. Lincoln had to do with outside
contacts. Dr. Patterson and Robert decided together to whom
she could write; remembering her campaign for a pension, Robert was nervous about what she might do with a pen. When,
along about the middle of July, she started talking about visiting
her sister, Mrs. Edwards, in Springfield, Dr. Patterson tried to
be gently discouraging. "Why would you want to do that? I
thought you didn't get along with her," he said. "It is the most
natural thing in the world to wish to live with my sister," she
replied. "She raised me and I regard her as a sort of mother."

If the logic in this was sound, there remained a good question as to whether she would be welcome in Springfield since Robert understood that, whatever her attitude might be about her sister, his Aunt Lizzie wasn't in the best physical condition. How, Mary Lincoln argued, could they ever know what Lizzie thought about the matter if they wouldn't let her write? The surest sign that both Robert and Dr. Patterson were misreading Mary Lincoln's busily working mind came toward the end of July when they not only agreed that Mary should write to Lizzie but that she should herself go down to Batavia in the carriage to post the letter.

As she had outwitted her guards at the Grand Pacific on the night after the trial, Mary had now outwitted her captors at Bellevue Place. Along with her letter to Lizzie in Springfield, she mailed two other letters that were unauthorized. Both landed in the mailboxes of Chicago area lawyers who would have every reason to be sympathetic and might find her plight more worthy of help than had Mr. Arnold. One of them, General John Franklin Farnsworth, carried with him the most searing of memories: a strong political supporter of Abraham Lincoln, he had been one of those gathered around the bed in the little house across from Ford's theater in Washington where President Lincoln died. He had been very affected by watching Mary Lincoln and her son, Robert, leaning on each other in anguish that night, and he had found the revelations in the newspapers about their present relationship all the more saddening. He responded to Mary Lincoln's letter at once, arriving unannounced at Bellevue Place and demanding to see his old friend.

A full-bearded man of impressive mien and credentials, General Farnsworth wasn't the sort of visitor that Dr. Patterson felt it wise to turn away. The mere act of refusing his request could raise doubts about Mrs. Lincoln's condition and treatment. But the general seemed quite reasonable when he sat down to talk to the doctor after his visit. He admitted that Mary Lincoln was seeking his help in obtaining her freedom, and he argued that she would not appear insane to anyone who had known her for as long as he had. In his view she had been "on the border of insanity" for years and would continue to do "*outré* things" if she were released, but he did not think that confinement was any more in order now than ever. He did agree, however, that it might be a good idea for Robert to keep control over her finances. Dr. Patterson discounted General Farnsworth's opinion because the general was a well-known spiritualist who probably thought Mrs. Lincoln's (alleged) hearing of voices was normal, but the mere fact of his visit was quite disturbing. Who else had Mary Lincoln reached?

Dr. Patterson did not have long to wait to find out. He had hardly seen General Farnsworth off to the station in a hired carriage before another carriage pulled up under the porte cochère and out stepped Judge James B. Bradwell and his wife, Myra. For Dr. Patterson, this was, indeed, an unfortunate development. The couple was not only politically powerful—until '69 Judge Bradwell had presided over the very same court in which Mrs. Lincoln was tried and was now a member of the Illinois General Assembly's lower house; Mrs. Bradwell was founder and publisher of the Chicago *Legal News*—but noted for using that power to make trouble. With her husband's support, Mrs. Bradwell was forever trying to get herself admitted to practice at the bar although there had never been a female lawyer in the state's history, and the Bradwells had been backers of that feminist agitator Mrs. Elizabeth Parsons Ware Packard, who had got herself out of Dr. McFarland's state asylum at Jacksonville and run a successful campaign to change the whole state law on commitment in the '60's. If this couple got the idea that Mrs. Lincoln's rights had somehow been violated there was no telling what they might do. Since Mrs. Bradwell was waving a letter of invitation from Mrs. Lincoln in her hand, Dr. Patterson had little choice but to let them see his distinguished patient.

At the time Dr. Patterson did not know how close the ties

between Mary Lincoln and the Bradwells really were. The judge was, in fact, the nearest thing that Mary Lincoln had to a personal lawyer; he had drawn up a will for her in '72. Although Mary was not a crusader for female causes like Myra Bradwell, she could appreciate Mrs. Bradwell's general view that women had brains that should be used and mouths that should be heard. Indeed, it was a widely held belief in the masculine circles surrounding Mr. Lincoln that Mary Lincoln had brought most of her troubles upon herself by stepping out of line and pushing her too compliant husband around in matters that should have been of no concern to a good little wife. Thurlow Weed had expressed this male resentment of her influence with the President most bluntly and cruelly in his editorial on the clothes sale, and Herndon had let his feelings on the same subject warp his whole view of Lincoln's domestic life. Even more temperate and discreet men around Lincoln like David Davis disliked Mary, although they apparently tried to conceal it from her. Writing home to his wife in the late '40's from Springfield where he was serving in the legislature, Davis said, "Mrs. Lincoln is not agreeable . . . Mrs. L., I am told, accompanies her husband to Washington City next winter. She wishes to loom largely . . ." For good measure, Davis added that he had been to a party at the home of Mary's brother-in-law, Ninian Edwards, and said, "I don't fancy his wife and the family of Todds." Davis's willingness to count Mrs. Lincoln a crazy when Robert appealed to him evidently came naturally to him.

Nevertheless Davis, the consummate politician, knew the value of cooperating with Mary Lincoln to stay in with her husband and, as a result, was more aware than most of how she, in his view, threw her weight around. Right after the '60 election there was the matter of how to pay off Norman B. Judd for his work as head of the Illinois delegation to the nominating convention about which Davis got an interesting letter from Mrs. Lincoln, who was shopping in New York: "Perhaps you will think it no affair of *mine*, yet I see it almost daily mentioned, in the Herald, that *Judd &* some few Northern friends are *urging* the *former's* claims to a cabinet appointment. Judd would cause trouble & dissatisfaction, & if Wall Street testifies correctly, his business transactions have not always borne inspection. I heard the report, discussed at the table this morning by persons who did not know who was near, a party of gentlemen, evidently strong Republicans, they were laughing at the idea of *Judd* being any way connected with the cabinet in *these times,* when honesty in high places is so important. Mr. Lincoln's great attachment for you, is my present reason for writing. I know, a word from you will have much effect." In the end Lincoln had solved the problem by making Judd his Minister to Berlin, and Davis had seen Mrs. Lincoln have her way in another affair with his help. Mrs. Lincoln had asked Davis to approach the President on behalf of her brother-in-law, Ninian Edwards, who was in temporary financial straits and wanted an appointment to the Commissary Corps. Springfield Republicans were indignant at the thought because Edwards, who had turned Democrat and had opposed Lincoln's election, would be taking up a lucrative post that should be the reward of a loyal Republican and was, they claimed, of doubtful honesty. Mrs. Lincoln thought that a soothing word from a solid gold Republican like David Davis would be helpful, and he had obliged her with a letter to Lincoln: "I know him to be an upright, honest & honorable gentleman, who will never soil his hands in any business that may be entrusted to him by the Government. If I was in your position & could find a place that I thought Mr. Edwards could fill, I would give it to him." Lincoln had made Edwards Captain and Commissary of Subsistence in which post he got back on his financial feet without scandal. Davis would have to admit that Mrs. Lincoln, herself, knew the rules of the game: when Leonard Swett was in Washington later promoting Davis's appointment to the Supreme Court, he called on Mrs. Lincoln at the White House and she told him, "I've been fighting Davis' battles with Mr. Lincoln. Tell Davis his matter is all right." Still, feeling as he did, it could be embarrassing to be owing to Mrs. Lincoln when you were never sure what she might do, and Davis at times envied the men like Weed and Seward and Chase and even Grant who had manfully, in his view, gone against her grain.

By the time the question of her sanity came up Davis had been around Washington long enough to know how goodly a company were the men Mrs. Lincoln mistrusted. If he had not heard horror stories about her interfering ways from the men themselves, he had read about them in that Keckley woman's book—a book that had to be believed, since Mrs. Lincoln had never disputed its truth, only the propriety of publishing it. In one vivid bedroom scene Keckley depicted Mrs. Lincoln standing while she basted a dress, Mr. Lincoln lolling in a chair and stroking Tad's head, when a messenger burst in with an urgent message from Secretary of State Seward, the man who had narrowly lost out to Lincoln for the nomination. The interruption prompted a family argument that began with Mrs. Lincoln's: "Seward! I wish you had nothing to do with that man. He cannot be trusted."

"Mother, you are mistaken. Your prejudices are so violent that you do not stop to reason," Mr. Lincoln said. "Seward is an able man, and the country as well as myself can trust him."

"Father, you are too honest for this world! You should have been born a saint. You will generally find it a safe rule to distrust a disappointed ambitious politician."

On other occasions Mrs. Lincoln warned her husband to inquire into the motives of Secretary of the Treasury Salmon P. Chase, described General George B. McClellan as a "humbug" because he talked so much and did so little, and opposed the appointment of Andrew Johnson as military governor of Tennessee on the grounds that he was a dangerous demagogue. But her most withering fire was trained upon General Ulysses S. Grant, whom she once called, heedless of Keckley's presence in the room, "a butcher who is unfit to be at the head of an army."

"But he has been very successful in the field," Mr. Lincoln replied.

"Yes, he generally manages to claim a victory, but such a victory! He loses two men to the enemy's one. He has no management, no regard for life. If the war should continue four years longer, and he should remain in power, he would depopulate the North. I could fight an army as well myself. According to his tactics, there is nothing under the heavens to do but to march a new line of men up in front of the rebel breastworks to be shot down as fast as they take their position, and keep marching until the enemy grows tired of the slaughter."

"Well, mother, supposing that we give you command of the army. No doubt you would do much better than any general that has been tried."

Keckley reported that there was a "twinkle in the President's eyes" but "a ring of irony in his voice." Reading all this, Davis' reaction must have been: imagine taking such talk from a woman! No wonder Mrs. Lincoln lost all sense of restraint!

Perhaps because she was a woman herself, Keckley gave Mrs. Lincoln high marks as a good judge of character who was trying to protect her too trusting husband and, through him, the country. Anybody who knew the inside of Washington politics knew, of course, how hard Lincoln had had to struggle to wrest control of the Republican Party away from Seward, its nominal head in 1860; how Chase had plotted to take the 1864 nomination away from Lincoln; how McClellan had resisted Lincoln's orders to the point of outright insult. While Mrs. Lincoln's sanity was on trial before the people in the newspapers of 1875, President Grant's intelligence and integrity were also on trial in those same papers through their accounts of unfolding official corruption. Some readers like Myra Bradwell would pick up such things, and she, for one, was an admirer of Mrs. Lincoln's shrewdness and courage in speaking her mind. From her own struggle to get permission to practice the legal profession she knew the kind of reaction Mrs. Lincoln must have provoked from most men. The fact that Mrs. Lincoln appeared to have been right about so many of the men around her husband would not be redeeming. It would be the most galling attribute she possessed to those masculine minds that could paradoxically consider freeing the blacks a cause worthy of sacrificing their lives for, but complacently insist that a woman be kept in her place. Myra considered herself lucky to have married a man as understanding as the judge, and she was sure that she would have found Mr. Lincoln the same sort of person. In the scenes Keckly reported, Mr. Lincoln did not always agree with his wife, but he never demeaned her as a woman who had no right to speak and, in fact, was quoted as saying directly to Mary: "I give you credit for sagacity." No wonder the poor woman complained of being left so alone and freely admitted talking still to Mr. Lincoln, wherever he was.

Even before they had received the letter that Mrs. Lincoln smuggled out to them from Batavia, the Bradwells had been debating what they could, or should, do about her situation. The judge hadn't been consulted, of course; all that they knew had come to them as a complete shock through the columns of the papers. With their legal knowledge, they had been struck at once by a glaring flaw in the procedure: there had been *no* defense for Mrs. Lincoln. The reason for this was not apparent in the newspaper accounts, but the participation of legal lights like Ayer and Swett and Arnold, and the acquiesence of Judge Wallace, would suggest that this was a matter of deliberation rather than omission and that Mrs. Lincoln, therefore, *was* probably insane. Nevertheless, the echoes of the Packard case were too loud for the Bradwells to ignore. The Bradwells had campaigned with Mrs. Packard in '69 for a law protecting the earnings of women and had had their sympathies aroused with respect to her crusade two years before to protect women from being "railroaded" into asylums, as she had been.

Wife of the Rev. Theophilus Packard, a Congregationalist minister in Manteno, Illinois, Mrs. Packard was forty-six and the mother of six children when her husband had her committed to the State Hospital for the Insane at Jacksonville in 1860. At that time Illinois state law decreed that married women who "in the judgment of the medical superintendents of the state asylum at Jacksonville are evidently insane or distracted" could be detained at the request of their husbands "without the evidence of insanity required in other cases." Taking advantage of this statute, the Rev. Packard, with the concurrence of Dr. Andrew McFarland, superintendent at Jacksonville, had his wife put away for her theological meanderings. In their native Massachusetts where the Packards had lived until 1857, Mrs. Packard had been interested in Universalism and phrenology; in Illinois she had become involved with spiritualism and Swedenborgianism. The last straw, in her husband's view, was an effort she made in 1860 to switch her formal allegiance from the Congregationalist to the Methodist church. To support his contention that this flitting around among the faiths was not normal, Rev. Packard dredged up the fact that his wife had briefly been treated as a young girl at the Worcester State Hospital in Massachusetts for alleged delusions that she was a third person in the Holy Trinity and mother of Jesus Christ.

Whatever her past, Mrs. Packard had become by 1860 a woman to reckon with. From the first, she charged that her husband, who was fifteen years older than she, resented the fact that her intellectual and religious interests, particularly her spiritualism, interfered with her cooking and cleaning for him and his brood and that he had committed her to punish her for this neglect of housewifely duty. An articulate person capable of self-dramatization, she managed to get her case before the public in newspaper articles and books by her own hand. She became such an embarrassment to Dr. McFarland, who had a reputation to protect as president of the Association of Medical Superintendents of American Institutions for the Insane, then the nation's most prestigious mental health post, that she was sent home to her husband in 1863. A year later a court declared her sane and she went on the road to sell her books and the revolutionary idea that women should have equal protection under the law. The subtitle of one book—*Christianity and Calvinism Compared with an Appeal to the Government to Emancipate the Slaves of the Marriage Union*—caught the wave of enthusiasm for emancipation in the wake of Lincoln's proclamation and brought sales in the thousands. Through her public appearances and lobbying she succeeded in changing the commitment laws in Massachusetts, Iowa and Illinois, where the statute under which Mrs. Lincoln was tried by jury was enacted. In view of Mrs. Packard's success and good sense in promoting her causes it was difficult for intelligent, open-minded people like the Bradwells to avoid questioning the whole matter of what insanity was and how its victims should be treated.

Women were particularly vulnerable to misunderstanding and mistreatment at a time when there were as few female physicians as lawyers, and Myra Bradwell was sensitive to that. The prevailing masculine medical view was that the female reproductive system made women weaker vessels prone to crack under the stress of hysteria and other nervous disorders. This point of view permeated the public consciousness to the point where advertisers of patent medicines used it to sell their wares—mostly to women themselves. At the time Mary Lincoln was undergoing moral treatment in Batavia, *Harper's Weekly* carried an ad by Dr. Pierce of the World's Dispensary, Buffalo, New York, that began: "MODERN WOMEN—It is a sad commentary upon our boasted civilization that the women of our times have degenerated in health and physique until they are literally a race of invalids—pale, nervous, feeble, back-achy, with only here and there a few noble exceptions in the persons of robust, buxom ladies characteristic of the sex in days gone by." But there was hope, according to the ad, since Dr. Pierce's Favorite Prescription, a vegetable extract, was good for "weak back, nervous and general debility, falling and other displacements of internal organs . . . very many other chronic diseases

incident to women, not proper to mention here . . ." Bombarded
with such unrefuted statements, members of any male jury
would be predisposed to find that the strains of life had un-
hinged any female.

With all this in the back of their minds the Bradwells were
shaken by Mrs. Lincoln's hastily scribbled note. It was a plea for
help that showed no signs of insanity. To be sure, it was full of
oddly placed commas and dashes and underlinings, but such
punctuation had been characteristic of all the letters they had
seen of hers over the years. The real message that came through
was that she was totally aware of the fix she was in and very
determined to get out of it. *She* did not think she was insane. The
only way for the Bradwells to know for sure what was going on
was to see Mrs. Lincoln and judge her condition for themselves.
Like General Farnsworth, they took the first train they could
catch to Batavia.

Being a woman, Myra Bradwell was able to get closer to Mrs.
Lincoln than could any man. During one of several visits in late
July and early August she stayed overnight in Mrs. Lincoln's
rooms. Like General Farnsworth, she told Dr. Patterson that
she did not believe that Mary Lincoln, whom she called "my
dear girl," ought to be confined, that what his patient needed
was the kind of tender loving care that she could get only in a
home—preferably that of her sister, Mrs. Edwards, in Springfield. To Dr. Patterson Myra Bradwell cannily conceded that
she found Mrs. Lincoln "not quite right," but to Abram Wakeman in New York, whose relationship with Mrs. Lincoln had
continued despite the adverse publicity during the clothes sale,
Mrs. Bradwell wrote that their mutual friend was "quite well
& as I think not insane." What the Bradwells thought was that
Mrs. Lincoln would surely *become* insane if she were kept behind
bars, however disguised, and in sight of people whose behavior
was openly and obviously lunatic. They decided to get her out.

Myra Bradwell added her voice to Mary's by writing to Lizzie
Edwards in Springfield proposing a visit. Then on August 7 she

laid the groundwork for using the Packard strategy if necessary. She arrived at Batavia with a man she introduced to the staff as Mr. Wilkie of Chicago, a friend of Mrs. Lincoln's from Washington days. She was only stretching the truth a little: Franc B. Wilkie, as a member of the Washington press corps during the war, had met the First Lady once. Mrs. Bradwell did not think it necessary to mention that Wilkie was now a reporter for *The Chicago Times;* his professional services would not be called upon unless her negotiations failed. The outlook was promising that day because Dr. Patterson revealed that her intervention had pried an invitation to Springfield out of Lizzie Edwards. Mrs. Bradwell insisted that the doctor share the news with Robert Lincoln at once, assuming that he would follow through on his agreement to let his mother go. She was wrong. Instead of finding a way out for her "dear girl," Mrs. Bradwell had set off a skyburst of emotional fireworks.

As a Chicago lawyer Robert Lincoln knew the Bradwells by reputation, and that reputation shocked his conservative nature. When he heard of Mrs. Bradwell's visits to Batavia, he was alarmed. Now he had a suspicion that Mrs. Bradwell had pried an invitation to Springfield out of his Aunt Lizzie by using misinformation for unworthy motives. The minute Dr. Patterson's note reached him on that August 7th, he sat down to write a confidential letter to his aunt that would frustrate the Bradwells' plan. Once his aunt knew the awful truth that had not come out in the papers, she would understand that the talk of letting Mary Lincoln visit Springfield was only a way of humoring her.

Robert started by warning his aunt that Mrs. Bradwell was "a high priestess in a gang of Spiritualists and from what I have heard it is to their interest that my mother should be at liberty to control herself and her property." Then he proceeded to reveal the kind of private domestic detail that only real fear could have dragged out of him. He confided that having his mother live with them after Tad's death had forced the young

Lincolns temporarily to "break up housekeeping," that when Mary Harlan finally did come back to Chicago in '73 his mother had become so violently angry with her over "some trifle" that the two women had stopped speaking to each other, and that when his mother had come to the house to visit Mamie she "had driven my servants out of the room by her insulting remarks concerning their mistress & this in the presence of my little girl." But the real shocker, according to Robert, came in 1874 when his mother "suggested to a lady (who told me of it in some alarm) the idea of running away with the child. Such a freak would be no more astonishing than a good many I could tell you that you have never heard of. I would be ashamed to put on paper an account of many of her insane acts—and I allowed to be introduced in evidence only so much as was necessary to establish the case."

Robert confessed that he had not asked for help from his Aunt Lizzie or the other Springfield aunts—Frances Todd Wallace and Ann Todd Smith—because of his mother's estrangement from them. If his mother did come to the Edwards' house he doubted that "she would receive a call from any one of her sisters. Keep this letter & see if I am not correct when the time comes." He also predicted that his mother would use her freedom to escape, to go off to Europe or somewhere, and he dreaded that possibility, as his conclusion would indicate:

> "I have done my duty as I best knew and Providence must take care of the rest—If you have in your mind any plan by which my mother can be placed under care and *some control which will prevent her from making herself talked of by everybody* [author's italics], I hope you will tell it to me—I do not know who is willing to assume such an understanding, nor do I believe anyone could succeed in it unless backed by the authority of the law, as is Dr. Patterson—He is a most excellent and kind

hearted man & as she knows his authority, he has absolutely no trouble with her."

While Robert was awaiting his aunt's response to this letter, he had a call in his office from Myra Bradwell, and he hastened to send another note off to Springfield on August 10. He said that Mrs. Bradwell had convinced him that he had been misinformed about her involvement with Spiritualists and that he had told her he had no objection to a visit to Springfield, pending his Aunt Lizzie's response to the earlier letter. But in an effort to make sure of what that response would be he wrote: "How completely recovered my mother really is is shown by Mrs. B's saying she was to take out to her samples of dress goods she wants to buy—She has with her *seven* trunks of clothing and there are stored here *nine* more—I told Mrs. Bradwell that the experiment of putting her entirely at liberty would be interesting to those who have no responsibility for the results. They can afterwards dismiss the matter with a shrug of the shoulder."

Robert's efforts were not in vain—a succession of letters that would let him blast the Bradwells came out of Springfield:

Aug. 11—Lizzie in responding to Robert's letter of August 7 apologized profusely for causing him "annoyance" by falling for Mrs. Bradwell's "plan" out of her "sympathetic nature." With respect to Mary, she acknowledged that "after hearing the facts from you—her position, and difficulties in your family—I do not see, that you could have pursued any other course." After assuring Robert that she would not interfere in the future, Mrs. Edwards declined his invitation to go with him to Batavia to see her sister as "altogether impractical owing to feeble health—and entertaining doubts also of the expediency."

Aug. 12—With Robert's letter of Aug. 10 in hand, Lizzie struck a note of alarm. She was beginning to believe that the Springfield visit was a plot to get Mary released, and she was not up to that. "When your poor Mother proposed a visit to me," she wrote, "I felt I must respond in a kind manner: supposing that if the visit, was permitted she would be in charge of a responsible person and taken back again for a continuation of treatment." She went on to admit that she had been aware of and understood the "peculiarities" of her sister all of their lives and had "not indulged in faintest hope of a permanent cure." Because her own health was "causing such nervous prostration, as would render me, a most unfit person to control an unsound mind," she said that she was "unwilling to urge any step, or assume any responsibility" for Mary.

Aug. 13—Rethinking her letter of the day before, Lizzie again wrote Robert to express her delight that, despite the unfortunate circumstance, Mary was again being "amiable" and plead with him not to let Mary know what she had said about her "peculiarities" in her earlier letter since it might again bring about a rift between them. Then it was Lizzie's turn to shock Robert with some very private information to let him know how and why she had become sensitive to the reactions of people with mental problems. In a postscript to her letter dealing with "a most painful subject" and marked "Private" she wrote:

> "Insanity, although a new feature, in our family history, first appeared within my knowledge, in the case of my own daughter, at the early age of thirteen— for six months, she was so decidedly flighty, as to be closely guarded—her back from irritants is scarred its length—At the birth of each child, the same symptoms were shown, and severely felt, particularly by her husband, and myself—At no time, has she ever been natural in her demeanor—God pity those who are the victims—and who are the anxious sufferers in such terrible afflictions!"

With these letters to back him up, Robert moved rapidly to put an end to any proposed trip to Springfield. He was in a hurry because he planned to take his family east on a vacation, and so on Aug. 14 he wrote to Myra Bradwell a letter that indicated shrewd suspicions as to her strategy:

"Madam

Your note came here in my absence—On yesterday I received a letter from my Aunt Mrs Edwards which I gave this morning to Dr. Patterson. I regret beyond measure that my aunt is not able to aid me, as she says that her health is such that she cannot assume the responsibility—I had hoped for a possibility of benefit from my mother's apparent desire to renew her proper relations with her sister—I hope my aunt may be able to come up here soon as I have invited her to do—

I visited my mother on yesterday and I could not help observing with pain, a renewal in a degree of the same appearances which marred her in May and which I had not noticed in my last few visits—I do not know of any outside cause for this unless it is the constant excitement she had been in since your first visit—I am persuaded that you wish only her good and that you recognize the responsibility which is on me and which I cannot shift or divide—When you asked me a few days ago whether I objected to your visiting her, I said I only desired that you would be prudent in your conversation with her and would not carry letters for her—In view of what I have seen and which I regard as a partial destruction of the good accomplished by two months and a half of quiet and freedom from all chance of excitement, I am compelled to request that you visit her less often and not at all with persons with whom I am not acquainted and especially that you do not aid her in corresponding with persons other than her relatives—As to them she (can give) Dr. Patterson with mail unopened as many letters as she desires to write—

Very respectfully yours,
Robert T. Lincoln"

Knowing how easily women could get excited, Robert had tried to be diplomatic in laying the law down to Myra Bradwell, but he had to be sure that there would be no eruptions while he was gone and, therefore, asked Dr. Patterson to spell the situation out to Judge Bradwell. In a letter dated Aug. 15 and addressed to Hon. J.B. Bradwell, Dr. Patterson wrote:

"MY DEAR SIR:
In regard to the case of Mrs. Lincoln, allow me to say that I see no good to her, but harm only in discussing *with her* the question of her removal from this place. It tends to keep her mind in a constant ferment over questions which should not be determined by an insane mind—questions which should never have been discussed with her. Promises should never have been made to her, the fulfillment of which could by possible circumstances pass beyond the control of those who made them.

I am quite willing to believe that the objects of your visits and the numerous letters of Mrs. Bradwell are well meant, and not designed to promote unrest and discontent. But I have become fully convinced that such is their tendency and result. My opinion is that, for the present at least, those visits be discontinued. Mrs. Lincoln may be written to assigning reasons for not repeating visits.

I understand that R.T. Lincoln, conservator of Mrs. Lincoln, will be absent from home about two weeks. I will suggest that, at least until his return, Mrs. Lincoln should be simply let alone.

I have written the above in no unkind spirit, but from a sense of duty only to my patient.

Mrs. Lincoln has repeatedly said to me that you have in your possession an important paper that belongs to her. She again alluded to it to-day, saying, 'Judge Bradwell has again forgotten to bring my paper.' If you have any paper that belongs to her *that she ought to have,* perhaps it may be well to send it to her or to me, and thus relieve her seeming anxiety.

Very respectfully,
R.J. Patterson"

If Robert had suspicions about what the Bradwells were up to, the Bradwells had similar suspicions about Robert and Dr. Patterson. They were not disturbed by the accusations that their efforts on Mary's behalf were undoing the beneficial results of Dr. Patterson's treatment. Mary had evidently confessed to them that her seeming docility was a deliberate act she had been putting on, ever since the failure of her suicide attempt, to keep restraints upon her at a minimum until she could figure out how to escape. Naturally, their confidence in her and willingness to help gave her cause for hope and, therefore, put new life into her. When Mary Lincoln, crushed and quiet again, showed Myra a letter from Robert explaining that the Springfield visit had to be called off because her sister Lizzie was not up to taking responsibility for it and hypocritically claiming that "there is nothing I want so much as to have you with her," Myra got on a train for Springfield to have a face-to-face talk with Mrs. Edwards. It worked wonders. By August 17 Aunt Lizzie was singing a very different tune in another letter to Robert. She expressed fears that a failure to yield to Mary's desire to come to Springfield would "greatly increase her disorder," and went on to say that "you misapprehend my intention, while willing to receive, I shrank from the responsibility, after your statement of her condition," and then added, "I now say, that if *you will bring* her down, *feeling perfectly willing,* to make the experiment—I promise to do all in my power, for her comfort and recovery . . ."

By the time Robert could have received this letter he was away, but, knowing its contents from Myra, Judge Bradwell was prepared to respond to Dr. Patterson, and on the 19th he wrote:

"My Dear Sir:

I have received your letter stating that you can see no good to Mrs. Lincoln but harm only of discussing with her the question of her removal from your place, that promises should never have been made to her, the fulfillment of which could by possible circumstance pass beyond the control of those who made them, etc., etc. Now, sir, who was it but yourself that told Mrs. Lincoln and also myself that she was in a condition to visit her sister, Mrs. Edwards, at Springfield, Ill., and that you had written a letter to her son Robert to that effect? Mrs. Bradwell, to carry out the expressed wish of Mrs. Lincoln, went to Springfield to see Mrs. Edwards to see if she would take her sister, and was assured by her that she would do so if brought by her son, and saw him day before yesterday. No, Doctor, if you have the good of Mrs. Lincoln at heart, I am sure you will see that she is taken to her sister. It is in accordance with your letter, I am satisfied, that Mrs. Lincoln does not require to be confined in a house for the insane, and that it would be greatly for her good to be allowed to visit her relatives and friends. She pines for liberty. Some of the best medical men in America say that it is shameful to lock Mrs. Lincoln up behind grates as she has been, and I concur with them. I believe that such confinement is injurious to her in the extreme, and calculated to drive her insane. Are you not going to allow her to visit her relatives to see if it will benefit her, or will you take the responsibility and run the risk of the American people saying hereafter that it was the restraint of your institution that injured Mrs. Lincoln and proved her ruin? Should you not allow her to visit Mrs. Edwards, and insist on keeping her in close confinement, and I should be satisfied that the good of Mrs. Lincoln required it, as I certainly shall unless there is a change in her condition, I, as her legal adviser and friend, will see if a habeas corpus cannot open the door of Mrs. Lincoln's prison house. I am, etc.

JAMES B. BRADWELL"

Before getting involved with the courts, however, the Bradwells decided that it was time to unleash the eager dogs of the press. The judge's correspondence with Dr. Patterson was released, Franc Wilkie was told to go ahead and publish the piece he'd been holding for further developments and the judge granted an interview that appeared in another paper on August 23:

"This morning, a representative of THE POST AND MAIL called at the office of the *Legal News*, and soon found the courteous and humane Judge Bradwell at leisure for an interview, though at first somewhat adverse to it. Only the strong feeling of his good heart that Mrs. Lincoln was

A WRONGED WOMAN,

and that, as a President's widow, the public were interested in her personal welfare, and had a right to know the facts, induced him to talk upon the lamentable theme.

The following dialogue ensued:

REPORTER—Judge Bradwell, is THE POST AND MAIL correct in inferring that yourself and Mrs. Bradwell are the legal gentleman and lady taking legal steps for the permanent release of Mrs. Lincoln from her confinement at Batavia?

JUDGE BRADWELL—Well, I have been to see Mrs. Lincoln several times of late, as also has Mrs. Bradwell; but no strictly 'legal' steps have been taken, as it is hoped that her release from

HER UNJUST INCARCERATION

can be effected amicably. Do you want to write anything on this?

R—Certainly; if you know anything about Mrs. Lincoln's condition and confinement at Batavia which the world doesn't know, and are disposed to tell it.

J.B.—Well, sir, I have no hesitation whatever in saying that Mrs. Lincoln ought not to be where she now is, and never ought to have been placed there. It was

A GROSS OUTRAGE

to imprison her there behind grates and bars in a place understood to be for mad people. Why to be so shut up and guarded and locked up at night, with the feeling that it may last for life, is enough to make almost any aged and delicate woman crazy. She is no more insane to-day than you and I are.

R—What makes you think so, Judge?

J.B.—I am as

THOROUGHLY CONVINCED OF IT

as of my own existence. I have had several business letters from her since she has been there, and Mrs. Bradwell has had letters of womanly friendship from her repeatedly; and she writes as straight and intelligible a business letter as she ever did, and as good, friendly letters as one need ask for. There is

NOT THE SLIGHTEST TRACE OF INSANITY

or of weak mind about any of her writings.

R—Well, a good letter is one of the best proofs possible of a sound mind. Will you permit one or more of her letters to be printed?

J.B.—I should hardly feel warranted in doing that without Mrs. Lincoln's consent; but you may take my word for it that they are good sane letters.

R.—When did you see and talk with her last?

J.B.—One week ago to-day.

R.—What did she say about herself?

J.B.—She sighed and plead for liberty like a woman shut up without cause. Said she to me: 'Mr. Bradwell, what have I done that I should be kept here in this prison behind these grates, my footsteps followed, and every action watched by day, and my bedroom door locked upon the outside at night, and the key taken away by my jailor? I am not mad, but soon shall be.

I WANT LIBERTY

to go among my friends.'

R.—Is it not a pleasant place then?

J.B.—Oh, yes; the scenery is fine, and Mrs. Lincoln eats well and sleeps well, and has a healthy look. But she does not well brook the idea of being a prisoner. I sat in the room with her and looked out upon the Fox River with the forests and flowers and the lawn, and said to her: 'Mrs. Lincoln, this is very nice.' She replied: 'Yes, it is very nice to you who have your freedom to go and come as you please, but not so to me who can see it only through those window bars. Everywhere I go those hateful bars are before my mind, if not my eyes.'

R.—She will be allowed to visit her sister, will she?

J.B.—We hope so. Dr. Patterson

HAS SIGNED A CERTIFICATE

of her fitness to go; but she has not got it, and I have not, but he told me he had signed it. Mrs. Edwards wrote to her that she could come and live with her, and it is expected that when Robert Lincoln returns from the East, about the middle of this week, he will go to Batavia and accompany his mother to Springfield. But I shall only feel safe when she is out.

DR. PATTERSON IS A VERY PECULIAR MAN.

I know that some letters she has sent have not been allowed to reach her friends, and some that have been sent her have not reached her. You can't tell what motives may tend to keep her there. Human nature is human nature. But if she is not soon out, there will be startling developments not to be mentioned now. Let her get out of danger first."

The very next morning, August 24, an unsigned article headed "MRS. LINCOLN—Her Physicians Pronounce Her Entirely Sane" appeared in the Chicago *Times:*

"Recently a representative of *The Times,* in quest of scientific facts by means of personal observation, visited the institution of Dr. Patterson at Batavia, and while there was introduced to Mrs. Lincoln by a mutual friend who happened to be there at the same time, not as a newspaperman, but as a gentleman who knew her history and who took a friendly interest in all that pertained to her welfare.

The lady appeared in very good spirits, and her mind was clear and sprightly. After some preliminary conversation she invited the gentleman to her room to obtain a view of the pastoral landscape from that source, and to pursue the interesting conversation already begun. This opportunity which had thus been presented by circumstances, was improved by the gentleman of the press, to discover the exact condition of her mind, so far as he was able to do so, by drawing her into conversation on all possible topics in which he deemed her to have been interested, either pleasantly or painfully during her life. If there were any weak points in her mind, he was determined to find out what they were. If she were brooding over any circumstance of her sad life, he was bent on finding out what it was. Her visit to London was alluded to, and thoroughly discussed. Little Tad was with her there, and she alluded to the child, now dead, but whose memory is very dear to her, with all the warmth and affection a fond mother might be expected to exhibit. There was not a sign of weakness or any abnormal manifestations of mind visible. She conversed fluently and rationally about her wanderings in England. She narrated her experiences in Germany, dwelling on the subject of her travels with much detail and interest to the end. During all this time she not only exhibited a sound and rational judgment, but gave evidence of the possession of uncommon powers of observation and memory.

Her attention was called to the time when the visitor had met her in Washington in 1862. The occasion she remembered. Knowing that the death of little Tad and the assassination of Mr. Lincoln were two incidents in her life that were known to have made the most powerful impressions on her mind of any events which had ever occurred to her, these circumstances were adroitly introduced into the conversation. During all this her admirable mind maintained its poise and perfection. Concerning Mr. Lincoln, she related anecdotes illustrating his extreme good nature. She conversed about the assassination. No mental weakness, under any possible test, could be discovered. She spoke of public men with whom she had become acquainted during her residence at the White House. She specially dwelt on the friendship which existed between Mr. Seward and Mr. Lincoln and herself. It was the habit of the secretary to dine with Mr. Lincoln and herself informally, two or three times a week. She alluded to the Motleys, whom she met in England and spoke with great sensibility of their kindness, and told how badly she felt when the minister was removed. She very keenly described the characters she had met abroad, showing that she possesses great powers of analysis. She gave her views of foreigners, and foreign matters, concerning which she exhibited great apprehension and acuteness of mind. She also spoke of the books she was engaged in reading, and the life she led. Her health at present, she observed, was superb. She had never been better. When she came to Chicago from Florida she had been suffering somewhat from fever, and her nervous system was somewhat shattered. She was prostrated, and any eccentricities she might have manifested then, if any, she attributed to this fact.

There were some light iron bars over the door, to which she called the attention of the gentleman. She said they seemed to menace her, and they annoyed her with the idea she was in prison. She was somewhat apprehensive that the prison bars, and the presence of insane people in the house, whose wild and piercing cries she sometimes heard, might affect her mind so as to unseat her reason, in time. She commented upon journals and journalists with great intelligence. The conversation took the widest possible range, and from this the representative of *The Times* became convinced that her mind was in a perfectly sound and healthy condition. She made no complaint of her treatment.

She thought she would like a little more liberty to drive out, and a little more liberty to receive her friends. She exhibited marvelous charity through the entire course of the interview for those by whose instrumentality she had been placed there. The gentleman departed thoroughly convinced that whatever condition of mind Mrs. Lincoln may have been in previously, she is unquestionably compos mentis now, and ought not to be deprived of her liberty."

This performance might have provoked something in the way of awe on the part of politically sensitive readers, particularly in the New York area. Whether the artist was Wilkie or Mrs. Lincoln herself, the effect of introducing Seward and Motley by name was brilliant. During the war Wilkie had worked for the New York *Times,* a pro-Seward paper, and she was evidently going out of her way to make amends for what had been said about her and Seward during the clothes sale and in the Keckley book. As for Motley, Mrs. Lincoln was simultaneously doing a favor for her late friend, Senator Sumner, and getting a dig in at President Grant. Grant had removed Motley as Minister to England because he had supported Sumner in opposing Grant's treaty to annex Santo Domingo. Deft dealing for an insane mind. However much was read into it, the Bradwell orchestrated publicity forced the other side out into the open.

With his motives and judgment so openly challenged, John T. Stuart, the mayor of Springfield, launched a very roundabout counterattack. In its editorial columns of August 28, the Chicago *Tribune* carried this curious item:

"A special dispatch from Springfield to the St. Louis *Republican* says:
'The relatives of Mrs. Lincoln here are greatly annoyed by the late obtrusion of her name in print and by the insinuations made that she is detained in the

Batavia Hospital unnecessarily. For some time after her arrival at the hospital her prospect for recovery was very good, and it was hoped her health would be premanently restored. It is known that a belief in Spiritualism was one form of her mental disorder, and a visit made her by a Chicago lady who professes that belief has caused a recurrence of the most distressing symptoms. Her relations here regret the late unpleasant exposé, but it is impossible to prevent such annoyances as long as the publication of sensational newspapers is a paying one.'

The comment of the above dispatch is a timely one and lacks only in severity. The scandal was set afloat by over-officious and intermeddling mischief-makers, who interfered in a matter which did not concern them, for purposes of sensation. The pretense made by them that she is sane and confined in the asylum against her will is an atrocious libel upon her son and friends. If she were really sane, they would be the first to know it, and remove her at once, and no one would rejoice more than they to find that this unfortunate lady had been restored to health in body and mind. There is no scandal in this case, except so far as the intermeddling scandalizers themselves are concerned. Inasmuch as there are plenty of other objects upon which they can exercise their slop-over philanthropy and maudlin sentimentalizing, it is inconceivable why they have chosen Mrs. Lincoln for the exercise of their talents in this direction, except that it affords them an opportunity to wound the feelings of her friends, and to libel them atrociously besides."

Not only did the *Tribune's* relentless Republicanism come through in that editorial but there was also a hint of jealousy at having been bypassed as the vehicle for the kind of sensation that people were willing to pay for. This was quickly rectified since Dr. Patterson, impressed by the *Tribune's* attitude, sat down on that same day and wrote the newspaper's editor an open letter that could be considered one of the biggest scoops in the unfolding case:

"BATAVIA, Ill., Aug. 28—It is no fault of mine that the sad case of Mrs. Lincoln has been again in all the papers of the land. But now that so many incorrect statements have been made, I deem it proper to correct some of them.

On the 19th of May last, Mrs. Lincoln, being in court, was declared 'insane and a fit subject for treatment in a State Hospital for the Insane.' The warrant for commitment was at the request of her friends, directed to the undersigned, commanding him, 'forthwith to arrest and convey her to Bellevue Place, Batavia, Ill.'

It has been publicly stated that I have 'certified' to the recovery, or mental soundness, of Mrs. Lincoln. This is not true. She is certainly much improved, both mentally and physically; but I have not at any time regarded her as a person of sound mind. I heard all the testimony at the trial, May 19, and saw no reason then to doubt the correctness of the verdict of the jury. I believe her to be now insane.

The question of Mrs. Lincoln's removal from this place, notwithstanding her mental impairment, has received careful consideration from her conservator, Mr. Robert T. Lincoln, and myself. The proposition having been made that she should go and live with her sister, Mrs. Edwards, in Springfield, I at once said that if she would do this in good faith, and thus secure a quiet home for herself, I should favor it, 'unless her condition should change for the worse.' This was written to Mr. Robert T. Lincoln in a letter addressed to him on the 9th inst. And this is all there is of the 'certificate' said to have been given by me of the 'recovery' or 'mental soundness' of Mrs. Lincoln. In accordance with the above conditional sanction of the proposition for removal, I have occasion to know that Robert T. Lincoln made efforts to perfect arrangements for the transfer of Mrs. Lincoln to Springfield.

It is well known that there are certain insane persons who need what in the medico-legal science is termed interdiction, which does not necessarily imply restraint. If time should show that Mrs. Lincoln needs only the former, without the latter, all will rejoice to see any possible enlargement of her privileges. And now, although the conditions upon which on the 9th inst. I favored her removal, have been modified by the presence of a greater degree of mental perturbation than at that time existed, I am still unwilling to throw any obstacle in the way of giving her an opportunity to have a home with her sister. But I am willing to record the opinion that such is the character of her malady she will not be content to do this, and that the experiment, if made, will result only in giving the coveted opportunity to make extended rambles, to renew the indulgence of her purchasing mania and other morbid mental manifestations.

In regard to the treatment of Mrs. Lincoln while under my care, it has been stated that she has been 'kept in close confinement,' 'virtually imprisoned behind gates and bars,' 'locked by her jailer as a prisoner,' 'incarcerated,' etc., etc. These and other harsh terms are not used in the interest of truth. They are unjust and do no credit to those who apply them to the case of Mrs. Lincoln. She need not remain in doors unless by her own choice more than two or three waking hours of any day. A carriage is always at her command.

She may ride or walk when and where she pleases, on condition that she shall return at proper hours, and be accompanied by some suitable person or persons. She receives calls from ladies of her acquaintance in Batavia, and may return them. She has been called upon by Gen. Farnsworth, of St. Charles, and by some of her relatives in Springfield. She has had, until the 16th inst., private unrestricted personal intercourse with Judge Bradwell, who, in a threatening and insulting letter to me, calls himself her 'legal adviser and friend.' The wife of Judge Bradwell, until the date above named, has been permitted repeatedly to visit Mrs. Lincoln, write her numerous letters, bear messages and packages of letters from her, and lodge over night with her in her room.

As to 'guarded windows,' I have only to say they are made as unobjectionable as it is possible to make them. A light ornamental screen was at first placed before Mrs. Lincoln's windows. These were subsequently removed. But when it is remembered that the same evening on which Mrs. Lincoln was declared insane she attempted suicide, all right-minded persons will agree that guarded windows were among the proper precautions against accident.

As to 'barred doors,' there are none at Bellevue Place. Mrs. Lincoln's doors leading to the outer world are never locked during the day time. The outer door only is locked at bedtime at night by her private attendant, and the key retained by the attendant, who sleeps in an adjoining room communicating with that of Mrs. Lincoln. This, to my mind, is the proper thing to do.

Mrs. Lincoln has been placed where she is under the forms of law, and, if any have a grievance, the law is open to them. This sad case has commanded the con-

stant endeavors of those who have the care of her un-
selfishly to do the best for Mrs. Lincoln.

R.J. Patterson"

By the time that Robert Lincoln got back to Chicago from his
vacation, it looked as if he had been outmaneuvered by his
mother's forces. Both in writing to him and in speech to Myra
Bradwell his Aunt Lizzie had gone on record as being willing
to take Mary into her home; Judge Bradwell and an impartial
observer, however anonymous, had announced to the world
their convictions from personal observation that the former
First Lady was of sound mind; despite some mumbling about
"rambles," her professional keeper, Dr. Patterson, had publicly
proclaimed his willingness to let her go to Springfield. It remained only for Robert, her conservator, to get Judge Wallace's
permission in accordance with his often stated desire to see his
mother visit her sister. But Robert could not bear the thought
of having all that he had undergone, the agony of public exposure, to achieve what he had achieved, be so quickly undone.
Once more he would need to worry day and night that his
mother would get herself talked about. With him it was not a
question of whether, but only when and how. On the other hand
he could not afford to appear to be some sort of unnatural ogre
of a son. In this crisis, as before, he sought support for his
position from sources that could not be faulted by the public.

On September 4 Robert Lincoln wrote a letter to Dr. Andrew
McFarland, whose reputation for defending the value of restraint he must have known from all the publicity in the Packard case. Dr. McFarland had left his state position to open a
private asylum, Oak Lawn Retreat, in Jacksonville, but he remained a leading figure in mental health circles. Robert asked
the doctor to see his mother at Batavia and render an opinion
on whether she should be taken to Springfield. "As a guest of
her sister, I do not think it possible that the same restraint could

be exercised over possible irrational acts, should they occur as if she remained under the care of Dr. Patterson, but I am anxious that she should visit my aunt, if it is not probable that harm to her may come of it," Robert wrote. No doubt impressed by the stature of the patient, Dr. McFarland, a grandfatherly looking man with a long beard and balding head, took the assignment with almost comical gravity. To keep his visit secret he told people he met enroute that he was going "East," and he registered under a false name in a Chicago hotel for an overnight stay before proceeding to Batavia. On Sept. 8, he wrote Robert Lincoln the kind of letter that Robert so obviously hoped to get:

"Sir,
Agreeable to your wish, I have this day visited Mrs. Abraham Lincoln, now under treatment at Bellevue Retreat, Batavia. My interview with her was protracted, confidential and such as to possess me of all the facts and features of her case. My opinion being especially desired upon the expediency of her making a visit to her sister at Springfield, I should doubt the safety of that step unless she was, all the time, under the care of some discreet and responsible person; and see no good results likely to follow beyond gratifying an ardent desire to go, in which she seems to have been prompted by others. My fears are, that a desire for further adventure, will take possession of her mind, as soon as beyond the control of the present guardians of her safety, that may be attended with hazard if gratified.

It is fully my opinion that all the steps taken, growing out of her unhappy mental condition, have been absolutely necessary for her interests, her safety, and her hope of restoration. All the measures now in use in her case are no more than her helpless and irresponsible state of mind render unavoidable, and will bear the fullest inspection on the part of her innumerable sympathisers, the country over.

I am pained to add that there are features of her case that give me grave apprehensions as to the result unless the utmost quietude is observed for the few ensuing months, beyond which all reasonable hope of restoration must be abandoned unless success within that period is achieved.

Andrew McFarland, M.D."

Robert had also requested Dr. A.G. McDill, superintendent of the Wisconsin State Hospital, for an opinion, but he didn't wait for Dr. McDill to work a visit to Batavia into his busy schedule. On Sept. 9, the day after he got Dr. McFarland's letter, Robert wrote an almost curt note to Dr. Patterson reporting the McFarland opinion but stating without explanation that he was going to try the Springfield experiment anyway and outlining details of railroad schedules, trunk storage and the like necessary to get Mrs. Lincoln to Springfield on Friday, Sept. 11. Robert's unexpected reaction to Dr. McFarland's prediction of disaster from the experiment took on the nature of a diabolical demonstration: let her crazy antics show all those people out there how right I am. Tucked away in the file he was already starting to keep would be Dr. McFarland's letter to produce if anyone accused him of dragging his feet on this experiment for mean or personal reasons; in view of this opinion, he was obviously using his heart instead of his head, wasn't he? He did, however, wire Dr. McFarland and ask him to engage a "discreet and responsible" person to accompany Mrs. Lincoln to Springfield. With many misgivings, Dr. McFarland sent a Miss Anna Kyle to join Robert and his mother on the 3:40 P.M. train from Chicago to Springfield on Sept. 11. Once again they rode in a private car provided by the railroad's president, but mother and son could have taken no pleasure in the journey.

CHAPTER VIII:

"That holy deluge . . ."

BACK IN SPRINGFIELD: a homecoming of sorts, but not the sort of homecoming Mary Lincoln could ever have imagined or ever would have wanted. Greeting her on the veranda of their house on the hill, Lizzie and Ninian Edwards did their best to give her a warm welcome. But misgiving, doubt, something close to fear stood in their eyes. It was not at all as heartfelt as their greeting of thirty-six years ago when they made her twirl around until her hooped skirts rose and flared and clapped their hands in delight at having such a beautiful belle arrive to turn their home into a center of gaiety. Just from the look of her, Lizzie's claims to "feeble health" were justified; she was thin and drawn, and her dark hair pulled back into a bun stretched the skin so tight across her high cheekbones that it made of her face a gaunt mask. Ninian's chin whiskers were white, and a slight stoop gave him the appearance of having shrunk from that great height that had entitled him, along with Mr. Lincoln, to be one of the admired "long nine" of the legislature in the happier days of her first coming. Even the house itself—one of the few in Springfield that deserved to be called a mansion back in the '30's—seemed to have shrunk despite an ugly addition they had built in the years of an expanding family. Ugly or not, it was a blessing in Mary's eyes since it once more made it possible for her to find shelter there.

Inside the Edwards house little had changed. There were fixtures for the gas lights Mary hated on the walls, and not far from the bedroom they assigned her a linen closet that had been enlarged and altered to accommodate the inside plumbing conveniences that were one of the true blessings of progress, especially for a woman with her ailments. But much of the furniture was the same. The long table at which her wedding party had been seated was set again for the full complement of relatives whom Lizzie had invited for a dinner to greet Mary and bolster her spirits. When Mary heard that her other sisters, Frances and Ann, were both coming, she did enjoy a small sense of triumph. During one of the sessions back at Batavia when Robert had tried to persuade her that going to Springfield wasn't a good idea he had been tactless enough to say that he doubted whether Frances and Ann would want to see her. Robert would never understand women. Her sisters, who had inherited as sharp Todd tongues as hers, had used them to lacerate Mr. Lincoln when they thought he wasn't good enough to marry a Todd. After Mr. Lincoln had far outpaced their respectable husbands—Frances' Dr. Wallace, the druggist and physician; Ann's Mr. Smith, the merchant—the sisters were not only jealous but embarrassed by their misjudgment. It had actually made matters worse with Frances when Mr. Lincoln had rescued Dr. Wallace from financial difficulties with a government job, as he had Ninian Edwards. Lizzie had been as adamantly opposed to Mr. Lincoln as a suitor as had the others, but the feeling of *noblesse oblige* conferred upon Lizzie by being an Edwards as well as a Todd and a motherly tolerance conferred on her by being the oldest had enabled her to maintain some kind of relationship with Mary. Lizzie, for instance, had put aside any sisterly differences to rush to Washington and be with Mary during the trying time after Willie's death. As for the others, Mary had not had the time or inclination to try to smooth their jealousy-ruffled feathers when she was riding high during the Washington years, nor the heart for it in the difficult times since. But she knew her sisters, knew that curiosity alone would bring them running, knew that her adversity would soften them. With places changed, she would be the same. She would feel at home in this house and in her family, but what about out there on the streets of Springfield?

The people of Springfield were full of sickening lies about her and Mr. Lincoln. Billy Herndon had seen to that. She had to hope, even pray, that she would not run into *him* in the streets, because she would very likely try to scratch his eyes out at the risk of being sent back to the asylum. Even more devastating than the attacks upon her loyalty to the Union during the war—attacks so vicious that she could not allow herself the humanity of mourning for her three half brothers and brother-in-law who died for the Confederate cause—had been Herndon's attacks on the most truly sacred thing in her life: her relationship with Mr. Lincoln. Mr. Lincoln had hardly been laid to rest before Herndon started giving those lectures full of nonsense about how Mr. Lincoln's heart lay buried in the grave with some New Salem girl named Ann Rutledge. It was an outright lie, but it was the kind of thing people wanted to believe to explain the deep melancholy in Mr. Lincoln's nature that they could not otherwise understand. Mary wasn't sure that she understood that aspect of him herself, but she was sure that it had nothing to do with Ann Rutledge, a name he had never mentioned in all of their twenty-three years of marriage. If his sadness had any personal cause, it could have been the death of his mother when he was only a boy, an early blow from life that she and Mr. Lincoln had both suffered. Even Herndon would agree with her description of Mr. Lincoln as "truth itself," and Mr. Lincoln had told her over and over again in those bedroom conversations that were just about the only part of her life still unpublished that he had never cared for anyone else. He had told the world, too, right at a White House reception. It always gave Mary a little thrill to think about that incident. She had been standing to the side and behind the President, as usual, and making conversation with some guests filing through the line when she noticed that the President was looking at her with a small smile and saying something to a correspondent from the *Christian Register*. Minutes later the correspondent was shaking her hand and saying, "You're a fortunate woman, Mrs. Lincoln. Do you know what your husband just told me? He said, 'My wife is as handsome as when she was a girl and I, a poor nobody then, fell in love with her, and what is more, I have never fallen out.'"

Mary couldn't imagine what had possessed Herndon to say that there was no love between her and Mr. Lincoln except that she had never given him an opportunity to observe them together in their home. The people who had bore different testimony. Her half sister, Emilie Todd Helm, an impressionable eighteen when she spent several months as their guest in Springfield, pictured them as veritable love birds. She liked to tell people how Mary would run out to the street to greet a homecoming Mr. Lincoln and return to the house with him hand-in-hand, how once when she lost her temper because he was late to dinner he scooped her up in his arms and kissed her quiet. The Rev. James Smith, her Presbyterian pastor in Springfield, was often with them in the house on Eighth Street in pleasure, such as the times when he and Mr. Lincoln would sit by the fire and discuss religion, and in pain, such as the time when he brought them spiritual solace after the death of four-year-old Eddie, their second son. The minister read of Herndon's Ann Rutledge lecture in a newspaper in Scotland where he had been appointed a consul by President Lincoln in his retirement years. He was so incensed that he released a letter he had written to Herndon to the Dundee *Advertiser*, and it was reprinted by the New York *Times* and the Chicago *Tribune*. The Rev. Smith made the point that a law office was not the best vantage point from which to judge a man's home life, related how he had been taken into the home and hearts of the Lincolns, and said, "Mr. Lincoln . . . was utterly incapable of withholding from the bride he led to the altar that which was her due, by giving her a heart dead and buried in the grave of another, but that, in the deep and honest sincerity of his soul, he gave her a heart overflowing with love and affection; and my intercourse with him and his family left the abiding impression upon my mind, by his demeanor toward her, that he was to the wife of his bosom a most faithful, loving and affectionate husband." If people had discounted the Rev. Smith's testimony on grounds that he was piously supporting holy matrimony, they couldn't have had the same reaction to the words that Senator Sumner, a most worldly and sophisticated man who knew their "home life" in the White House, spoke during the debate on her pension: "Surely, the honorable members of the Senate must be weary of casting mud on the garments of the wife of Lincoln: those same garments on which one terrible night, a few years ago, gushed out the blood and brains of Abraham Lincoln. She sat beside him in the theatre and she received that pitiful, that holy deluge on her hands and skirts because she was the chosen companion of his heart. She loved him. I speak of that which I know. He had all her love and Lincoln loved, as only his mighty heart could love, Mary Lincoln."

Herndon chose to ignore this kind of testimony, chose to ignore, too, what she had told him back in '66 during an interview she granted him at the St. Nicholas Hotel on one of her trips down to Springfield from Chicago to visit the grave. Because Mr. Lincoln had put such trust in his "Billy," she had thought him to be at least honest in his quest for information to write a book about the President, or she would never have talked to him, especially when he came to her reeking of liquor. What she had told Herndon then was that Mr. Lincoln "was the kindest man, most tender husband, and loving father in the world. He gave us all unbounded liberty, saying to me always when I asked for anything, 'You know what you want, go and get it,' and never asking if it were necessary. He was very indulgent to his children. He never neglected to praise them for any of their good acts. He often said, 'It is my pleasure that my children are free and happy, and unrestrained by parental tyranny. Love is the chain whereby to bind a child to its parents.' " In taking his own view of their domestic life, Herndon had twisted hers around to interpret Mr. Lincoln's kindness as weakness in the face of her wrath, his concept of love as carelessness in the raising of children. He viewed the Lincoln boys as brats and complained of Mr. Lincoln's bringing them to the office on Sundays while she was at church and letting them make a shambles of the place by scattering papers around and spilling ink. No doubt they did that, but then the office that Herndon was supposed to tend was such a shambles anyway that Mary could remember dirt staying in a corner so long that the seeds within it sprouted.

Except in emergencies when Mr. Lincoln was away, Mary stayed out of that office since its disorder disturbed her. She had such a drive to keep things neat and tidy, to keep schedules and be on time, that Mr. Lincoln with his casual disregard for these things could send her into a rage or give her a blinding headache. Those temper tantrums and headaches were beyond her control, part of her nature, a cross that she and those who loved her had to bear. Acutely aware of them herself, she always tried to make up for whatever she had said or done with warm apologies, which in Mr. Lincoln's case were often of the private and passionate sort. Far from being afraid of her wrath, Mr. Lincoln sometimes teased it out of her to enjoy the fireworks that lighted up her eyes and spirit. As he would tell friends after one of her eruptions, "It does her a power of good, and it doesn't hurt me any." His tolerance of her imperfections was the tolerance of love as was her tolerance of his. She never did cure him of the habits of coming late to meals, of stretching out on the floor with his head propped against a chair to read while the boys crawled over him, of lounging around in shirtsleeves and slippers and even answering the door in such attire. Mr. Lincoln could be as stubborn as she could be explosive. As she had tried to explain to Herndon, "none of us, no man or woman, could rule him after he had once fully made up his mind. I could always tell when in deciding anything he had reached the ultimatum. At first he was very cheerful, then he lapsed into thoughtfulness, bringing his lips together in a firm compression. When these symptoms developed I fashioned myself accordingly, and so did all others have to do sooner or later."

One thing that Herndon had missed completely was the intellectual companionship that she and Mr. Lincoln had shared from their very first meeting. It was a rare thing in marriage, she knew, and she doubted that Herndon enjoyed it with either of his wives. She was so involved with keeping abreast of the latest thinking in books and lectures that her own sisters called her a "blue stocking," but Mr. Lincoln appreciated the fact that she was far better educated than he in these matters. In the calmer times of their hectic lives she would read to him from the poetry that they both loved, from such classics as the plays of Shakespeare, from modern novels that she thought to be of value. Contrary to popular misconception, Lincoln was not much of a reader; having had so little formal education, it came hard to him. Of all people, Herndon had to know this. A wide reader himself, particularly in philosophy, Herndon expressed irritation at Lincoln's lying on the couch in the office and reading newspapers aloud. Mr. Lincoln, however, could hardly get enough of the theater; he and Mary went together to every play or opera that managed to reach Springfield and nearly every performance of any worth at all in Washington. When it was inappropriate for them to go out, as in the time of mourning after Willie's death, Mr. Lincoln thoughtfully tried to bring cultural entertainment to her in the White House. She could remember especially the visit of Madame Patti. On a trip to Chicago in '53 Mr. Lincoln had heard Patti, then only ten, in concert with the Swedish violinist Ole Bull, and he wanted to be sure that Mary could enjoy her wonderful voice when he read that she would be in Washington. While Patti trilled her way through some intricate arias, the performance was a pleasant diversion, but when she sang "The Last Rose of Summer," Mary was so overcome with memories of sweet Willie that she had to jump up and look out the window to hide the stream of tears on her cheeks. Mr. Lincoln hadn't helped matters much by asking for "Home, Sweet Home" next, and they were all in tears when Patti left. In memory that experience was no longer tied to the specific hurt of Willie's death; it represented Mr. Lincoln's sensitivity and their shared emotional response to art and to life.

While ignoring the Lincolns' mental compatability and the fact that Mr. Lincoln took more advice than abuse from Mary—for instance, Herndon had to be quite well-acquainted with the circumstances when she argued her husband out of taking an appointment as governor of the Oregon territory that would have ended his political career—Herndon did credit her with the making of a President in his queer and bitter fashion. He said that by making Mr. Lincoln, a fundamentally lazy man, so uncomfortable at home, Mary had driven him out to the office and judicial circuit where he made a name for himself. Unfortunately young Henry Rankin who had read law in the Lincoln and Herndon office in '56 and spent a good deal of time in their home wasn't trying to cash in on what *he* knew by making speeches. But it had come to Mary's ears that, after hearing Herndon talk, Rankin had told people that it was a "cruel, bitter, false charge" that Mr. Lincoln spent so much time out on the Eighth Circuit to escape home. In Rankin's view, Mary pushed Mr. Lincoln out onto the circuit—at great inconvenience to herself in keeping house alone—so that he could accumulate the money and wide acquaintance he needed to realize his political potential. Rankin saw Mary as "a stimulus to Lincoln's intellectual life." Far from causing his periods of moody silence, as claimed by Herndon, Mary was the only one who could pull him out of them, according to Rankin. "Her sprightliness of spirit, her keenness of wit, the brightness of her versatile mind, lit up many times—as I personally know—the gloom and self-centered moodiness of his spells of melancholy," he reported. Sister Emilie would agree. She liked to recall a time when Mr. Lincoln, in one of his moods, sat staring into the fire while she and Bob played checkers and Mrs. Lincoln sewed. "Your silence is remarkably soothing, Mr. Lincoln, but we are not quite ready for sleep just yet," Mary told her husband, and when he didn't seem to hear, she got up and took his hand and added, "I fear my husband has become stone deaf since he left home at noon." That brought Mr. Lincoln around. "I believe I have been both deaf and dumb for the last half hour," he admitted, "but now you shall not complain." He then told an anecdote that broke them all up in laughter.

Nobody who knew anything about the Lincoln of Springfield days, including Mary, would argue with Herndon's claim that Mr. Lincoln was in need of prodding from time to time, especially when he fell into one of his funks. Mary was proud of the fact that she had been the one to do most of this. From the time when, as a little girl, she had talked of going to the White House with Mr. Clay, Mary had never tried to disguise her ambition. Early on in their courtship confidences, she discovered that Mr. Lincoln had a similar ambition, and her belief that he would realize it probably helped keep her constant during the very uncertain time that their engagement was broken. Thinking of that reminded her painfully of another Herndon lie—that Mr. Lincoln had deserted her at the altar, so to speak. No wedding had yet been planned when he came to her with his doubts— doubts that he could support her because of his debts, doubts that he was worthy of her because of his background. She knew that they were doubts that he had to work through on his own, and so she let him go. But she believed that he *would* work them

189

through, because that instinct of hers about people had led her to sense the strong stuff of which he was made. Once they were married she seized every opportunity to talk of his prospects. When Mr. Lincoln's Vermillion County partner, Ward Hill Lamon, first came to their Springfield house for dinner he told her, "Mr. Lincoln is a great favorite in the eastern part of the state." She replied, "Yes, he is a great favorite everywhere. He is to be President of the United States some day; if I had not thought so I never would have married him, for you can see he is not pretty. [The lady had a sense of humor, not popular in those days.] But look at him! Doesn't he look as if he would make a magnificent President?" On the train going east for the first inauguration, Lamon, who came along as Mr. Lincoln's body-guard, confessed to her that he had thought her to be indulging in wifely vanity that night, that he had then considered Mr. Lincoln "about as unpromising a candidate as I could well imagine the American people ever likely to put forward." Mary wasn't surprised: until '58 when Mr. Lincoln engaged Douglas in their famous series of debates, nobody in Springfield but his wife saw Lincoln as a President.

This was particularly true of the relatives with whom she would now be living. Aside from having turned Democrat, Ninian Edwards was by preference and nature an aristocrat. The son and inheritor of the first governor of Illinois, well-educated at Transylvania College, tall and handsome, Edwards lived the life of a true lord of the manor on his Springfield hill, well-complemented by a wife he had plucked out of a similar aristocracy in Lexington. As a man, Edwards enjoyed Lincoln's funny and sometimes crude stories, appreciated his skill in the courtroom, but he simply could not picture this ungainly back-woodsman as *his* brother-in-law. Nor could his wife. Aside from the likelihood that Lincoln couldn't support a Todd in the manner to which Todds were accustomed, he was an uneducated boor as far as Lizzie Edwards was concerned, a man deficient in just about all the attributes that interest women. Sister Frances, who had gone out with Lincoln a few times while she was husband-hunting from the Edwards house, felt the same way. Frances discovered that, although Mr. Lincoln would go to parties when invited, "he was never much for company," whereas Mary, a true Todd, was, in the words of a young man in their set, "the very creature of excitement, you know, and never enjoys herself more than when in society and surrounded by a company of merry friends." The sisters let their icy feelings about Mr. Lincoln be known to Mary and apparently to him as well; the chill he felt on his visits to the mansion on the hill was one of the reasons Mr. Lincoln gave for breaking off the engagement—he didn't want to come between Mary and her family.

However much he was put off by their attitude, Mr. Lincoln was never really awed by the Todds, which allowed Mary to respect him. He was not the type to be bitter or hold grudges, but he couldn't resist wielding the weapon of humor. When one of the Todds, in boasting of the family lineage, revealed that the name had originally been spelled T-O-D, Mr. Lincoln said, "One *d* was good enough for God, but not for the Todds." Once on the circuit when Lincoln arrived at an inn with a group of lawyers, including John Todd Stuart, the landlady said, "Stuart, how fine and pert you look! But, Lincoln, whatever have you been doing? You look powerful weak." Lincoln laughed: "Nothing out of common, Ma'am, but did you ever see Stuart's wife—or did you ever see mine? I just tell you, whoever married into the 'Todd' family gets the worst of it." In the opinion of the other lawyers, Lincoln had won another case, because they couldn't think of a Todd spouse with much meat on the bones, other than Frances' Dr. Wallace. If Herndon knew of this story, which he probably did since it would have been passed around among all the lawyers of the town, his insinuations that Mr. Lincoln married just to become part of the "aristocratic" Todd family were all the more calculated and nasty.

How could Herndon claim he knew Mr. Lincoln's motives when he himself admitted publicly that Mr. Lincoln was a mysterious man who kept his real thoughts to himself. But Herndon was made up of gall, in every sense of the word. He assumed that he could read Mary's mind, too, and the most hurtful of his claims—broadcast to the world through press accounts of his lectures—was that she had married Mr. Lincoln to make his life miserable in revenge for his jilting her. Talk about insanity! The whole thing—Ann Rutledge, desertion at the altar, domestic hell—was a product of Herndon's drink-befuddled imagination. Mary would have to say this for Robert: he had gone right down to Springfield and confronted Herndon in an effort to get him to stop spreading those lies. Since Herndon's obvious dislike of all the Lincoln boys extended to Robert, the effort had been futile and, in any case, too late. One of the many reasons she could not understand why Robert had taken her to court was that he had thereby played right into Herndon's hand. If she were a crazy woman, she was quite probably an impossible woman to live with, as Herndon charged. So who would believe her word against Herndon's now?

If by painting her as a heavy cross to bear, Herndon intended to make Mr. Lincoln look more of a saint, there was bitter irony in what he had done just this past year. Not content with pretending to disclose the secrets of Mr. Lincoln's bedroom, he came up with another lecture revealing what he thought to be the secrets of his famous partner's soul. An unbeliever himself, Herndon insisted that Lincoln was also one. As evidence he cited the interview in the St. Nicholas hotel when Mary had been distraught after visiting the grave, and he quoted her as saying that Mr. Lincoln was "not a technical Christian." She could not remember any of the precise words she had used on that emotional occasion. Trusting Herndon then, she probably had admitted that Mr. Lincoln was not, unlike herself, a member of any church, and that he had often of a Sunday taken care of their rambunctious boys so that she could have a peaceful time to worship herself. But she was certain that it would never have occurred to her to suggest that Mr. Lincoln was not a

Christian. He paid the family's pew rent, attended church on ceremonial occasions, but, more than that, he took down the Bible and searched it for inspiration and advice whenever he was confronted with difficult decisions during the War. He used it, too, to lean on in their personal tragedies, first with the loss of Eddie and then of Willie. It was after Eddie died that they got to know the Rev. Smith, who gave Mr. Lincoln something he had written in which he set forth the arguments for and against Divine authority and the inspiration of the scriptures, and in his letter to Herndon, Smith wrote: "To the arguments on both sides Mr. Lincoln gave a most patient, impartial and searching investigation. To use his own language, he examined the arguments as a lawyer who is anxious to reach the truth investigates testimony. The result was the announcement by himself that the argument in favor of the Divine authority and inspiration of the scriptures was unanswerable. Immediately after the above avowal, Mr. Lincoln placed himself and family under my pastoral care, and when at home he was a regular attendant upon my ministry." Armed with Smith's statement, Mary denied Herndon's version of their interview when a reporter came prying into the story. Herndon responded with a broadside that was sold on the streets of Springfield and reprinted in papers all over the country in which he transcribed the notes he claimed to have taken right after the interview, called her an out-and-out liar and a victim of "spasmodic madness." Now, and again thanks to Robert, the public would have good reason for believing Herndon instead of her.

Mary had been as sure of Mr. Lincoln's fundamental faith as she had been sure of his love. One of the depths within him that he allowed very few people other than herself to glimpse was a respect for the unexplained mysteries of life, including those of religion. Unlike those smug and "scientific" doctors in Chicago who had made fun of her being in touch with people who could not be seen, Mr. Lincoln took a serious interest in the séances she attended after Willie's death and sat in on them with her when they were in the White House. He was quite aware that other men of intellect in America like Horace Greeley, William Cullen Bryant and James Fenimore Cooper made earnest efforts to get in touch with the spiritual world. Once, however, the skeptical lawyer in Mr. Lincoln balked at the performance of a certain "Lord" Cochester who claimed that the tappings that could be heard during the darkened séances he held for Mary at the Soldiers Home were coming from Willie. Mary had so dearly wanted to believe him that she had suspended her usual good judgment about people, but this time Mr. Lincoln had spotted the humbug. He asked Dr. Joseph Henry, superintendent of the Smithsonian Institution, to investigate Colchester, with the revealing result that the noises were found to be coming from the medium's flexing his muscles through an instrument strapped around his arm. Still, Mr. Lincoln did not ridicule her for claiming to have seen Willie and Eddie at times, because, in fact, he was given to more strange dreams and visitations than she.

One of the reasons Mary had such confidence in Mr. Lincoln's future was that he had told her about what he called a "presentiment" that he'd had from earliest youth that he would rise to a high station where he could do something to benefit mankind. For a long time he concealed from her the other half of his presentiment, which was that he would be brought down from that high station in tragedy. But a vision he had in Springfield just after his nomination so affected him that he had to share it with her. Lying on a couch fully awake he saw a double image of himself in a looking glass—one image was glowing with health, the other pale and ghostly. Tying this in with his old presentiment, he decided that the meaning of the vision was that he would be elected to two terms but die during the second. Overwhelming events caused both of them to forget about that vision when they got to Washington. It did come back to mind when Mr. Lincoln's hat was shot off, on that summer's night ride to the Soldiers' Home, but it enabled him to shrug away

Samuel A. Schreiner, Jr.

that incident in view of its timing. Mr. Lincoln continued to
have prophetic dreams, but they were good ones. Before each
battle won by Union forces, he saw in his dream a battered ship
sailing away with a trim Union ship in hot pursuit, and then he
saw enemy land forces running in ragged retreat while Union
troops held the high ground. But after the second inaugural
came another sort of dream which was one of the things Hill
Lamon published about them that she could recognize as true.
Perhaps that was because Lamon, as Marshall, felt responsible
for the President's life and had the good sense to take down
notes right after the event at which only the three of them had
been present:

"The President was in a melancholy, meditative mood,
and had been silent for some time. Mrs. Lincoln rallied
him on his solemn visage and want of spirit. This
seemed to arouse him and without seeming to notice
her sally he said in slow and measured tones:—

" 'It seems strange how much there is in the Bible
about dreams. There are, I think, some sixteen chapters
in the Old Testament and four or five in the New in
which dreams are mentioned; and there are many other
passages scattered throughout the book which refer to
visions. If we believe the Bible, we must accept the fact
that in the old days God and His angels came to men
in their sleep and made themselves known in dreams.
Nowadays dreams are regarded as very foolish, and are
seldom told, except by old women and by young men
and maidens in love.'

"Mrs. Lincoln here remarked: 'Why, you look dread-
fully solemn; do *you* believe in dreams?'

" 'I can't say that I do,' returned Mr. Lincoln, 'but I
had one the other night which has haunted me ever
since. After it occurred, the first time I opened the
Bible, strange as it may appear, it was at the twenty-

195

eighth chapter of Genesis, which relates the wonderful dream Jacob had. I turned to other passages, and seemed to encounter a dream or a vision wherever I looked. I kept turning the leaves of the old book, and everywhere my eye fell upon passages recording matters strangely in keeping with my own thoughts—supernatural visitations, dreams, visions, etc.'

"He now looked so serious and disturbed that Mrs. Lincoln exclaimed: 'You frighten me! What is the matter?'

" 'I am afraid,' said Mr. Lincoln, observing the effect his words had upon his wife, 'that I have done wrong to mention the subject at all; but somehow the thing has got possession of me, and, like Banquo's ghost, it will not down.'

"This only inflamed Mrs. Lincoln's curiosity the more, and while bravely disclaiming any belief in dreams, she strongly urged him to tell the dream which seemed to have such a hold on him, being seconded in this by another listener. Mr. Lincoln hesitated, but at length commenced very deliberately, his brow overcast with a shade of melancholy.

" 'About ten days ago,' said he, 'I retired very late. I had been up waiting for important dispatches from the front. I could not have been long in bed when I fell into a slumber, for I was weary. I soon began to dream. There seemed to be a death-like stillness about me. Then I heard subdued sobs, as if a number of people were weeping. I thought I left my bed and wandered downstairs. There the silence was broken by the same pitiful sobbing, but the mourners were invisible. I went from room to room; no living person was in sight, but the same mournful sounds of distress met me as I passed along. It was light in all the rooms; every object was familiar to me; but where were all the people who were grieving as if their hearts would break? I was puzzled and alarmed. What could be the meaning of all this? Determined to find the cause of a state of things so mysterious and so shocking, I kept on until I arrived at the East Room, which I entered. There I met with a sickening surprise. Before me was a catafalque, on which rested a corpse wrapped in funeral vestments. Around it were stationed soldiers who were acting as guards; and there was a throng of people, some gazing mournfully upon the corpse, whose face was covered, others weeping pitifully. "Who is dead in the White House?" I demanded of one of the soldiers. "The President," was his answer; "he was killed by an assassin!" Then came a loud burst of grief from the crowd, which awoke me from my dream. I slept no more that night; and although it was only a dream, I have been strangely annoyed by it ever since.'

" 'That is horrid!' said Mrs. Lincoln. 'I wish you had not told it. I am glad I don't believe in dreams, or I should be in terror from this time forth.'

" 'Well,' responded Mr. Lincoln, thoughtfully, 'it is only a dream, Mary. Let us say no more about it, and try to forget it.' "

They had said no more about it, but of course she had not forgotten it, and she doubted that Mr. Lincoln had either. Now she did believe in dreams and visions, but the days immediately following his revelation were much too full of activity and promise to be blighted by a dream. Nevertheless, it must have left within her an uneasiness, a subconscious fear of losing Mr. Lincoln, that could account for the way she had behaved down at City Point. She had never tried to deny that an element in her love for Mr. Lincoln was fierce jealousy. This hadn't caused much trouble back in Illinois where, far from being interested in Mr. Lincoln, most of the women around her, including her own sisters, seemed almost to pity her for being married to such an uncouth creature. But in Washington she discovered very quickly that power in men is an aphrodisiac for women. She watched ladies who would have looked upon him with scorn when he was a humble lawyer fawning over him, flirting with him, and her gorge rose. Although she never really doubted her husband's love for her, she did observe that he enjoyed the novelty of this often insincere female flattery and feared that it could affect his judgment. Before large gatherings she would warn him away from certain women like Kate, the beautiful daughter of Secretary Chase, who would willingly commit murder, not to mention lesser crimes or sins, to see her father in Mr. Lincoln's chair. She also changed the social custom of the White House so that she would be on the President's arm during the promenades instead of yielding the honor to some other ambitious woman. What with people calling her a spy in the White House because of her Confederate relatives—a charge so serious and persistent that at one point Mr. Lincoln had to go personally to the Hill and plead with a Congressional committee not to "investigate" her—she could not have endured even the slightest hint of a sexual scandal. Although she could control things when they were together in Washington, she worried when Mr. Lincoln went off to visit the troops—and not entirely without cause.

One correspondent after visiting the headquarters of the Army of the Potomac wrote that "it was a place to which no self-respecting man liked to go, and no decent woman would go; it was a combination of barroom and brothel." This being the case, Mary was suspicious of the officers' wives who *did* insist on being in the field with their husbands and would not have been surprised in such an atmosphere at whatever wiles they would use on the visiting Commander-in-Chief who controlled their husbands' destinies. In view of her feelings about this, Mary and Tad went with Mr. Lincoln as often as possible, but even their presence was no restraint on some of these bold

women. On one occasion General Sickles, who as her friend
should have known better, proposed that the women at a reception in his headquarters cheer up a gloomy looking President by
gathering around him and kissing him. Most of them had sense
enough to refuse, but one attractive woman with the improbable
name of Princess Salm-Salm tripped over to Mr. Lincoln, stood
on tip-toe, pulled his head down and planted a kiss on his cheek.
Furious, Mary told Mr. Lincoln what she thought of him for
letting the woman get away with such effrontery and, at dinner,
refused to talk to him or General Sickles. But, as always, Mr.
Lincoln knew how to handle her.

"Sickles," he said to the general, "I never knew you were such
a pious man until I came down this week to see the army."

"I am quite sure, Mr. President," Sickles replied, "I do not
merit the reputation if I have gained it."

"Oh, yes," Mr. Lincoln said. "They tell me you are the
greatest Psalmist in the army. They say you are more than a
Psalmist—they say you are a Salm-Salmist."

That time Mary had to get over her peeve, but with the
underlying anxiety induced by Mr. Lincoln's dream working in
her she was beyond the reach of humor at City Point. Riding
with Mrs. Grant in a field ambulance over a road so rough that
their heads were striking the top, she arrived at the parade
ground after the President's review of the troops was already
under way. Trotting beside Mr. Lincoln on a spirited horse was
a lovely young woman identified as the wife of General Ord.
Knowing that the President's wife was visiting them, what
would those thousands of soldiers think? When Mrs. Ord rode
over to the ambulance to pay her respects, Mary let her know
in the strongest language at her command what *she* thought of
such an indiscretion. Mrs. Ord burst into tears, and Mrs. Grant,
trying to smooth things over, talked to her as if she were an
idiot. But she thought that General Ord should be relieved of
command for having a wife so brazen, and told General Grant
her view. Then, before Mary could get around to apologizing in

some manner, as she usually did after too forcefully speaking her mind, one of her headaches took over and she secluded herself in her cabin on the *River Queen*. Sensitive to the embarrassment she had created for herself, Mr. Lincoln got her out of it by having another of his dreams—that there was a fire in the White House—and sending her back to check up on things in Washington. Of course she knew now that he had made up that dream. She had found everything in perfect order, but the return to Washington had given her an opportunity to calm down and round up some real friends like the Harlans and Senator Sumner for a second visit to City Point that went off without a hitch.

In retrospect, she thought of the few days left to them after their return from City Point as fittingly like true April days—switching from sun to shadow, shadow to sun. She remembered well riding in the carriage from the *River Queen* to the White House, looking about her at people passing in the streets and being overcome with that ominous feeling that she could not shake off. Suddenly she shivered, as when clouds cut the warmth of the sun, and said, "This city is filled with our enemies." She knew instinctively that Mr. Lincoln felt much the same way when he said to her in a tone of angry denial that he would normally never use in front of a friend like Senator Sumner, "Enemies! We *must* never speak of that." The sun came out the next day with news of the victory at Appomatox, and by Friday it was quite possible to believe that it would stay out.

That morning Mr. Lincoln was more cheerful than he had been on any day since they had arrived in Washington. On top of all that week's good news, he had had what he considered a version of his pre-victory dreams. As he told his Cabinet at their morning meeting, something momentous—possibly surrender of the remnants of the Southern forces—was about to happen, because in his dream he was "in some singular, indescribable vessel, moving with great rapidity towards an indefinite shore." When Robert, home on leave, came in to show him a picture of

General Robert E. Lee, he looked at it, smiled and said, "It is a good face; it is a face of a noble, noble, brave man. I am glad the war is over at last." It was that afternoon that he insisted on riding alone with Mary so that he could impart to her all of his plans for a happier future together.

The day had been so busy that neither of them really wanted to go to the theater. She had the beginnings of a headache, and he was bone-weary. In view of their feeling about omens it was rather upsetting that none of the people they had invited to accompany them would accept. Their first choice, General Grant, begged off because of "family problems" somewhere out of town, like Baltimore—problems that Mary had long since realized had to do with the fact that Mrs. Grant was avoiding her after the incident at City Point. Even at dinner they were still debating whether or not to go when they thought about the fact that their appearance had been announced and decided that they could not let either a headache or weariness cause them to disappoint the public in this week of general jubilee. At the last moment suitable companions in the form of Miss Clara Harris and her fiancé, Major Henry R. Rathbone, were rounded up, and by eight-thirty they were all settled in the flag-draped Presidential box hanging out over the stage of Ford's Theater to watch a performance of the comedy, *Our American Cousin.* It was not a brilliant play, but Mr. Lincoln was in a mood to relax and enjoy a laugh, and the actors *were* brilliant in taking full advantage of his presence. It was only much, much later when the extreme shock of that night's events subsided a little that Mary, in reconstructing them, could appreciate what turned out to be a precious last gift to Mr. Lincoln in the form of the wit he so loved.

It had been a blustery day with winter lingering into April's spring, and there was such a cold draught in the box that she'd persuaded Mr. Lincoln to get up and put on his overcoat. No doubt the actors on stage had seen this, and, of course, they had to be aware of the fact that, with the war winding down, the most hated measure of the administration—the military draft—had been canceled. In a garden scene Mr. Sothern, playing the role of Lord Dundreary, came in with the American cousin, Miss Meredith, on one arm and a shawl on the other. When she had settled herself on a rustic seat, Miss Meredith gave her companion an inviting smile and said, "Melord, will you kindly throw my shawl over my shoulders—there appears to be a draught here." Sothern minced his way over to her, glanced at the Presidential box to telegraph his punch and adlibbed, "You are mistaken, Miss Mary, the draft has already been stopped by order of the President!" Mr. Lincoln let go with the high-pitched, whinnying horse laugh that he could no more suppress when his mind was tickled than she could suppress the kind of rage that had come over her at City Point.

During slack moments in the play and between acts Mr. Lincoln had reverted to their conversation on the ride and had reaffirmed his desire to travel. The one city he really wanted to see, he told her, was the Biblical city, Jerusalem. For her, his hearty laugh at the punning joke on the draught was a sure sign that he really was beginning to shuck the burdens of the war that had so interfered with their personal lives. In a warm gush of hopeful affection she nestled up to him and took his arm; he folded one of her small hands into one of his large ones. Then she had a thought about the proprieties of such a public display of affection. "What will Miss Harris think of my hanging on to you so?" she asked. "She won't think anything about it," he said, giving her a smile of promise for the time when they would be alone together.

At that precise moment, there was a kind of crack as John Wilkes Booth, who had eased his way into the box behind them without their seeing him, fired his pistol. She could never clearly recall actually hearing the snap of that shot; what she could never forget was the sudden clutch of Mr. Lincoln's hand;

the sight of his eyes rolling up into his head as he slumped forward; the warm and sticky feel of his life's blood on her hands and on her legs as it strained through her skirts. She could not remember screaming, either, although everybody said that she had. God was kind and let her faint dead away and miss the sight of the murdering actor Booth jumping onto the stage and limping away.

The rest of that night, after they had revived her and led her up the winding stairs of the Peterson house across the street to a small room where Mr. Lincoln lay crisscross on a bed too small for him, gasping for breath, was too full of horror to bear keeping in memory. On her knees by the bed she had implored him with every endearment they had ever shared to stay with her, and then, sensing him going, to take her with him.

Gray light was filtering through the skies that were actually weeping when death brought release to that man whose goodness she knew more intimately and had probed more profoundly than any of his millions of admirers could ever imagine. She had a release of a kind, too. She had been immediately drained of all strength, all true vitality, and Robert had at least been right in telling the jury in that courtroom that never since had she been the same as once she was. Few people realized the enormity of what had transpired that night. Although he did not write the kind of poetry her classical education had taught her to admire, Mary had to admit that one of those few was Walt Whitman, a shaggy tramp of a man whom she had seen nursing soldiers a few times on her hospital rounds in Washington:

"O powerful western fallen star!
O shades of night—O moody, tearful night!
O great star disappear'd—O the black murk that hides the star!
O cruel hands that hold me powerless—O helpless soul of me!
O harsh surrounding cloud that will not free my soul."

For a while right after her arrival at the Edwards house she sat alone in her room looking west over Springfield disappearing in the creeping dark and summoning strength to go down and prove to her relatives that she was not crazy. She let the remembered words of Whitman roll over her and over her, let herself weep a little and then said, *Well Mr. Lincoln, I'm home. I know you're here with me. You're the star I see there; you've never fallen. You won't let me fall, either, will you?* She heard no voice, no actual words, but she must have felt a presence that gave her strength to get up and call for Miss Kyle in the room next door to take her down to dinner.

On the eve of her husband's election to the presidency, Mary Todd Lincoln,
proud matron of Springfield, poses with her sons Willie, left, and Tad. Courtesy
of The Lincoln Museum, Fort Wayne IN (Ref. #3155).

Ninian Wirt Edwards, Elizabeth's
husband, was the son of an Illinois
governor and a leader of the Springfield
aristocracy; he appeared for Mrs. Lincoln
at her second trial. Courtesy of The
Lincoln Museum, Fort Wayne IN
(Ref. #1352 [Edwards]).

Only Mary Lincoln saw future greatness in the lean, melancholy face of this circuit riding lawyer, whom she married against the wishes of the Todd family. Courtesy of The Lincoln Museum, Fort Wayne IN (Ref. #o-37 and #o-14).

(*Above*) Abraham Lincoln stands in the front yard of the modest Springfield home from which he was catapulted into the White House and to which he would never return. Courtesy of The Lincoln Museum, Fort Wayne IN (Ref. #0-38).

(*Opposite*) Billy Herndon, Lincoln's law partner, as he looked when he created the myths of Lincoln's lost love, Anne Rutledge, and Lincoln's "domestic hell" from the lecture platform. Courtesy of The Lincoln Museum, Fort Wayne IN (Ref. #62).

The Edwards "house on the hill" in
Springfield, where the Lincolns were
married and where Mary Lincoln died,
was regarded in its time as one of the
town's finest mansions. Courtesy of
The Lincoln Museum, Fort Wayne IN
(Ref. #609).

CHAPTER IX

"Affectionately yours . . ."

F̲OR A MONTH NOW, Robert Lincoln had begun to think that he had been wrong in ever opposing his mother's visit to Springfield. She was apparently accepting the situation in which she found herself with good grace, and he was able to focus his attention on his wife, who was going through the last stages of a difficult pregnancy with their third child. But by November he began receiving disturbing letters, letters that often conveyed more information and emotion between their lines than on the surface, letters that frequently belied their polite salutations and protests of affection. Shining through these letters, although written by her relatives, were Mary Lincoln's mind and will. Robert soon sensed that he was in danger of being outwitted again by his "crazy" mother, and began keeping a file of the most important letters and blotted copies of his answers. They told the unfolding story so well that, he thought, he would need no other witnesses to exonerate *him* when the disaster he saw in the making struck.

"Springfield Nov 5th 1875

Dear Robert

I have not written to you recently, wishing to wait, until I could better understand your Mother's, mental condition. I have no hesitation in pronouncing her sane, and far more reasonable, and gentle, than in former years—She bears up with quiet patience under the oppressive weight of restraint, which to her proud spirit, is very galling—awaiting the time, when the right of person and property, will be restored to her. Surely, the evidence of derangement exhibited last Spring, must have arisen from physical disorder—she informs me that her health was poor before going to Florida, and during her stay there, and on her return, was often conscious, of the presence of fever—moreover, had used Chloral very freely, for the purpose of inducing sleep—Those causes, had doubtless much to do, with producing the sad result.

As far as I can judge, she is capable of taking care of her interests. She assures me that from the income of every year, she has largely added to her principal. To a person of my plain practical ideas it is surprising to look upon unnecessary purchases, but I have been startled, so often by the extravagance of persons of small means, as to judge leniently of those who can afford. Whatever her habits are in that respect, I would advise that you hereafter assume indifference, by doing so, you can quietly and unconsciously to her, gain such influence, as to keep her pecuniary affairs, in a proper state.

Above all, do everything, that will conciliate, and make her as happy, as it would be possible to render her —for she has indulged her morbid ways so long, that it is impossible to prevent frequent reactions, to extreme sadness. The reunion with her family, receiving the calls of former acquaintances, and returning visits, has already had a very beneficial [effect] upon her spirits.

As you desired me to be the judge of her necessities, I will state, that she is too much *herself,* to allow many suggestions. I quite agreed with her that her dust-soiled veil bonnet & shawl, were too shabby for *her* to wear visiting or church going—She stated, that she had no fresh substitutes in her trunks. You understand her sensitive nature, and know why I hesitate to presume to oppose what I really think, she is entitled to enjoy—If I have ventured too far in giving my impressions, I hope you will pardon, and believe that I am intensely interested in your Mother's future, hoping that it may be soothed with your tenderest love and forbearance—and occasionally refreshed, with pleasant intercourse with your dear household—

I will not dwell long on this painful subject, and hasten to a conclusion requesting you to enclose a reply to Mr. Edwards address—she knows nothing of my intention to write to you, and may be present, on the delivery of the mail

With sincere love
Your Aunt Lizzie"

"Springfield, Nov 12th 75

My Dear Robert—

I received your letter on yesterday, and after a careful reading with much reflection, must say, that I am convinced, that the only alternative in this case, for the sake of peace and quietness, will be to yield your Mother the right to control her possessions—You will understand, that she is now proposing this matter, until the unpleasantness is such that I am constrained to make the plea. She assures us, that she will pledge herself to place her bonds with Mr Bunn to be undisturbed during her life—In a conversation, some time since, she mentioned that she had left a will with Judge B [Bradwell]—had set apart $20,000 for little Mamie, leaving the remainder of her property to you. I cannot believe that she would ever divest it from you—and should she in resentment do so by will—you can well understand that your interest would not be injured.

With regard to Spiritualism she is wholly reticent— I would infer that she had no ideas upon the subject, and that it would not be an acceptable subject to one of her timid nature—She told me of a gift of plated ware, used in her early home marked "Lincoln," that she presented to some charitable home, which a friend of hers, *Mrs Farnell* I believe was the name, felt interested in. It may be, that was, the silverware you referred to, and the destination, may have been misrepresented to you.

I perfectly understand you, with regard to her reckless expenditure of money, for the purpose, of adding to the contents of her trunks—It has always been a prominent trait—in her character, to accumulate a large amount of clothing, and now that she has the means, it seems to be, the only available pleasure. Is it not best, that she should be indulged in it, as a matter of expediency? There is no evidence of derangement— at this time, that would justify confinement in an asylum—and to impose restraint of any kind, would involve more contention, than could be endured.

As to what she would do in her future movement, I do not know, and will not predict—Should she show again a roving propensity—I would advise, that she should not be interfered with—If you determine, to become indifferent—to what you cannot prevent—you will insure yourself, a greater degree of repose of mind, than you have known for years. Excuse me for making such suggestions, as the experience of long years, has taught me the most availing remedy in life's trials, where others are interested—Let them alone when you have done what you could.

I am desirous to retain your Mother's kindly feeling, *on her account,*—realizing the loneliness of her situation, and believing that if any persons can influence her, we may find it possible—I do not know, that she desires any change—In dreading the approach of winter, she regretted that her plans for spending the cold months in Florida, had been hindered. She is usually cheerful and enjoys everything, which interests us, as riding, visiting, etc. If she would take more pleasure in society, she could overcome the morbid state of mind, so long indulged. This is the place, where she is drawn out of herself and I would be glad to see her better prepared to enjoy surrounding circumstances.

Even if I weary you, I am certain that you will appreciate my kind intentions. Remember me kindly to your wife, hoping that she will soon be well.

Very affectionately, your Aunt Lizzie"

"Chicago Nov 16 1875

My dear Judge (Davis)

I know you will pardon me for again troubling you.

I enclose two letters from my aunt Mrs Edwards and one from Mr Edwards & a copy of my reply to Mr Edwards. The trouble that my aunt is in is plain and of course she is to be relieved of it—In reference to her letters I want to note that by permission of Judge Wallace I long ago told her that it was not necessary to scrutinize my Mother's expenditures so long as they were not palpably outrageous, so that there was no need of her mentioning the bonnet & shawl purchases. I merely mention it to you to say that one of the last deliveries of goods when before she went to Batavia was four new bonnets all of which are in her trunks at Mrs Edwards & none of which she has ever worn—It is an indication to my mind that no radical change has taken place since last spring but only opportunity is wanting to develop the same trouble—Her remark in her letter of Nov 12th as to my Mother's will was caused by my saying in my reply to her first letter that I did not desire to limit her expenditures beyond the point where she would have neither capital or income to live upon, as I had no interest after her death understanding (as I did, and I must say still do) that she has by will otherwise disposed of her property.

My aunt is also misinformed about the silverware matter—the stuff is owned by a 'Clairvoyant' woman who has a ranch on a side street a few blocks from my house—This I have been told of by three different persons—How gravely she misjudges on the general subject of my mother's devotion to spiritualism, I think you know. She hardly thinks of anything else and almost her only companions were spiritualists—One other remark of my aunt and my 'notes.' She says that experience has taught 'that the most availing remedy in life's trials where others are interested—Let them alone when you have done what you could.' The trouble in my case is that I cannot abandon the matter if I would—The time will not come when I can end the trouble by saying I have done what I can & if I let it alone, it would not let me alone.

You will of course keep this letter privately. I would not discuss my aunt's letter with anyone else—I cannot help feeling that she is taking a pretty short turn on me to relieve herself at all hazards of the trouble—How great the trouble is I well know, but last summer without speaking to me my aunt sent my mother a letter by the hand of Mrs. Bradwell inviting her to visit her. Of course I could only acquiesce.

Mr. Swett has been to see Judge Wallace—The Judge says (and we all concur) that under the statute he cannot 'entertain an application for relief from the disability until the expiration of one year from the date of the appointment of the conservator' & that he has frequently so decided. That if he should entertain the application before that time (next June) his opinion is that his order would not discharge the obligation on the Bond, of the Conservator or his sureties.

The judge's authority as to maintenance seems sufficient to authorize almost anything—and practically he will order whatever Mr. Swett and I think best—Mr. Swett and I are discussing this proposition—

1. I to remove all restraints on travel and residence
2. To pay to her to be expended by herself without scrutiny of any kind her whole income in monthly instalments—At the present rate of gold & including a payment from me to her of $125 per month which will end with 1881, this monthly income will be about $700
3. To have a competent person make an estimate on the annuity principal of what monthly sum can be paid her during her life so as to leave nothing at her death and if Judge Wallace will consent to pay such sum to her monthly
4. In addition to 1 & 2 or to 1 & 3 to deliver when as being necessary for her comfort all of her personal effects which consist of clothing & jewelry.

The trouble with No 3 is that her pension is to be regarded and personally I consider its payment for many years as uncertain.

If you have time to consider this whole matter & to counsel me you will add to the many obligations I am now under to you—

Please also to return to me the enclosed letters—

Most Sincerely yours
Robert T. Lincoln

Hon David Davis
Washington DC

(1875, Nov. 16)

P.S. Mr. Swett makes this further suggestion—Both he and I regard her as unsound in mind and not to be trusted with the power of impoverishing herself—Her course since the inquisition has shown that in general she is able to control her impulses if she has an object in doing so—She has constantly kept in view her discharge and her aberrations during that time would make no case against her discharge probably. Supposing her to be insane, is it not better to utilize the six months which must intervene before she can be discharged, in giving her every opportunity (at least to the extent I have indicated) to develop her vagaries if she still has any than to have her restrained and watchful with no opportunity, & then get her discharge & break out fully again & perhaps ruin herself before I could stop it?"

"Washington D.C.
Novr. 20, 1875

My Dear Robert

You do right in always addressing me when in difficulty—No one sympathises with you more or is more willing to share responsibility with you in whatever concerns your mother.

218

The present posture of affairs is not encouraging, but I was not unprepared for it—

I expected from the first the intermeddling of officious people who do things in ignorance of the real situation—Mrs Edwards brought the difficulty about when she sent a letter to your mother inviting her to visit her without consulting you in advance of the proposition—And I think your comments on her letter are eminently just and proper—She has no conception of your mother's real condition & evidently does not believe that Spiritualism has anything to do with it while you & I know differently—And her advice of indifference by you, though doubtless well meant, is, to say the least, grounded on a total misapprehension of the relations between parent & child—

You cannot escape responsibility if you wanted to and it would be esteemed by the world bad conduct if you should try—The trouble is on you & would not let you alone even (to suppose an impossible case) you were willing it should.

The embarrassments growing out of the visit to Springfield must be met altho you had an agency in creating them—Your mother has evidently convinced Mrs Edwards & her other relatives that she is unjustly restrained of her liberty—Persons in her condition can generally restrain their impulses when they have an object in view—And I have no doubt yr mother from the first has acted in a way to convince all who have been brought in contact with her that she ought not to be confined.

You cannot now send her back to Batavia and Mrs Edwards must be relieved of the trouble—

It seems to me to be the right thing to remove restraints on travel and residence and to pay her monthly the amount of her income—The six months which must intervene before she can be discharged & you relieved will develop her insane vagaries if they still exist which we all believe.

If she had remained undisturbed at Batavia, there might have been a chance for her recovery but I fear the intermeddling will prove disastrous to her as it has already added to yr troubles.

If she spends no more than her monthly income it is no matter—Should she contract debts beyond this with persons who do not know her to have been adjudged insane, it is now clear that they could not be recovered, because of her being discharged from the asylum & being left to go free & unrestrained. But this must be risked—

The annuity principle I dont think I would apply— There is no necessity for it & the Judge would hardly be justified in paying her more than monthly income—If she is not insane, she would never expend as much as this—If the insanity remains, you cant tell what she will do—The six months can as you say be utilized for the purpose of ascertaining what is best to be done for the future—of course her personal effects, including jewelry, she will want & it is best to give them to her—If she gives away any part of her clothing or jewelry, it is a small matter—

I think yr mother w^d rest satisfied if unrestrained, paid her income in monthly installments. At any rate it is the only practicable thing to do in the present emergency so far as I can see—

I took all day yesterday to reflect on the matter & I cannot see any other course to pursue in justice to yourself & the future of your mother—She must not be impoverished & she may live as long as you do—There is no other way left since the Springfield visit—You could not get her back to Batavia & it is best to try freedom from restraint—I am glad that Mr Swett is taken into counsel—Do nothing without his sanction—He is a wise counsellor & a sympathetick man—You know you have my sympathy

Write me what you do

> Yr friend
> David Davis"

"Washington DC
Nov 30

Dᵣ Robert

I have been so incessantly occupied for ten days & past that my correspondence is way behind—Mᵣ Edwards' first letter is not near so explicit as the last—I cant appreciate Major Stuart's reticence—I return you both of Mᵣ Edwards letters—

I congratulate you upon the birth of another child (a daughter)—If I had a large family, I should be very happy provided the children behaved *cherubly*

This is a very important *proviso*—

Let me know the result of yr visit to Springfield—I expect to be at the Pacific Hotel in Chicago over Sunday (the 12th Decᵣ)—

> In haste
> Yr frnd
> *D Davis*"

"Springfield Dec 1st 75

My Dear Robert

I read last evening your note to your Uncle giving a statement of your Mother's expenditures since she has been in our home—The recent demand surprises me—I had supposed, from her assurances, that she was *fixed* for the winter, that her shopping was over. She has protested against asking you to send her winter wraps, and has consequently provided herself with new *water proof* shawls etc—I do not really know anything about her purchases—we have never been with her in a store, and have never seen her open a trunk, therefore could be wholly ignorant of her needs. A few days ago, she said, that she had purchased a shawl and dress, to present to Mrs Wallace (Mary's sister, Frances) for Christmas—the two articles were purchased for less than $40—I told her she would find it difficult to have them accepted, and it proved so—You understand the proud nature of that Aunt—It is only in the seasons of her darkest sorrow, that Mr Edwards Mr Smith and their wives have been able to contribute in a substantial way to her necessities. Let me here say, that the music box sent by you, was presented to Frannie W. (Mrs. Wallace) who was exceedingly pained believing that it had been withdrawn from you—We intend as far as possible to prevent any distribution of her money in our midst—and will not encourage any generous inclinations. At the time of the fair for the home of the friendless recently held here, Mrs Lamon caused a sofa cushion, flowers etc to be made a complimentary present to her—It gratified her, and in response, she enclosed $25 for the benefit of that charity.

The checks you have sent, have been enclosed to herself, she invariably requests Mr E to hand her the amount, when cashed. We intended to receive her as our guest, not boarder, but she insisted that she could not feel contented, or make herself at home, without we received a board bill from her—She demanded from you $150 a month for that purpose, although she knows, that I consented to $100 only—Amanda (woman hired to replace Miss Kyle) left at the end of her first month—and I felt that so liberal a sum for my trouble justified me in hiring the third female servant—Thus she has her washing and every service rendered her—We hire when necessary additional assistance for our grounds, to be enabled to place our carriage at her disposal, at all times.

I am glad to state that she is unvarying in a polite, amiable, and affectionate manner towards everyone.

I would gladly look forward to the pleasure of protecting her for life. It is only, when discussing the restraints imposed upon her that she exhibits the slightest impatience. I have ventured in a previous communication to express myself upon the subject of restraint, and the degree necessary—May I beg of you to regard my letters as confidential. I of course wish you to understand matters—In haste

Your affectionate
Aunt Lizzie"

"Springfield Ills. Dec 18/75

Dear Robert

I inclose receipt of box which was on yesterday delivered by express agent to your Mother—In yours of the 16th inst you ask me to give you the best aid and advice I can for your Mother's good and seem to think hard of both Stuart and myself for not having done so before. I have not done so because in several of your letters you said you would be governed by the advice of Judge Davis, Mr Swett, Stuart, and *others* of your father's friends.

Thus far you have done everything your Mother has asked with the exception of restoring to her her bonds and you have with the approbation of Judge Wallace written to me that you would give to her the entire income to do as she pleases with it—As the delivery of bonds is the only point of issue I will confine myself exclusively to it—It is true that the 39th section page 689 of the . . . Statutes provides that 'no application shall be entertained for the removal of a conservator within less than one year from the time of this appointment' and if the judge is unwilling with the consent of both parties to entertain such a motion within the year, of course nothing can be done until then—If your Mother could know this from him, she would probably not fret over it, nor find fault with you for not yielding to her wishes—As soon as she can legally do so, she says she will apply to have all her rights restored to her, and that she 'is a fit person to have the care and custody of her property,' she says she will prove before the court, how well she has managed it, how much she has given you, and how much she has added to the principal, and that she has already within a few days past requested you to invest $2,000.00 of her income in bonds—she says she will show to the court how much she would have lost if she had acceded to your request to allow investments to be made by you and John Forsyth—I wish if possible to prevent all this—and I would therefore advise as soon as it can be done for you to consent to what she proposes to do—that she shall by deed of trust place her bonds and monies in the hands of a trustee to pay over to her the income only and to hold the principal to be paid on her decease to those persons entitled by law to receive it—She has said she would do this and would consent that Mr Bunn should be her trustee. Your Aunt and myself both think that all her property should at death go to you and your children—Judge Bradwell has at her request sent her the will she made two years ago and she has shown it to me—In it she left $20,000.00 to your daughter Mary,

about $5000 of the income to you until the year 1781
(sic)—to be paid annually and after 1781 (sic) the entire
balance is left to you and your children—Whether she
would do this now in a deed of trust I cannot say, as
she is so much exasperated against you. If she has to go
to law she will summon a good many witnesses from
here—and she is waiting for Governor Palmer [a former governor of Illinois and political supporter of
Abraham Lincoln in the '50's] to return for the purpose
of seeing whether she can have her funds restored to
her now—I think she will consent that Mr Bunn shall
hold in trust the principal when this is done. I think it
is fair to say to you, that I believe she will go to Europe
to remain there.

You mentioned in one of your letters that such a
deed of trust couldn't be made—In this I think you are
mistaken—C.C. Brown is trustee under such a deed of
trust for my daughter Mrs Baker—I would under no
circumstances advise that her bonds should be given up
to her or placed under her control unless such a compromise is made—It is important however that whilst
she is with us that she should not know that I have so
advised—I have therefore written this in confidence—
We fully sympathise with you and believe that you
have done what under all the circumstances you
thought it best.

Very affly yours
N. W. Edwards

When you write—send two letters one of which I may
hand to her—as she always asks to see them."

As the autumn darkened into the short days of December
Mary Lincoln began to lose patience with her enforced residence in Springfield. Although she no longer had actual bars

standing before her eyes or in her mind, she was nonetheless a prisoner. When she would sigh over missing the warmth and sunshine of Florida that she could otherwise be enjoying, she would be reminded by Ninian or Lizzie that she ought not to be thinking about such things since she wasn't, after all, at liberty to go; indeed, she ought to be grateful for being where she was instead of in that asylum at Batavia.

Having never been anywhere far from home themselves, the Edwardses could not understand her wanderlust. This was nothing new for her. She had always thought of Springfield as a stage rather too small. Way back when the White House was still only an improbable dream a lucky stroke of business had enabled her to accompany Mr. Lincoln to Niagara Falls and on to New York, and she had yearned then to be rich enough to travel. That Mr. Lincoln had understood this yearning in her was evident in his talk on that last day of their lives together. He had promised to take her to places they had glimpsed through the window of literature, especially the Jerusalem of his beloved Bible and the Scotland of their jointly beloved Bobby Burns. She had made that Scotch pilgrimage with Taddie, but it had been a bittersweet experience. The scenery had been all that she had anticipated, and it had evoked lines that she and Mr. Lincoln had read together, lines that life had made unbearably true, like those about the rose which she had found herself reciting to Taddie with her voice breaking all the while:

> "Oh my luve is like a red, red rose
> That's newly sprung in June;
> O my luve is like the melodie,
> That's sweetly play'd in tune.
>
> As fair art thou, my bonnie lass,
> So deep in luve am I;
> And I will luve thee still, my dear,
> Till a' the seas gang dry.

> Till a' the seas gang dry, my dear,
> And the rocks melt wi' the sun;
> And I will luve thee still, my dear,
> While the sands o' life shall run.
>
> And fare-thee-weel, my only luve!
> And fare-thee-weel a while!
> And I will come again, my luve,
> Tho' it were ten thousand mile."

As fate would have it, it was Taddie who had come the thousands of miles from where they were then to join her love here—here in Springfield. This was causing another kind of torment that the Edwardses and the rest of her family and friends who must never have known such love could not appreciate. Everybody had said that the sensible thing for her to have done after the assassination was to have moved back into the Springfield house, which she still owned and rented out. After that one visit to the vault at Oak Ridge Cemetery in '66 she had known that being here so near and yet so unreachably far would only keep reminding her of all that she had lost, as she had written then to Mrs. Welles. It was worse now with Taddie in the same ground, and a lament by Burns that she had once recited mostly for the fun of using her skill at mimicry in catching the Scotch accent had suddenly become a true expression of her own feelings:

> "Drumossie moor, Drumossie day,
> A waeful day it was to me!
> For there I lost my father dear,
> My father dear, and brethren three.
> Their winding-sheet the bluidy clay,
> Their graves are growing green to see;
> And by them lies the dearest lad
> That ever blest a woman's e'e!"

She just had to get out of Springfield, had to go somewhere. For a while she toyed with taking another of those trips that Mr. Lincoln had had in mind—to California by rail. It would be easy enough now . . . it had been six years since they had driven the golden spike at Promontory Point, Utah, to join the rails of the Union Pacific going west with those of the Central Pacific coming east. What a moment of history to have witnessed, as they surely would have had Mr. Lincoln lived. The making of America into one was the substance of his hope. They were saying now that a train could make it clear across the continent in a little more than eighty hours and in perfect comfort in one of Mr. Pullman's sleeping cars. What with General Custer driving the Indians back into the wilds of the Dakotas, the journey would be safe too. She could remember Mr. Lincoln's talking of how much he admired George Custer, one of the youngest of the brigadier generals, for the way he had handled his cavalry at Gettysburg and in the Shenandoah Valley under Sheridan. Yes, since they said that the climate of California was very like Florida, a trip west was a distinct possibility if only she could get control of her money, if only she could get Robert and the court to leave her alone.

Mary knew that Lizzie and Ninian were in touch with Robert, and she gathered from what she saw of the correspondence that they were doing what they could on her behalf. But she was beginning to doubt how effective they would be. It was distressing to observe how the Edwardses' power and prestige, which had once made their house on the hill something like the palace in one of those medieval European towns, had eroded away. Actually in Mary's view their decline had set in not long after she and Mr. Lincoln had married; Lizzie became so serious about religion that she stopped holding the banquets and balls that had made their place the social center of town, on the grounds that such expensive frivolity was an affront to the Lord. Money could have had something to do with it too, as it turned out when Mr. Lincoln had to bail Ninian out of debt with a government job. But the real reason was probably that Ninian had been fool enough to turn Democrat just when the new Republican party was seizing a power they hadn't yet lost. Of course, Ninian being Ninian, he could never admit to being wrong. Much as she disliked Grant, Mary was nevertheless irritated by hearing Ninian gloat over the news that the president's private secretary, General Babcock, was involved in this year's "Whiskey Ring" at St. Louis, where government revenues were skimmed into private pockets, and over the further fact that the first Congress with a Democratic majority since 1859 was convening this very month of December, 1875, in Washington. "Our time is coming," Ninian would keep saying, but it had not come yet, and Ninian was beginning to look too old and too feeble to take advantage of it if it ever did.

With this in mind Mary did a little pointed gossiping on her shopping trips to town and discovered that the lawyer with the fastest growing practice in Springfield was former governor John M. Palmer. Unlike Ninian, he undoubtedly had sufficient Republican connections in Chicago to impress Robert and the people around him. To be sure, Palmer was a Liberal Republican in revolt against the Grant administration, but so were Judge Davis and Attorney Swett—and so would have been Abraham Lincoln. Mary had good feelings about Palmer because it had been he who, twenty years ago, had tried to get Mr. Lincoln the vice presidential nomination during the very first Republican convention. As soon as she heard that Palmer was in town she went to see him, and a new voice was added to the deceptively polite correspondence between Springfield and Chicago.

"Springfield Dec 21—1875

Robt T Lincoln Esq
Chicago Ills

Dear Sir
    At the request of Mrs. Lincoln I beg to call your

attention to her situation and inquire whether in your judgment it is not possible to relieve her from her present situation which causes her so much annoyance.

It will occur to you readily that I write to you on the subject with great hesitation (feeling) that you will do nothing but dictated by the best considered views of duty but at the same (time) you will understand that I am only anxious to promote the comfort of your mother for which many of (us) feel a degree of Solicitude only less than your own. She feels herself to be entirely competent to manage her own affairs and her conduct since she came to this city seems to justify a belief entertained by her friends that she is correct and my principal object in writing you is to inquire whether your consent can be obtained to allow her to do so.

Of course this enquiry implies that you will at once or at the earliest day possible allow the proceedings in the County Court of Cook County to be set aside and her conservator discharged.

I wish to be understood in calling your attention to the wishes of your Mother to mean no more than to urge the matter upon you as one that causes her much uneasiness and in regard to which very much should be risked to relieve her.

She understands me to represent her professionally but I write under the influence of motives of a different character.

Respectfully
John M Palmer

P S Since writing Mr Edwards showed me your letter to him. I find you are naturally embarrassed in regard to this subject. I hope you will regard this in the light of a Suggestion and answer me in such way that I may lay it before your Mother.

J M P"

"Springfield Illinois
Dec 22 1875

Dear Robert

I have received yours of the 21st instant—Your Mother for the last two or three weeks has been very much embittered against you and the more you have yielded the more unreasonable she seems to be—She is threatening to withdraw all her possessions in your house—but your Aunt is pleading with her not to do so, urging the inconvenience and expense of storing them elsewhere—I do not now believe she will consent to the compromise she requested me several weeks ago to propose to you—As you propose to see Judge Davis consult with him as to what is best to be done in the event of her insisting unconditionally on having her bonds restored to her. I believe on reflection, and knowing her as I now do, and as in any event she will have her pension for life, I would give them up to her provided nothing else will satisfy her.

Gov Palmer has shown me a letter he has written to you—Neither he nor I have any doubt but that the court would be justifiable by consent in allowing the order appointing a conservator to be vacated—and we also entertain no doubt but that she could make such a deed of trust as she proposed sometime since to make—If it should turn out that she was insane when she made it, it could be set aside on her decease. I am very anxious that there should be no controversy either before the courts or in the newspapers—I would also advise that she should know as soon as possible what she may expect. As I said in one of my letters I do not believe she will remain with us a week after her bonds are restored to her—If any papers are to be executed by her I would advise that they should be either prepared or approved by Gov. Palmer.

Very affectionately yours
N.W. Edwards

Robt. T. Lincoln
Chicago Ills"

"Chicago Dec 23. 1875

Hon J.M. Palmer
Springfield Ills

My dear Sir:

Your letter dated Dec 21st reached me only this morning—I have tried to the utmost limit to which Judge Wallace, our County Judge, would allow, to satisfy every wish of my Mother since she has been at Springfield.—On the question of her discharge I have already written to my uncle Mr Edwards the opinion as expressed to me entertained by the Judge of his power under the Statute—I called on him today and asked permission to say to you that he will write to you his views on any points you may suggest—He said he would do so—I did this because what I have said heretofore seemed to be taken as *my* opinion of his power instead of his own.—I wish you would write to him (Hon M.R.M. Wallace) and learn from him his views.

I will be very glad to resign my office—and relieve my sureties from their responsibility and myself from embarrassment and perplexity in endeavoring to do my duty, which are nearly overwhelming.

Mr. Henry F. Eames and Mr Isham are on my bond for $150,000 and they are in no way (indemnified) of me under the views which Judge Wallace has expressed to me. I see no way for my relief except by resigning—This I will do at any moment—I suppose it would not be accepted until my successor qualified and I will be grateful to you for aid in finding a successor—

If you are confident in your view that the (matter) of vacating the proceedings in the County Court depends upon the consent of the Conservator, will you not as I resign take my place as conservator and then act on your own proposal as representing my mother's interests?

Very truly yours
Robert T. Lincoln"

"Springfield Ill. Jan 14/76

Dear Robert

I am sorry to say that your mother has for the last month been very much embittered against you and has on several occasions said that she had hired two men to take your life—On this morning we learned that she carries a pistol in her pocket—we also hear from others that she has had a great many dresses made and is still purchasing largely for her *own* use—She has everything she buys sent direct to her rooms—She says she will never again allow you to come into her presence—We do not know what is best to be done—Your aunt says nothing will ever satisfy her until she has possession of her bonds, and her advice is that all her rights should be restored to her as soon as possible.

She does not believe that she will expend her income—and she can never come to want as she has her pension for life—Nothing else will satisfy her—Gov

Palmer advises me to inform you of her threats and of her carrying the pistol—He is of opinion that by consent her bonds may be restored to her—If you think it best to come down you had better not come direct to our house but advise me where to meet you—Except on the subject of the restoration of her bonds and her purchases she is as rational as I ever knew her—Please do not let her know that I have written to you on the subject—The information in regard to the pistol you can learn from others.

Yours affly,
N.W. Edwards

She spends nearly 1/2 of every day with dressmakers & in the stores."

Robert had at last received the letter that he had been expecting, even wanting. The panic it reflected suggested that the Edwardses were now seeing for themselves that his mother was, indeed, insane. He sat down and drafted a stern reply to his "dear Uncle" in which he shrugged off the "pistol business" as just one of the "possible freaks" that the doctors had predicted would "take possession of my mother." He said again that his hands were legally tied with respect to giving her back her bonds. Saying that he'd heard from another source in Springfield that his mother was purchasing so wildly that she was giving merchants her "notes," he predicted that things would go from bad to worse. He then complained that she had been removed from Batavia against his judgment. He pointed out that the doctors thought that his mother should be put "where no catastrophy could happen" and that, aside from the "idea" of it, Batavia was a pleasant place. Although he stopped short of proposing that his mother be returned to custody, such a move was implied. Before mailing it, Robert showed his letter and the Springfield correspondence that prompted it to his legal partner, Isham. He was advised to bury it in his file; it might aggravate the situation to the point of prodding Governor Palmer into formal action.

Palmer had, in fact, written Judge Wallace and by early February had a reply that he could show his client and ease her mind about Robert's position to the point of putting her pistol away. Lizzie Edwards wrote to Robert that her sister had become "much calmer, since she was informed, in a positive way, that she would entertain no hope of release until *May.*" Picking May as the month of deliverance was an unfortunately false assumption made by nearly everybody in Springfield, based on figuring a year from the date of her court trial. Judge Wallace had failed to make it clear that Robert's appointment as conservator did not take place officially until June 14, 1875, and that, therefore, he couldn't be relieved until after that time in 1876.

This false assumption would cause trouble, but for the moment, having given up on getting immediate control of her bonds, Mary Lincoln decided to use her waiting time to recover some of her other possessions. Robert at first tried to humor his mother by sending down some items she requested, but he soon discovered that he was upsetting his Aunt Lizzie in the process. The Edwardses were eager to have Mary get her bonds, which she was promising to lodge in the safekeeping of Mr. Bunn, but, with a room already so filled with Mary's trunks that the the floors were threatened, Lizzie expressed a rather natural reluctance to accept more in the way of goods. This time Robert did send a letter written in anger.

"Feb 12 6

My dear Aunt

Your letter of the 9th was only received by me late on yesterday—I am sorry the things I sent down incommode you—I believe I have told you that my house is filled with all sorts of things—presents from my mother to my wife and myself during the past eight years—In a letter of Feb 3rd she asked to send her a few books, she named, a clock & half a dozen pictures—all (intended) for her room—although I considered these things as much my own as though I had bought them, I gave them to her desiring to satisfy her as far as I can. Then came at once from her another letter more than a dozen pages long filled with demands for 'my this' and 'my that,' almost without end—Everything that we can recognize was a present at one time or another—many things neither my wife nor I remember ever seeing—many others (dress goods & the like) are worn out & forgotten—Apart from these considerations the whole demand is so unreasonable in the light of my service that the things could (be returned) or that she could properly (make use) of them in her situation that the letter is plainly irrational and the emanation of an insane mind—Even if the things were not my own, I agree with you that they should not be sent—

In the hope of making her more contented and thus aiding her mental condition, I have with great trouble obtained from the Probate Judge the permission from time to time to relax in various ways the legal restraints imposed upon her & I am so satisfied that so doing has worked harm instead of good that I do not propose to go any further—Her demands have gone on from one thing to another as you know, until they indicate such a state of mind that it is a serious question whether we will not have to take the back track—

> Affectionately your nephew
> Robert T. Lincoln"

"Feb 16 6

My dear Aunt
    I did not reply to the letter of my mother which I

mentioned in mine to you and I have not since heard from her—I glanced at her letter again today and I find on one of the crossed pages [having written horizontally, Mary Lincoln would often turn the page and write vertically to squeeze more on each sheet] that she asks for a number of things, a whip, some shells, some engravings . . . as being at 375 Washington St—her old residence. I ought to mention to qualify what I said about *all* the things she sent for being presents—as the things at 375 were stored there by her at various times in a . . . room which I have not been in for a year and a half. Those things now there are her own and were never given to me—They are of little value and perfectly safe & I propose not to go near them—& certainly do not intend to send them down to lumber you with them—

Affectionately yours
Robert T. Lincoln"

Possibly because his aunt put her foot down about storing any more stuff, Robert's "benign neglect" of his mother's requests seemed to work. He stopped getting demands from her for a month or more, and by early April his Uncle Ninian was informing him that his mother was "very happy and contented." It was another calm before a storm. With the Springfield misunderstanding about dates, excitement began to build in Mary Lincoln toward the end of April, and she began pressing her attorney, Governor Palmer, and the Edwardses to get assurances from Robert and his advisers that she *would* be allowed to go free with all rights restored.

Palmer sounded apologetic in sounding out Robert and his counsel, Leonard Swett, about how they would react to a request that Robert be discharged as conservator. He expressed his own doubts as to her ability to hold onto her money if she got it (which hardly made her unique) but he warned that the Edwardses would testify as to her competence. Meanwhile, the Edwardses, still under the impression that action could be taken in May, began to share Mary's impatience and prod Robert. Still sure that his mother was insane and fearful of granting her freedom, Robert blew up again.

"May 17 6

My dear Aunt

Your letter was delivered at my home so that I did not receive it until last evening—

You entirely misunderstand my powers—A year ago my mother was so out of her mind, showing it in many ways, that it was absolutely necessary for her personal safety that she should be placed for a time under proper care—Under the laws of this state no person could (take) this care without the order of the County Court. When this was had, the law compelled the Court to appoint a conservator of her property and it appointed me on June 14, 1875.

The same law provides that the Court *shall not have* any application for the removal of the Conservator for one year—I had to give a bond of $150,000 with two gentlemen here as sureties to deliver up all her property at the end of the year—It would not only ruin me but besides be a heavy loss to my friends on my bond if next month I should for any reason whatever not be able to place these bonds (being in value more than $70,000^{00}) in the hands of the Court.

From what you say about her expressed intention to throw away everything she has and to depend upon the government for support I should hardly think her as sound in mind as you do, as the sane way of punishing me for trying to take care of her, would be to make a will and give me nothing. If she is so unreasonably exasperated against me, her anger might now easily lead her if she had the power, to waste or give away her property and then next month call on me and my sureties to account for and pay over every cent—I think anyone would admit that I would be very foolish to run such a risk, with no possible good to come from it. I send her every penny of her income as fast as it comes in . . . and nobody has ever suggested my sending them (the bonds) to her except Mr Edwards—I have repeatedly urged that someone should become Conservator in my place who might be more daring in running risks than I but I get no reply and there is nothing for me to do but await my discharge.

No scandal or trouble will be avoided by my doing or not doing anything—Plenty of it will probably come and I can only hope that my Aunts, who now have charge of her, will have less trouble on that score than I have had for many years—

> Affectionately Yours
> Robert T. Lincoln

Robert's angry letter was upsetting to everybody in the house on the hill in Springfield. Along with the flowers starring the surrounding prairies, spring brought on a new fever of impatience for the ordeal to be over. Mary Lincoln's frustration at the invisible bonds that bound her was considerably increased when she couldn't go to Philadelphia for the opening of the Centennial Exposition in Fairmount Park on May 10. With exhibits from fifty countries, it was the sort of thing she would have thoroughly enjoyed. The Springfield people who did go came back so full of the wonders they had seen that it was hard to have any other conversation. There was, for example, a machine for talking through a wire called a telephone and another machine for tapping out letters onto a sheet of paper called a typewriter and a huge hand for a Statue of Liberty that was being made in Paris as a gift to America from the French people. Even though it might have galled her to watch little Grant acting as if he owned the whole show while he was guiding Dom Pedro II, the emperor of Brazil, around the grounds, Mary Lincoln thought that she would have enjoyed seeing the wonders. But it wasn't so much what she may have missed but the circumstance that she, a former First Lady of the land who might have easily presided over such a celebration, could not even attend because she was legally a dangerous lunatic.

Although Lizzie and Ninian did not share the substance of Robert's letter with Mary, they did feel obliged to inform her of the only possible date of release which meant waiting another month at the very least. What worried them most was that it might not happen even then. From Robert's tone, they had the feeling that they could no longer sit back and just hope for the best.

The implication that he was doing nothing to guarantee what they considered a fair and necessary solution to the "trouble" with Mary Lincoln prompted the Edwardses to seek a powerful ally in Robert's camp. With the Supreme Court in summer recess, Judge Davis would be home in Bloomington, and Ninian Edwards, who had known Davis back in the days when he himself was practicing law on the Eighth Circuit in Illinois, made an appointment to see him. Ninian Edwards made a persuasive case. When Robert found himself deserted by the man whose public stature and unconditional support had vindicated what otherwise might have seemed an act of filial cruelty, he felt that his worst fears were in the process of coming true. About all that Judge Davis left him with was another series of exculpating letters for his growing file.

"Bloomington, Illinois
May 22, 76

My Dear Robert
—By appointment Mr Edwards came to see me today, and I am satisfied that you had better consent to the discharge of your mother at the end of the year— This is my advice on the theory that her money is squandered by her. She cannot come to want, as the pension of $3000 will in any event be enough for her support—

—Mr Edwards & his wife both believe her to be sane, and that she ought to be discharged—They will testify to her sanity—Can we oppose it? Ought we to oppose it?—Can we afford to have a (general trial) which is sure to come?—I think she has enlisted Marshal O. Roberts in her behalf who has employed a lawyer in New York to assist Gov Palmer if the discharge is resisted—Mr E. says she still purchases things, chiefly dresses that she does not need, but he says she always did this—Mr E. does not believe that your mother will squander the principal—He says she intends to spend her income hereafter but not to trench on principal—

I have after mature reflection, come to the conclusion that it is better for your happiness to give a free consent to the removal of all restraint on person or property—and trust to the chances of time—

And I would suggest that you see the Judge of Probate to ascertain what evidence he needs to grant the discharge—Edwards' testimony would be enough—Of course the ten days notice . . . you could waive—I have heard nothing from Gov Palmer—Let me hear from you or you can write Mr Edwards—In haste,

> Yr fnd
> D Davis"

"Chicago, June 4

My Dear Robert

I do not believe that any raid on you is contemplated. It may be that Edwards did not know that any reply was necessary. He wrote me so pleasantly after his return home and spoke so encouragingly, that I am not prepared for any change of front—

What do you say on my reaching Madison I write him and ask him if you have arranged things satisfactorily.

This will draw his fire. Write me at once, whether or not I had better do this.

> In haste
> Yr fnd
> D Davis"

"Springfield Illinois
June 8th 1876

Hon. D. Davis
Madison Wis.

My Dear Sir

Yours of the 6th inst is received—Immediately on the receipt of your letter to Robert, he wrote me that he would waive notice and that I might present his mother's petition for his discharge as her conservator to the court on the 15th inst at 2 o'clock P.M. no one being present except the Judge, Clerk, him & myself—

This I will do and I have no doubt that the order will be granted. There will be no opposition to it. When it is obtained I will write you.

> Truly yours
> N.W. Edwards"

> "Madison, Wisconsin
> June 9

Dear Robert—

This letter rec^d fr Mr Edwards shows that everything is going on smoothly—Of course you will be careful not to let him know I sent it to you—

> In haste
> Yr friend
> D Davis"

After he had read these letters Robert put them in his pocket and went out to pay a call on Leonard Swett. There was nothing left to do but to meet his uncle in court and try to let his mother go. He was glad that there was no mention of his mother's being there, too. He had no idea of precisely what she would do in the event that the court's control was set aside, but he remained very certain that the "trouble" was not over. He was by no means as sure as Judge Davis, for example, that there would not be a raid on him. His mother was turning out to be a tough and resourceful fighter who was at least worthy of his respect, and the only person who had proved tough enough to stand up to her was Leonard Swett. There could be a long, hot summer ahead.

CHAPTER X:

"Wickedness against me and High Heaven . . ."

T HE CROWD THAT GATHERED at the Union Park Congregational Church in Chicago on the evening of Thursday, June 15, 1876, to hear the Honorable Leonard Swett deliver his lecture on Abraham Lincoln got more than their twenty-five cents' worth. The tall, chin-whiskered Swett, who some said looked much like his subject, let his audience in on a bit of news that the rest of Chicago and the world at large would not learn until the following day: that very afternoon a jury in County Court had found the late President's widow, Mary Todd Lincoln, to be sane. It was a legal proceeding of which he, Leonard Swett, could boast since he had played an important part in seeing that justice was done to the woman his great friend Abraham Lincoln had so dearly loved. Swett felt that he hardly had to remind an Illinois audience that the towering Lincoln had established an ideal in marriage as he had in so many other affairs by having the ring he gave his bride inscribed "Love is eternal." He was sure that Mr. Lincoln's kindly spirit would be rejoicing this night in the happy outcome of the day's events. The audience applauded the announcement and then settled comfortably back into their seats to hear Swett run through his usual stock-in-trade—anecdotes of the rugged days that he and Lincoln had spent together riding the Eighth Circuit in Illinois.

It was a strange coincidence that Swett would have the opportunity to break the news himself that night. The lecture had been scheduled and advertised well before the astute maneuvering of Ninian Edwards and Governor Palmer in Springfield had forced him and his client, Robert Lincoln, to go against their convictions and agree to offer no opposition if Edwards petitioned the court to discharge Robert as his mother's conservator. Swett had to wonder whether David Davis, Supreme Court justice or no, had understood all the legal implications when he had advised this course of action. He was sure that Edwards, too long retired from active practice to be up on such things, had not. The old man had looked more surprised than pleased at what his day in court had wrought. It was one thing to have custody of Mary Lincoln's bonds transferred from Robert Lincoln to Jacob Bunn; quite another to have her pronounced sane.

Swett had boned up on the law and had discovered that a jury would have to reverse the verdict of insanity before the court appointed conservator could be discharged. He could undoubtedly have summoned the doctors as witnesses and rewon his case, but it wasn't worth the effort when his client, deserted by Judge Davis, had lost heart for a fight. But, sensitive to the strong light of doubt that this proceeding might cast on the earlier one in the public mind, Swett did the next best thing: he made it look in court, as he later did for his audience at the church, as if the whole business had been his and Robert's idea. He did not have to wait long to know how well he had succeeded. On the way home from the lecture he stopped off at the Grand Pacific to have a relaxing nightcap and go through the early editions of the morning papers. The *Tribune*, its Republicanism forever embarrassed by Mrs. Lincoln's plight, ran only a few paragraphs under the wooden heading

"MRS. PRESIDENT LINCOLN—HER RESTORATION TO REASON AND PROPERTY," but they did fall into the trap he had set by saying, "Mr. Swett appeared for her . . ." Evidently proud that its sneak attack had helped get Mrs. Lincoln out of Batavia, the *Times* had crowed with a full bank of headlines:

A HAPPY DENOUEMENT

MRS. ABRAHAM LINCOLN RESTORED TO HER
REASON AND FREEDOM

AND BY ACTION OF COURT IS AGAIN
PLACED IN POSSESSION OF HER
PROPERTY

WHICH AMOUNTS TO THE SNUG SUM OF EIGHTY-ONE
THOUSAND THREE HUNDRED AND NINETY DOL-
LARS AND THIRTY-FIVE CENTS

It was Swett's idea for Robert to file his accounting right there on the spot since he had long noticed how bemused underpaid reporters were by money. It had certainly worked. Even before getting down to an account of the case, the *Times* noted that Mrs. Lincoln's estate had grown during the year of Robert's trusteeship by the purchase of some $4,000 worth of additional bonds and added: "The property is quite large, when it is considered that generally the relicts of the presidents of the United States are left only a small pittance, and amply sufficient to enable her to live in an elegant and comfortable manner." After absorbing that information no reader would be disposed to pity Mrs. Lincoln on account of ill treatment. The *Times* said that the action had been initiated by unnamed friends who were "highly gratified over the indications of a restored mind." Although the *Times* did not identify Swett as Mrs. Lincoln's counsel, its report of the actual case could hardly have been improved from his point of view . . .

"The gentlemen who appeared in court on yesterday afternoon were Hon. Leonard Swett, counsel for the conservator, Mr. Ninian W. Edwards, her brother-in-law, and her son, Mr. Robert T. Lincoln. Mrs. Lincoln remained at home in Springfield, and left the consummation of her desires to the above gentlemen.

After Judge Wallace had disposed of several small cases, he rested his eyes upon the gentlemen, who had a lien upon the clerk's desk, and awaited their pleasure.

Mr. Leonard Swett said that if the court pleased, Mr. Edwards, of Springfield, desired to present a petition from Mrs. Mary Lincoln.

MR. EDWARDS

adjusted his eye-glasses and proceeded to read the following:

'STATE OF ILLINOIS, COOK COUNTY—In the County Court—to the June term, A.D. 1876—To the Hon. M.R.M. Wallace, Judge of the County Court of the County of Cook, State of Illinois—Your petitioner, Mary Lincoln, respectfully represents unto your honor that on the 14th day of June, at the June term of 1875 of the county court in and for said county that Robert Lincoln, whom your petitioner prays may be made defendant to this petition, was appointed under the provision of chapter 86 of revised statutes of said state now in force, her conservator, your petitioner showeth to your honor that she is a proper person to have the care and management of her own estate. Your petitioner therefore prays that her said conservator may be removed and that your honor may enter an order fully restoring her to all the rights and privileges enjoyed by her before her said conservator was appointed, and that her said conservator may be required to restore to her all the money, estate, title and pension papers, United States bonds, leases and all other effects with which he is chargeable as her conservator.

MARY LINCOLN"

Mr. Swett then stated that the friends of the petitioner had been anxious to restore her to the management of her estate some time ago, but as that could not be done under the statute until the expiration of a year, they had deferred making the application until this time. Her friends had conferred together upon the matter, and now asked for a jury to pass upon the case.

A JURY

was accordingly selected and Mr. Edwards was sworn. He made a statement which was short-handed by a reporter and subsequently put into the form of an affadavit.

The statement is as follows and rather singularly contains a number of repetitions:

'STATE OF ILLINOIS, COOK COUNTY—In the County Court, June Term A.D. 1876—Mrs. Lincoln has been with me for nine or ten months, and her friends all think she is a proper person to take charge of her own affairs. She has been with me about nine months and her friends all of them recognize that she is a right person to take care of and manage her own affairs. That she is now in such condition that she can manage her own affairs. She has not spent all that she was allowed to spend during the last year, and we all think she is in a condition to take care of her own affairs.

N.W. EDWARDS'

THE COURT

said that unless the conservator waived process the discharge could not be made until the expiration of ten days.

Mr. Lincoln replied that he waived the service of the usual notice, and desired immediate action. To that end he had prepared his final report of the account of the estate, and therein asked to be relieved from further responsibility.

The jury then retired and returned shortly with the following

VERDICT:

'STATE OF ILLINOIS, COOK COUNTY—County court of Cook county—We the undersigned jurors in the case wherein Mary Lincoln, who was heretofore found to be insane, and who is now alleged to be restored to reason, having heard the evidence in said case, find that the said Mary Lincoln is restored to reason and is capable to manage and control her estate.'

The verdict was signed by R.H. Paddock, M.D., D.J. Weatherhead, S.F. Knowles, Cyrus Gleason, W.J. Heren, D. Kimball, R.F. Childs, W.G. Lyon, C.H. Chapin, H. Dahl, W.S. Dunham and W.W. Roberts.

Mr. Lincoln then filed his

ACCOUNT OF THE ESTATE

from the 19th day of May, 1875, to the 16th day of June, 1876. The receipts were $11,140.35 and the disbursements $6,875.97 for personal expenses of Mrs. Lincoln and $4,264.38 for investments in United States bonds. The inventory of the property of Mrs. Lincoln when it was placed in his hands on the 14th of June showed that in cash there was $1,029.35; United States stocks and bonds $58,000; personal obligations of conservator, $8,875; lace curtains, $549.83; wearing apparel and personal jewelry, $5,000; other items, $7,936.17. Total, $81,390.35.

THE ACCOUNT

was approved and an order was entered discharging him as conservator of the estate.

The parties then left the court room and immediately a dispatch was sent to Mrs. Lincoln by Mr. Edwards as follows: 'All right. We shall send them.' "

Reading through this, Swett must have had to chuckle over how incensed old Edwards, the aristocrat, would be at the implication that he was sort of a bumbling fool. Actually he *had* been amazingly nervous for a man with so much court experience in the past, and his aging voice had turned so thin and reedy that Judge Wallace had had to ask Edwards to repeat himself to make sure that the jury heard him. The short-hand reporter had just put down every word without explanation. Edwards was plainly stunned by a verdict that let his sister-in-law completely off the hook. Swett was certain that Edwards considered Mary Lincoln as deranged as he did, but he figured the poor old fellow was tired of living with her and hearing her plaints. All Edwards had been hoping for was that her condition would *improve* a little, once she had Robert off her back. Swett shrugged, tossed off his brandy and muttered aloud, "Sow the wind, reap the whirlwind . . ." He could hardly wait to show the papers to Robert in the morning. Whatever Edwards had got himself in for, Swett had managed to get Robert out of it with his reputation very much intact of a dutiful son doing his sad duty . . .

By the time that Ninian Edwards got back to Springfield he found that Mrs. Lincoln had already made good on her promise to deposit with banker Bunn the bonds he had sent down. She had been as surprised as he by the verdict. In her anxiety to be rid of Robert as her conservator she had not thought much about the judgment of insanity against her. Why should she? *She* knew that she was not insane. But unlike her brother-in-law she was delighted with the new verdict and the way it was played in the local papers. She had the stories telegraphed to New York. Except for the most assiduous readers it was largely a wasted effort. In their editions of June 16 the New York *Times* ran a single paragraph, and the New York *Tribune* confined its coverage to a single sentence: "A jury has decided that Mrs. Abraham Lincoln is restored to reason." Aside from running into the press's predilection to ignore good news, the account of Mrs. Lincoln's brief trial was overwhelmed by reams of copy coming out of Cincinnati, where the Republican Party that day nominated Rutherford B. Hayes, the three-time governor of Ohio, as its standard bearer in the coming presidential race. At almost any other time, when her own personal affairs were not so absorbing, Mary Lincoln would have been the most avid consumer of all the political comment surrounding the event. In this instance, however, she was content with knowing that the Stalwarts, like her son Robert, had had to abandon the idea of renominating Grant in view of the scandal that broke in March when his Secretary of War, William Belknap, resigned one step ahead of impeachment by Congress for taking money from the trading post sales in Indian territory. There would be no more fancy weddings like the one that had brought seventy carriages and 200 guests to the White House when Nellie Grant married Algernon Charles Frederic Sartoris—a nothing in British society, a nephew of an *actress,* Fanny Kemble, as Mary knew well from her sojourns in England. She hoped that the Grants would now get a taste of what she had been put through, but she doubted it: all those rich friends he had allowed to rob the treasury would take care of them. She had entertained the Grants in the White House, and they could have thought to entertain her, but of course they had not: she was an embarrassment.

For a few days the relief of knowing that Robert could no longer boss her about was such that Mary began to think that some sort of reconciliation might be possible. She missed seeing Mamie and little Abraham, and there was now a baby she had not laid eyes on. But as she went over Robert's meticulous accounting, which everybody, including Ninian and her own lawyer, Governor Palmer, praised, the anger she had tried to suppress in order to win her freedom began to burn bright. Correct or no, how cold and calculating and cruel it was to have taken out of *her* money $151 for wages and $64 for board at the hotel for the detectives whose spying on her *had* nearly driven her crazy. Whether the expenses were properly hers or not, it took a mind on the order of Mr. Dickens' Scrooge to record items like "September 9, 1875: paid several telegrams in arranging for visit to Springfield—$1.92" and "Sept. 16: paid express charges on trunk from Springfield—$1.15." Even though a private car had been donated for their comfort, Robert managed to deduct $36.30 on September 10 and 11 for "expenses of Mrs. Lincoln and myself going to Springfield and my return." One listing especially boiled her blood: the fees that Robert paid out of her estate to the doctors who had condemned her:

"*June 2.* Paid Dr. H.A. Johnson for professional service
in consultation   15.00
July 7. Paid Dr. N.S. Davis for professional services in
consultation   50.00
July 13. Paid Dr. R.N. Isham for professional services
in consultation   50.00
July 23. Paid Dr. J.S. Jewell for professional service in
consultation   15.00
July 24. Paid Dr. C.G. Smith for professional services
in consultation   15.00
Sept. 8. Paid Dr. A. McFarland for professional service
and expenses in going from Jacksonville, Illinois,
to Batavia   100.00"

Where had Robert acquired such a mean spirit? How could he be any kind of son of hers? How could he act this way when she had been nothing but generous, when she had virtually set them up in housekeeping, when she had showered them for years with gifts, when in last year's spring she had offered him her all? To humiliate her before the world with that trial was bad enough, but to *charge* her for it was unpardonable. Now that she was free again and no longer had to hold her temper for fear of being put back behind bars, she sat down, dashed off a letter and ordered the Edwards' carriage brought around to take her to town to post it before she could have a change of mind—or of heart . . .

"Springfield, Illinois.
June 19th—1876

Robert T. Lincoln

Do not fail to send me without *the least* delay, *all* my paintings, Moses in the bullrushes included—also the fruit picture, which hung in your dining room—my silver set with large silver waiter presented me by New York friends, my silver tête-à-tête set also other articles your wife appropriated & which are *well known* to you, must be sent, without a day's delay. Two lawyers and myself, have just been together and their list, coincides with my own & will be published in a few days. Trust not to the belief, that Mrs Edwards' tongue, has not been *rancorous* against you all winter & she has maintained to the very last, that you dared not venture into her house & our presence. Send me my laces, my diamonds, my jewelry—My unmade silks, white lace dress—double lace shawl & flounce, lace scarf—2 blk lace shawls—one blk lace deep flounce, white lace sets 1/2 yd in width & eleven yards in length. I am now in constant receipt of letters from prominent, *respectable,* Chicago people such as you do not associate with. No John Forsythes & such scamps . . . Two prominent clergy men, have written me, since I saw you—and mention in their letters, that they think it advisable to offer up prayers for you in Church, on account of your wickedness against me and High Heaven. In reference to Chicago you have the enemies, & I chance to have the friends there. Send me all that I have written for, you have tried your game of robbery long enough. On yesterday, I received two telegrams from prominent Eastern lawyers. You have injured yourself, not me, by your wicked conduct.

Mrs A. Lincoln

My engravings too send me. M.L. Send me Whittier
Pope, Agnes Strickland's Queens of England, other
books, you have of mine—"

When this letter reached Robert in Chicago he took it right
to Leonard Swett. The "raid" that Judge Davis had considered
unlikely had begun almost immediately. Along with this most
recent letter Robert brought a collection of letters and fragments of letters that his mother had written to his wife from
Europe in the late '60's and early '70's. They were letters overflowing with motherly and grandmotherly sentiment, but they
were also letters rich in detail about the gifts that she was acquiring in Europe and sending back to them as well as about the
possessions she had left behind in Chicago and thought they
should, or could, use. In view of the relations between the
women, it seemed now something of a miracle that Mary Harlan
Lincoln had kept these letters instead of trashing or burning
them, as Swett realized immediately when his eyes perused
them. "This is all I need," he said. "You stay out of this, Bob.
Let me take care of it. When I get through with them down
there you won't have a thing to worry about."

Despite his show of confidence, Swett knew that there was a
good deal to worry about; the smugness he'd nursed only a few
days ago at the outcome of the second trial was gone. The situation was, in fact, far too dangerous to allow Robert, who was,
he felt, sometimes confused by misplaced sentiment for his
crazy mother, to try to handle it. If Mrs. Lincoln actually did
get hold of some cheap ambulance chasing lawyer, or the other
way around, there would be plenty of grounds, what with that
second verdict, for a publicity-generating suit that could ruin
them all. No matter how a trial actually turned out, the mere
conduct of one would leave in the public mind an image of
Robert as some form of monster, of himself and Judge Davis as
conniving incompetents, of the doctors as quacks. Mrs. Lincoln
had to be stopped. Dealing with her directly now would be like

fooling around with an enraged tiger just freed from its cage. The only real hope lay in her handlers. With the kind of ammunition he had in these letters to Mary Harlan Lincoln, Swett thought that he could scare a nervous Nellie like Ninian Edwards into keeping Mrs. Lincoln under control.

Before composing what would be one of the more important letters of his life, Swett sat back and went slowly through Mrs. Lincoln's letters from Europe to make certain that his first impression of their value was correct. It was, he decided, so much so that, if he had been given to sentiment, the glimpses he got of Mrs. Lincoln through them might have unnerved him for his task. Bits and pieces leapt to the eye:

From Frankfort, March 22, 1869: "I wish my dear Mary, you would gratify me, by taking any lace or muslin waists you may see—as of course, I shall never need them again—Also take any lace of any description—for it is all yours—or any thing you see—Every thing is only getting soiled, by being laid aside—There are also needle worked kchfs with "M L"—worked in them, which are pretty—do oblige me by considering me as a mother—for you are very dear to me, as a daughter. *Any thing & every thing* is yours—if you will consider them worth an acceptance—I have the loveliest white Paris hat to send you—with the Sweetest white & green wreath—Flowers are altogether worn on these hats—a lovely apple green & white silk—for a costume a green malachite set of Jewellry & one or two other things, I found in Italy—all simple and not very expensive—but very pretty. If I only could meet with an opportunity, *now* of *sending* them—I never see, any thing, that is *particularly* pretty—that I do not wish, it was yours . . ."

Undated fragment: "I hope, dear Mary, you will immediately—get the *box* from the bank—near the Tremont House—either of the partners will give it to you—the contents is yours—also at 375 (Washington St., Chicago)—is a new set of plaited silver—very neat for you—you will find it, (the set) in a large basket—all the ornaments you can find take—the books too—also the large horn chair—if you like shells—you will find plenty of them—in a large red bowl—they were gathered together, in my own happy Springfield home—when life was very different to me—from what it is now—broken hearted as I am . . ."

From Kronberg, Sept. 4, 1869: "I suppose, dear Mary, you are just settling *yourselves* at housekeeping, feeling tired enough I dare say, at the close of each day, superintending the arrangements. Dear child, I wish I wish I was there to assist you, but alas a wide & stormy ocean separates us—you must be very careful of yourself, but I hope even now, your Dear Mother, may be with you to enjoin ALL THAT caution upon you. Robert, I am sure, will be quite as exacting in that respect, as will be necessary. *Twenty six* years ago my beloved husband, was bending over me at the birth of *your* husband, with all the affectionate devotion, which a human being is capable of, it appears *so short* a time since, and now, my son, will be enacting over the same scene—with HIS darling little wife—Such are time's changes—When I left Frankfort—I left some *baby* work, in the hands—of two different parties—2—*very* handsome long dresses are promised me *made & tucked* by hand—3 weeks hence. . . ."

Undated fragment: "There is also a large & very fine fur carriage rug at 375—I prize it very much, as it so often covered my dear husband—please guard that carefully—in the box—by the front room door up stairs—is a box of woollens—2—elegant sofa cushions. I hope you will make yourself very comfortable—be sure & have the rent of this month handed you—for your own particular use—Also the Nov rents of the 2 houses—you must receive into your own hands—I only wish it was more I hope *some day*—I may be able to do better by you. Heaven bless you, my dear child . . ."

From London, Nov. 22, 1870: "Robert writes that you were quite frightened, about the baby clothes—Certainly they were made of the simplest materials & if they were a little trimmed there was certainly nothing out of the way—The *baby* is *not* supposed to be able to walk out in the street this winter & being carried in a nurse's arms, certainly a simple embroidered cloak—is not too much, for people in *our station* of life—The very *middle classes* in Europe, dress their children quite as much & as I do not consider ourselves in that category, I would not care what the MEAN & ENVIOUS, would say. However, I will send no more be assured. Only Robert intimates, that you have no drawing room curtains, & I do not wish Christmas, to come, *without* those windows being suitably draped. You have never mentioned to me if you had two parlors or how many windows you had. But I wish *the day* you receive this, to go & get *silk* biscatelle, *not worsted* curtains, to match the colour of your carpet, a piano cover—& lace curtains—cornices &c. charge to my account . . ."

From London, Jan. 26, 1871: "I am very glad, that you are pleased with your diamonds. The style of their setting, I think, very pretty & effective—certainly the *pendant* form is the decided fashion, NOW—Therefore if I were in your place, I would not change it—They may need cleaning, but *that*, Bob, in *his* lawyer style, will tell you *is* a *risk*—for fear the diamonds, *might be changed.* I agree with him there . . . I have my eye & *occasionally* my mind, on a beautiful *baby* chain for the neck links of gold & turquoise, which would go beautifully with *the* turquoise locket—nous verrons, before long. I picked up a chain and a dainty little pair of gold, acorn earrings—They were little loves—That blessed, darling baby, how I long to see it & you all— . . ."

There was more—much more—twenty-five letters or fragments in all. Swett shook his head over the collection. How could all of that obvious love and generosity have misfired so badly? These female things baffled him. He could only guess that, since he had always thought of Mary Todd Lincoln as crazy, Mary Harlan Lincoln had come to the same conclusion at some point and had been tactless enough to let her mother-in-law know it. Robert and his wife were still too young to have learned the uses of tolerance and deception in human relationships; on the other hand, Mary Lincoln was too old to be behaving like a spoiled child—unless, of course, she *was* insane. Well, if people were perfect, there wouldn't be any law business. Whatever he *felt* about the situation, Swett knew very well what he had to *do* about it as a good servant of his client. Picking up a pen, he reached for a clean sheet of paper, scratched June 20, 1876, in the upper right hand corner, addressed it to N.W. Edwards in Springfield, and let himself go:

"The recent attitude of Mrs. Lincoln towards Robert and her . . . intentions expressed in letters and verbal conversations have induced him to consult me as his and his father's friend in regard to attacks which she proposes to make upon him. I therefore take the liberty of addressing to you this note. Prior to her recent mental troubles Mrs. Lincoln was exceedingly kind to her children. She had an income larger than she needed herself and . . . since the death of her husband she has been (generously undertaking) presents to them. About the time Robert was married in 1868 she was in England and feeling kindly towards him and his wife she sent them a great variety of personal gifts. She accompanied these by letters full of affectionate regard and presenting them. And fortunately most of the letters have been preserved.

While Mrs. Lincoln was in Chicago in 1866 she bought and furnished a house but soon tiring of this mode of life she broke up her house and stored most of her household ornaments, some furniture and a large number of trunks containing a great variety of personal articles. As Robert contemplated housekeeping after his marriage Mrs. Lincoln wrote to him and his wife repeatedly saying that she had no imaginable use for her household goods and asking them to go where they were stored and take such articles as they might need and buy nothing which they could find of use there. Her letters also name certain specified things such as unmade material for dresses and these they are asked to take and use. As this afforded Robert an opportunity to save expenditures in commencing his housekeeping it was a material matter and they, as young people would do, took these things as they were directed. Such of them as are not worn out are now scattered through Robert's house. About 1873 Robert collected for his mother five thousand dollars and at her request kept it a while she saying that she would determine by and by what to do with it. Finally she said she had no use for it and gave it to him and he used it largely in purchasing his law library and for other purposes.

After leaving her house bought in 1866 she in 1874 at her own urgent request took from Robert a contract to pay certain installments for seven years and deeded to him the house, it being practically a handsome gift to him. These payment have been made for the two years that have expired and thus the matter stands. The title to this property is now involved in litigation, a certain grantor in the chain of title insisting that her deed was forged. (If this) shall be established a subsequent deed to Mrs. Lincoln of course will be void. At the death of Taddy his estate by law descended two thirds to Mrs. Lincoln and one third to Robert, Mrs. Lincoln generously insisting on dividing this evenly. It was done. About 1867, Mrs. Lincoln bought a house upon speculation. This was found difficult to rent and was finally traded for among other things a vacant lot. In 1873 she gave this lot to Robert and he still owns it.

Notwithstanding these acts she harbors towards Robert an insane hatred because he caused her to be pronounced insane. For about two months she's been demanding from him the return of personal gifts described in this letter at first specifying certain things which she desired. All that were asked for in her first letter were sent but as he yielded she demanded more and finally has said to him by letter and verbally that he must immediately have "all her things," things which she says to Robert "you remember." Otherwise she says "my lawyers" will immediately commence suit and that unless the things are received scandalous publications will be immediately made. A moment's reflection will show that very many of the things cannot be returned. A part of them are baby clothes and dress materials which have worn out and household ornaments broken or gone. The watch presented to Mrs. Robert Lincoln before her marriage which is especially demanded was a beautiful gift presentation being engraved on the inside of the case. But in a railroad car years ago a thief stole it.

Both you and I know that we have committed acts of doubtful propriety in causing to be returned to her what has been returned already. Recently through our agency, you in asking it and I at the request of Robert in not opposing it, more than seventy thousand dollars in value in securities has been handed over to her which there is great danger will never be of any benefit either to her or to her friends and that, too, upon the distinction which you drew in your testimony and in your letter received today that while she is not in her right mind she is able to manage her business. What ought to have been done, as common prudence most glaringly dictated, was to place the bonds in some safe deposit and let her spend the income and all principal she needed. What she does as we both know is to buy dresses and be almost constantly employed in making and fitting them and then folding them in trunks never to be again unfolded or taken out. In this way much of her income for the past six months has been spent. Now this is very harmless and as long as she has the money she should be gratified in it for it does her good in employing her mind and does good also for those who are paid by her. I have always advocated therefore that she should have monthly all her income which I understand to be about seven hundred dollars per month and if she could spend enough of the principal also each month so that at such a time as her life would terminate according to ordinary calculation it would be all gone.

Robert is her only heir and he has had enough to give him a start and now let him for his own good work his own way. He is in a most excellent law firm, has now an assured permanent business which must give him, I should think, five thousand a year and such a position is improved more by giving it work than giving it money. Now assuming that we have done right in our doubtful experiment of giving to her her [whole] fortune in bonds have we not gone far enough in that line? If any misfortune happens to her Robert [will have] to support her and is it not proper that [having] given her seventy thousand dollars to experiment on when we all [agree] that she is not in her right mind, we should keep something for her in case of misfortune. Besides Robert cannot now pay back the money she has given and turn over to Mrs. Lincoln a law library which he needs and which she can have no need for. [Wouldn't] you prove her to be insane and ourselves very weak and foolish in permitting it? . . .

Robert is a young man of whom his mother might well be proud. He is [making excellent progress in his profession]. He demands the respect and confidence of the whole community and is growing, I think I may personally . . . say, as fast as his father was growing at his age of life. Now with such a son bearing patiently for ten years after all his past sad family history the terrible burden of his mother's approaching insanity, putting off any steps restraining her until seven of the most prominent physicians say to him professionally there is danger of her jumping out of her window to escape from him and from imaginary rebels, visiting his mother every week while at Batavia, permitting her to be rational the first day the statute permits it mainly at your request and when you yourself say that she is not in her right mind, giving her also mainly at your request every dollar of the principal and all the interest accrued when it was his judgment that it would be better to have it in monthly installments, I say with such a son and such a mother [shall] we friends of the family permit her to go about with a pistol avowing her purpose to shoot him, shall we permit her to break him down and ruin him by harassing and annoying him?

If Mr. Lincoln could speak to us, what would he say? If Mrs. Lincoln who in her right mind was the kindest of mothers with proper reason could see herself trying to ruin her son, would she not cry out, 'Hold me, hold me.' The question with us is not one of judgment but one of courage. We yield to her step by step when we know it is wrong and make the situation worse simply because we are afraid of her and afraid while we are trying to save her from herself we ourselves will be misrepresented and misunderstood by the public because the public don't understand the facts. Now for one I am determined to do this no longer and therefore I write you this note.

If Mrs. Lincoln wishes specific articles of property such as pictures or ornaments or things of like character which she has once given Robert or his wife and

will ask their return recognizing the gift and not demanding them as a right we will return them if it can
reasonably be done. But we cannot return them upon
the theory that they were improperly procured, improperly detained, or under denunciation and threats.
There has been an effort by meddlesome people to cast
upon Robert, because he wanted money saved for his
mother so that it might be spent by his mother, the
imputation of selfish motives. I am happy to say however that this feeling has been universally disavowed
by all persons who know him and who know the facts
and especially by you and your family who on all occasions have expressed to him your sympathy and confidence. He cannot therefore for his own reputation
allow his poor insane mother to charge him with getting the things improperly and then half acknowledge
the charge by yielding to her in returning them.

You may ask what can I do about it? I will tell you
what I will do about it. We both know that the removal
of civil liability from Mrs. Lincoln is an experiment. It
has been done to err upon the side of leniency towards
her if we should err at all. It has been done with the
hope that she would be quiet. If she will it is all right.
If she will not but turns upon her only son . . . to
destroy him, knowing that she is insane, I shall as a
citizen irrespective of Robert or anyone in discharge of
what I know to be my duty to her and her dead husband at the proper time have her confined as an insane
person whatever may be the clamor or the consequences. Please state to her kindly and firmly my intentions.

Since writing the above, I have conferred with Judge
Davis who happens to be in town and he approves of
this letter. Since this writing also Robert has received

another . . . letter in which . . . she characterizes him
as a 'monster of mankind.'

> Yours truly, Leonard Swett"

Swett was confident that, however it was conveyed to her, his
threat to put her back behind bars would throw the fear of God
into Mary Lincoln. Since she had watched him do it once, she
could not doubt his ability or willingness to do it again. And as
for Ninian Edwards or Governor Palmer or any other lawyers
she might try to bring into the affair, they would appreciate
right away that Mrs. Lincoln's letters of gift to her daughter-in-
law cut the ground out from under a suit. He had also made sure
that this time there would be no running to Judge Davis. It was
not therefore a surprise to Swett to receive almost immediate
word through Edwards that "all she [Mrs. Lincoln] asks Robert
to return to her are some paintings she left in his house for
safekeeping, and her case of silverware." Even more satisfying
was Ninian's report that he now had reason to believe that "the
story in relation to the pistol was not true" and that Mrs. Lincoln had promised him "in the presence of her sister and niece
Mrs. Clover, that she will neither bring any suits against Robert
nor make any attacks on him."

Leonard Swett, the lawyer, could again boast of a firstrate job
of work: his client would no longer be "troubled" by his mother.
Indeed, it was not long before word filtered up from Springfield
that Mrs. Lincoln was making plans to go abroad as soon as
possible. It would be a relief to Swett and his client to have what
Mrs. Lincoln herself called "a wide and stormy ocean" between
her and the Chicago courts. If, as his letter showed, Leonard
Swett could not comprehend Mary Lincoln's rage at being
branded insane, it was to be doubted that he could ever comprehend her sorrow, either. When a sister tried to talk her out of
going on a long, lonely journey, Mary Lincoln said that she

could not be comfortable in Springfield—or anywhere in America. "I cannot endure to meet my former friends," said the former First Lady of the land. "They will never cease to regard me as a lunatic. I feel it in their soothing manner. If I should say the moon is made of green cheese, they would heartily and smilingly agree with me."

CHAPTER XI:

"... *simply an* exile"

The REST OF MARY LINCOLN'S STORY needs a different kind of telling. Whereas the year of struggle with her son in and out of court, in and out of the asylum, in and out of Springfield provides the stuff of almost daily drama, the years after she embarked on a ship for Le Havre in October, 1876, were comparatively quiet. Large gaps in all but the most routine correspondence and a merciful disappearance of her name from the public prints make it impossible to reconstruct these years in the form of detailed on-going narrative. But there remains enough record to let us see that the trials of Mrs. Lincoln were over only in the most literal sense when a jury found her to be sane. A great many did not accept that verdict, and she knew it. Whether she actually saw Attorney Swett's threatening letter or not she quite obviously felt the attitude that he so brutally expressed. And so she felt obliged to put herself through the trial of proving her sanity through her conduct while enduring at the same time the trial of failing health.

The place where Mary Lincoln chose to face these trials was

a spa in the French Pyrénées name Pau, a place she had evidently seen and liked during her first visit to Europe. With its fourteenth-century castle hung with Gobelin tapestries, its many-bridged ravine, its view out over the Gave de Pau, the little town had the touches of quaint charm that Mary Lincoln appreciated and the kind of climate that her body with its multiple ailments craved. One reason for going there that she gave to Springfield relatives worried about her being alone was that she would have friends—members of the Orléans family, a branch of the royal house of Bourbon. In this she was probably stretching the truth only a little. One of the special delights of the "Republican Queen" in the White House had been working her wiles in French on representatives of Napoleon III's court in which the Orléans dukes were prominent, and she had undoubtedly met members of the family resident in England during her sojourn there. It is to be doubted that she saw much of these royal personages, for all the evidence would indicate that she led a hermetic existence.

In fact, Mary Lincoln's true and only friend in those days lived thousands of miles away—in Springfield, Illinois. He was an eighteen-year-old named Edward Lewis Baker, Jr., and he was her grandnephew, grandson of Elizabeth and Ninian Edwards. Since his parents were abroad on a diplomatic mission young Lewis was living in the Edwards' expanded mansion on the hill when Mary came down from Batavia. That these two could develop a sympathetic relationship seemed unlikely. Even though Mary Lincoln would have been the most famous and talked about relative in the Todd family for most of his life, a boy of that age would normally shy away from an aging, black-gowned lady who had been called by the scary name of lunatic and who, it was said, spent most of her time pawing through trunks full of uninteresting dress goods. On her part, Mary Lincoln might well have carried her dislike of Lewis' parents down to another generation. With a Todd-like tongue and pen that could be as tart as Mary's own, Julia Edwards Baker had made critical remarks about her famous aunt during the White House years that had caused a permanent rift with Mary, who might have been more sympathetic had she known of Julia's mental condition—a family secret imparted only to Robert during the negotiations over Mary's own release from the asylum. As for Lewis' father, he had virtually assured the failure of Mary Lincoln's New York clothes sale when, as editor of the *Illinois State Journal*, he chose that time to disclose the full details of Mr. Lincoln's estate and—almost worse—Lewis' very presence in the Edwards house was due to his father serving President Grant, for whom Mary Lincoln had a feeling close to loathing. But there was something like a chemical attraction between Mary Todd Lincoln and young people in general that proved as powerful in this instance as it had through the whole of her life.

Almost without exception people who knew Mary Lincoln when they were children were close to ecstatic when they recounted their experiences with her—and with Abraham Lincoln as well. A shared attitude of lenience and camaraderie with children was one of the glues of the Lincoln marriage, and it seems to have affronted their more conventionally minded, spare-the-rod-and-spoil-the-child contemporaries. Billy Herndon based much of his charge that the Lincoln household was a "domestic hell" on the fact that the children were, in his view, undisciplined brats, and Judge David Davis' reaction to a child-centered Lincoln household in Springfield, not to mention in the White House, might be guessed from his comment that children were all right as long as they behaved "cherubly." Possibly out of suppressed envy, even women disapproved Lincoln's sharing the chores of child-rearing with Mary, and one of them called him down in the streets for wheeling a baby carriage instead of going to the office where he *belonged*. Lincoln ignored such carping, and was rewarded for his behavior—a neighbor tells how the neighborhood children would run and jump and hang from his hands and arms when he walked home for meals. That Mrs. Lincoln was equally attractive to children comes through in the testimony of those who liked to play or visit in her house. Although some of them witnessed displays of her famous temper, it was never directed at them—or at her own children.

"I was at their home a great deal of the time. I played there more often than any other place," Julia Isabelle Sprigg told an interviewer in 1928 when she was seventy-six, "and I do not remember ever seeing her angry even when we planted flowers and put the tops in the ground, leaving the roots in the air. She never talked cross, and was very gentle. She was always kind. She was the kind of woman that children liked, and children would be attracted to her." The reason children liked to play at the Lincolns' becomes apparent in these recollections of Mary's half-sister Emilie from her visit with them in Springfield as a teenager:

> "Governor Matteson had a beautiful daughter Lydia. Coming home from church one morning my sister said to me, 'Emilie, you are just as pretty as Lydia, but I do not like your bonnet.' The next Sunday 'Little Sister's' head was crowned with a white velvet bonnet smothered in lovely white plumes, a gift from my sister and brother Lincoln. We often went for long drives beyond the limits of the town, and Bob, who was quite a little Chesterfield, due to his mother's careful training, would help us out of the carriage and we would gather wild flowers and carry home great armfuls.
>
> Mary was reading the novels and poems of Sir Walter Scott to Bob that spring. One day hearing sounds of strife, we ran to the window. Bob and a playmate were having a battle royal. Bob, with his sturdy little legs wide apart, was wielding a fence paling in lieu of a lance and proclaiming in a loud voice, 'This rock shall fly from its firm base as soon as I.' Mary, bubbling with

laughter, called out, 'Grammercy, brave knights. Pray be more merciful than you are brawny.' "

Another happy glimpse of Mary Lincoln interacting with children comes from Julia Taft, who as the teenaged sister of boys who played with Willie and Tad was often in the White House. "I have a very tender memory of Mrs. Lincoln who was always so good to me," she wrote. "More than once she said, 'I wish I had a little girl like you, Julia.' She always called me Julia, although the boys, like their father, usually changed my name to Julie. I think both she and the President would have been glad to have a daughter. She told me about her little son Edward, who was between Robert and Willie, and who had died in infancy, and we wept together as she told me about his death. Once, a long time after this, I spoke of a boy friend who had joined the Confederate army and she said, 'Yes, dear, it is sad when our friends are in the rebel army.' I had heard that two brothers of Mrs. Lincoln were in that army and she may have been thinking of them when she comforted me but I never heard her actually speak of them. She said rebel army, not Southern or Confederate but 'rebel.' Mrs. Lincoln was wickedly maligned by people saying that she was in sympathy with the South, but I am sure she was unreservedly for the Union and at one with her husband. I showed her an impassioned appeal from this boy friend to, 'fly with me to the Southern clime before Washington is destroyed.' I would not have dared to annoy my lady-mother with such trivial things, but the First Lady was not too exalted to sympathize with my story and give me kind advice."

Since three of the four Lincoln boys died before they could reflect on their relationships with their parents and write about them, much valuable testimony in this area is not available. Eddie, at four, was too young to have left much of an impression; sadly but rather fittingly for a time when the taking of a photograph was a major production, not even a picture of Eddie survives. Willie was universally held to be the sweetest and most promising—he had, for instance, written creditable verse at the age of eleven—of the Lincoln boys, and he was the acknowledged favorite of both parents, a no doubt difficult acknowledgement for Robert to accept. Tad, who lisped badly and may have been mildly retarded, was something of a family pet and no threat to anybody, even Robert. He could handle his mother as expertly and tenderly as Mr. Lincoln had. In the immediate aftermath of the assassination, Tad alone could persuade her to stop weeping and cope with some of life's demands by lying on her bed and empathizing with her, and Mary Lincoln's letters from the years she and Tad spent together in Europe contain many touching scenes of young Tad bringing her food and nursing her when she was sick, of Tad's looking on her with eyes as full of loving concern as those of Mr. Lincoln in similar situations.

The slim record with respect to Robert indicates early distancing from his parents. There is no question that Robert admired—and probably felt overawed by—his towering father, but there is also no question that their very different temperaments and Abraham Lincoln's busy life during Robert's growing up years prevented any closeness. Reticent in everything, Robert was truly clam-like about his childhood, which he seems to have regarded as difficult, whether from enduring the taunts of peers about his crossed eyes or from bearing the brunt of his mother's efforts to create a "little Chesterfield." Nowhere does Robert describe his early feelings about his mother, but in her letters Mary makes transparent her feelings about Robert—she was proud of her creation but found it a difficult thing to like. This may have been because Robert was never very much of a child. Consider Julia Sprigg's memory: "Robert was very fond of books; he would pay no attention to anyone or anything; we always called him 'Rob'; he was a great student; he was away at school, but when at home *sometimes* [author's italics] he would play with us. I think he looked more like his mother." Or take a White House scene: Like the rest of America, Mrs. Lincoln and her husband were bemused and amused by the most famous pair of the times—Mr. and Mrs. Charles Sherwood Stratton, the midgets whom P.T. Barnum had press agented to fame as Mr. and Mrs. Tom Thumb. When the midgets took a wedding trip to Washington in February, 1863, the Lincolns, partly to relieve the strain of war, invited them to a White House reception. Home from college at the time, Robert stayed upstairs, telling a miffed Mary Lincoln: "No, mother, I do not propose to assist in entertaining Tom Thumb. My notions of duty, perhaps, are somewhat different from yours."

For a woman who had squandered so much emotional investment in the love of children, what she saw as a betrayal by Robert and the accompanying separation from her own grandchildren must have been even worse than the indignity of the trial. So perhaps it was in the nature of a compensating gift from God that circumstances provided Mary Lincoln with the opportunity to work her old magic on Lewis Baker. Since no account of them has been given, the happy hours that this young man, eager for knowledge of the great world with its great affairs and great people, must have spent listening raptly to the former First Lady can only be imagined. The consequences of his evidently sincere interest in her are documented. Lewis escorted his great-aunt to New York and saw her safely aboard ship. It was not a duty trip; it was a fun trip. Mary Lincoln was ever an enthusiastic sightseer, and she and Lewis took advantage of the journey east to stop and visit the Carlsbad Caverns. So sympathetic and understanding a companion was this remarkable eighteen-year-old that Mary Lincoln, through her letters, shared with him everything that happened to her, everything that was in her mind and heart, during the next four years.

These were years when, internally as well as externally, things seemed to calm down for Mary Lincoln. For whatever reason, the searing headaches had apparently gone and possibly taken with them the emotional firestorms. She was not, however, well. She lost a great deal of weight and reported symptoms that have since suggested the onset of diabetes to some medically trained minds. When she was up to it physically she visited favorite old haunts along the Riviera or in Italy, but for the most part she stuck to her modest lodgings in Pau. A measure of how quiet her life was there, how far she had sunk out of the world's sight, is the account of the visit that the Grants made to Pau on their triumphal post-White House round-the-world trip. In a biography intended to depict his grandparents in the best of lights, U.S. Grant III wrote: "After brief stops at Valencia and Barcelona, they then proceeded to Paris via Pau, where they learned (just before leaving) that Mrs. Abraham Lincoln was stopping there. They regretted very much they had not learned this sooner so that they could have made a call on her, but they had their tickets and a train scheduled, and a party going with them, and could not change their plans."

Pride and still smouldering jealous anger would, of course, have kept Mary Lincoln from seeking *them* out. In the days when she was fighting for a pension she had resented the gifts of houses and money bestowed by admirers, generally Republican, on the Grants. Since one of her chief occupations at Pau was going to the library to keep up with the papers she could not have missed the glaring comparison between her own abstemious, anonymous European existence in walk-up boarding-house rooms and the lavish living provided the Grants. There was, for instance, notice of how Mrs. John W. Mackay, with a killing from the Comstock silver lode to spend, rewarded the President of the rich with a dinner and ball in her Paris home on the Place de l'Étoile at which the menus were printed on silver tablets and the guest list included the Marquis de Lafayette and M. de Rochembeau.

Although not mentioned specifically, Mary Lincoln's reaction to something like that can be guessed from the tone of her letters to Lewis. She may have calmed down, but she did not necessarily mellow. She remained outraged by the injustices meted out to her by the nation in general and her son in particular. In one typical letter, Mary Lincoln paints a full-rounded, indelible self-portrait:

"Pau, France
June 22, 1879

My dear Lewis:

It is impossible for me to express to you, the great pleasure your beautiful letter of the 1st of June, afforded me. . . . I loved you all very much whilst I was with you, but in this strange land, so *far* removed from you, my heart and thoughts revert continually to your little circle, and very frequently, I wish myself in your midst—*Very* reluctantly, I left you all, and it was only for *self protection,* that I did so. Of this, dear Lewis, you are *fully* aware. The great God, removed from me my idols & when my last worshipped one, who so completely filled my heart & thoughts, & who idolized me as much in return, was taken THEN my heart broke—Your Grandma is indeed blessed to have *you* remain with her— . . . 'Love crowned you at your birth,' it would be almost sacrilege, if you left Springfield, with your many friends there. I remember, whilst in Washington in the Summer of 1861—I sent your Mother a bottle of *Jordan* water, which had been sent me from Palestine, as she had mentioned that she was going to have her children christened. I believe that face of yours, loved by so many persons, *so* abounding in intelligence, good looks, & sweet sympathy, was watered by this same Jordan water—Yet, it required, my dear Lewis, nothing of the kind, to beautify that nature of yours, that gladdens, so many hearts . . . *This* is a fete day, among the Catholics & the grandest procession, quite a mile in length, passed this street, half an hour since. Two or three bands of music, were interspersed in the line. Can I say to you how much I wished your Grandma and yourself, had witnessed it. From *little* girls of 3 years of age, to those of 30—all dressed in pure white—then came a long line of nuns, priests, and an indescribable array of gilt glitter—*Music* such as would have rejoiced your brother Willis greatly. Has the latter yet left you? What a comfort you must have found in him, the past winter! I trust the *benign* influence of J.T. Stuart [John Todd Stuart, whose part in her trial had soured Mary on this cousin and playmate of her youth, who had been the agency of her meeting Mr. Lincoln] had nothing to do with the difficulty concerning your property & that of your good Grandfather. In J.T. Stuart—I have not the *least* faith. It is a great pleasure to me to hear that your Grandpa is in a measure recovering the use of his right arm & hand—the latter in damp weather, I fear he will often find painful—please remember me to him, with much love. Fannie Wallace [Mary's sister], *now* writes about *twice* a year— . . .

There is a paper published at Pau, called the 'American Register,' which is issued once a week, & which I sometimes see. Recently, I had the privilege of seeing a short article in it, mentioning that Robert T. Lincoln and Stephen A. Douglas [Jr.] were practising law in Chicago, both prominent in their respective political parties, with *quite a certainty* of being at no distant day, candidates for the Presidency. You can imagine how elated I felt, in my quiet way, over such a prospect the triumph of the *'just' slightly different* from the great & good father, however who was kind to *his stepmother*— I began to study over in my own mind, with such a *CERTAINTY* in view, what never once occurred to me in my good husband's time notwithstanding articles that often appeared in the papers, that 'Mrs Lincoln was the power behind the throne' I found myself revolving in my own *feeble* mind, of what superior persons the *Cabinet* would consist . . . & *Little Mamie* with her charming manners & presence, in the event of *success*, will grace the place. By the way, dear Lewis, should I again enclose any thing for this dear child again, I will not trouble your good Grandmother— only if you will write R.T. Lincoln—a formal note— remitting what is sent. *The* young man, who makes *no* concessions to the *Mother*, whom he has so cruelly and unmercifully wronged—So that he will be a *temperate* man is the boon, for which I *daily* kneel. How terrible is the death of young Lewis [sic] Napoleon [Son of Napoleon III and Eugenie who was killed in an ambush by native warriors while a member of a British expedition to Zululand]! Cut to pieces after receiving the fatal shot, in so unnecessary a cause. Write to me frequently, my dear Lewis, I write so rapidly, that I fear my letters are not easily read. Please present my best love to all friends. Always, your very affectionate Aunt,

Mary Lincoln

Please burn this letter, so hurriedly written that I dare not read it over. Write *very frequently*, dear Lewis—

Aff
M.L."

Just about every contradiction in Mary Lincoln's complicated emotional attachment to Robert, her son, can be read into this letter. Pride, hurt, anger—all tumbling over each other and spilling onto the page. The pride was warranted since, while she was living out her life in obscurity in Europe, Robert was carving out in Chicago the very kind of career for which she had groomed him.

Granted that, as the son of the most illustrious President in American history, Robert Lincoln had opportunities and advantages not enjoyed by most other young men, he showed himself capable of making maximum use of this head start. If he was quite different from his famous father in talent and temperament, he did share with Abraham Lincoln—and with Mary Lincoln, too—a certain knack for riding the tide of history. Before the Civil War, politics was the consuming passion of America, and the society's shining stars were performing in the political arena. The names that inspired Mary and Abraham Lincoln in their growing-up years were those of the Founding Fathers, only a generation removed—Washington, Jefferson, Adams, Madison, Hamilton, Franklin—who had created a new nation, and in their own time the likes of Jackson, Webster, Clay, Calhoun, Sumner, Douglas, who were shaping its future. But the war changed everything. Quite aside from the fact that it settled the major political question of the times, as Lincoln had hoped it would, the war so strongly stimulated economic growth in the north that power shifted from the hands of political leaders to those of men who became known as "Captains of Industry." Power confers glamor; the holders of power become the current heroes. The post-war stars in young men's eyes were Vanderbilt, Rockefeller, Carnegie, Morgan, Mellon, Pullman, Huntington, Stanford, Gould, Harriman, Armour. As it was made clear in the scandals of the Grant administration, political leaders of the day, including luminaries like Vice-President Colfax and the silver tongued Senator Blaine of Maine—the "plumed knight"—were little more than paid hands of the men with money. So Robert Lincoln, inheriting the parental instinct for power, decided to make money and, as his father had been in *his* time, he was becoming very nearly an incarnation of the American ideal in *his* time.

It was not easy for Robert to follow that path. Astute Republican politicians looked on him as a potential asset from the day he set up in the practice of law in Chicago. The two strongest vote-getting emotional appeals that the Republicans used to keep themselves in power, despite a depression and scandal, for all but eight of forty-seven years after the war were "waving the bloody shirt"—reminding everyone that it was the predominantly Democratic South that was on the wrong side of the conflict—and evoking the Lincoln legend. As a living part of that legend, Robert's appeal was self-evident. But except for serving in 1876 as supervisor of the town of South Chicago, a civic duty roughly equivalent to being president of the local PTA today, Robert expressed a disdain close to dread of political involvement. Nevertheless, as his mother noted in faraway Pau, he was being seriously proposed as a Presidential candidate from the moment he reached the statutory age of thirty-five in 1877. Those who kept pressing him chose to ignore both his outspoken disgust with politics and the nature of his personality, which was totally unsuited to running for office. Shy and publicity-shunning, he was in his way as uncompromising as his mother, and he created the impression of arrogance. Although over-colored by his personal aversion to Mary Lincoln and all of her sons who were competitors for the time and affections of his law partner, Billy Herndon's view of Robert showed the kind of impression he could often create. "He has the insane rage of his mother without the sense of his father. Robert Lincoln is a wretch of a man," wrote Herndon, who added for good measure that Robert was "little, proud, aristocratic and haughty—his mother's 'baby' all through." If Robert Lincoln thus lacked charisma as a people's candidate, another aspect of his character doubtless made up for that lack in the minds of the political pros: he was "safe"—that is, without so much as a whispered hint of personal dishonesty, moral turpitude or liberal leanings. Although he had so far kept his name off national ballots, Robert was carrying too much in the way of political baggage to unburden himself completely.

In Mary's letter, a rather justified pride in Robert's public image quickly dissolved into an equally justified and prideful refusal to go crawling to him. But her instruction to Lewis to communicate with "R.T. Lincoln" by formal note was moving further in the direction of some sort of reconciliation than was Robert from his side. Once she had wriggled herself out of his grasp with the aid of her relatives, his mother had virtually ceased to exist for Robert, as judged by his public utterances. When, about the time of this letter, a New York minister pressed Robert for news of her, he wrote testily, "My mother is now somewhere in Europe but she has, for unfortunate reasons, ceased to communicate with me, and I do not know her present address although, of course, I can by writing to some of her friends obtain it in case of need." Quite obviously Robert had felt no need for any direct communication in three years, has made *"no* concessions," as his mother acknowledged.

Posterity would be the poorer if the recipients had burned all the letters that Mrs. Lincoln instructed them to. That she did so shows, however, that she was very sanely conscious of her sometimes rather too hasty and frank confidences. Most of her correspondence with Lewis, though, is innocuous and given over to quite sound auntly advice. She urges him to go to college and to travel—"I am so pleased also that you will visit the White Mountains next summer, lake George, & pass a day or two at Niagara falls—I have visited all those places & have always returned to Niagara with renewed interest—I think *24*—hours, *however* will suffice you, on the Tip Top house." Warming up, she said she felt strongly that he shouldn't follow his father into journalism because it would lead to a love of politics *"that is anything, but* desirable in a young man." In that same letter she typically—and rather ironically—reveals her own life-long in-

terest in politics by criticizing President Hayes for appointing
David M. Key, a Tennessean who served in the Confederate
army, as Postmaster General. Repeatedly, she makes it clear that
she feels she was driven from home by fear of what Robert
and/or Leonard Swett might do to her. One such passage also
reveals that Mary Lincoln's love of the good things in life was
not limited to clothes and jewels. "How much I long to see you
all—to have a taste of your dear Grandma's good food—*waffles*,
buttercakes, egg corn bread—are *all* unknown here—as to bis-
cuits, light rolls &c. they have never been dreamed of—*not* to
speak of *buckwheat* cakes—It needs no assurance of mine, to
convince you, that a long period of absence from America, is not
agreeable—but to an oppressed, heartbroken woman it is simply
an *exile.*"

Mary Lincoln moved to end that exile after a severe fall. In
December, 1879, she was expecting guests at her lodgings when
she noticed that a picture over the mantle was not hanging
straight. In her fashion, instead of waiting for help she tried to
climb a ladder to fix it and a rung of the ladder broke. In falling
she hit the edge of a sofa with the middle of her back and
suffered what the doctors of the time called "inflammation of the
spinal cord and a partial loss of power in the lower extremities,"
a condition for which they prescribed bed rest. She did improve
enough to try a trip in search of greater warmth, got as far as
Nice, realized that she was not getting any better and headed
back to Pau to make plans for sailing home. Her deteriorating
condition was starkly described in another letter to Edward
Lewis Baker, Jr.:

"Pau, France
June 12, 1880

My dear Lewis,
    . . . I shrink from writing almost to day, dear Lewis,
having so poor a report to make of myself. On my

return here, the day afterwards being utterly exhausted with the sufferings of my back & left side, & the journey, I was compelled to send for the physician, who insisted upon perfect rest, outward applications & resting on the lounge, the greater part of the time for two months—Allowing me a drive of an hour once a week. In my desire to regain my former strength, I think I *faintly* promised him to do so—But in my great wish to leave four days since, I sent for a bonne, who had sometimes been of service to me—took her arm and *painfully* wended my way to the 'Hotel de la Paix' closed & deserted—I wished to take a survey of broken trunks & see how many had to be replaced. Alas, for my weakness, on attempting to *descend,* my left side gave way, she had to call the Concierge to lift me down, place me in a carriage, although my present Hotel Henry Quatre is as near to the Hotel, where I went, as Mrs. James Lamb's is to you. The bonne, went for the physician who ordered a warm bath, the bonne placed me in bed, & gave me a cup of warm soup, the physician returned towards evening with fresh plasters & I am now sitting propped up, on my lounge. This is a weary recital to you dear Lewis, but with your great, good heart perhaps it will not be amiss, to write you the exact truth. But I feel assured, that I shall be completely cured, by following the directions of my physician. But it is a curiosity to see *how* angry these French people can become. The *most unprincipled, heartless, avaricious* people, on the face of the earth. With the exception of a *very few,* I detest them all . . . *To this hour,* I do not know who is nominated for the Presidency [it was Garfield], you must write and enclose me, *all* news —I have been thinking over a good deal, dear Lewis, the last two or three days, in my darkened, solitary room and I think IF I DO NOT regain my health, a little more rapidly than I am now doing, *instead* of the trip to the White Mountains as I proposed to you several months since, a trip to Havre and a run down to Paris, the latter a journey of four hours to meet me, with a visit of ten days or two weeks in Paris—would be more pleasant to you *in the late autumn. Of this,* more hereafter. I shall never feel satisfied until you see the beautiful Pyrénées . . . But I must first return to America, straighten out my bonds and settle down, THEN, I shall be only too pleased if you will undertake the journey by yourself . . . I write you very sincerely, since last autumn, owing to illness and thieving generally by the *French physicians* &c. I shall be *better* enabled to carry out my wishes, after *my* RETURN. You wrote me that your kind, good Grandfather had letters that would pass me through the Custom House . . . I will write in a few days to your dear Grandmother further particulars. I *so* long to be with you all. In ill health & sadness quietude & loved faces, are far the best. Have *perfect* confidence, in what I write you & *future movements best* love *to all.* Your Grandmother will understand every thing.

Most affectionately,
Your Aunt
Mary Lincoln"

In addition to what it says about bodily health, this letter says a lot about Mary Lincoln's thinking. Management of her money was still of great concern, hardly a cause of wonder in view of all that had happened to her. Until the assassination she was an indulged "child wife"—Lincoln actually liked to call her that. With supreme confidence in her husband's generosity out of at least four years of Presidential income, she had contracted debts that she had every good reason to believe would easily be discharged. When Lincoln's income was chopped off as surely and swiftly as his life, Mary Lincoln was left with a fearful insecurity with respect to future money. This accounted for much of the behavior so embarrassing to her son—the clothes sale, the no-quarter fight for a pension, the bonds in a petticoat pocket. This also accounted for her frightened rage when, through the agency of the insanity trial, her resources were taken away from her control. Driven by fear that the bottom could again drop out from under her and determined to demonstrate her financial competence, Mrs. Lincoln devoted considerable time in Pau to staying in constant touch with her Springfield banker, Jacob Bunn. In all, she wrote him more than ninety notes and letters in which she showed a remarkable command of every detail of her investments and income. Like her headaches, her shopping sprees were a thing of the past. Her generous impulses such as offering to fund Lewis on a European tour were accompanied by cautions such as insisting that she first had to come home and put her financial house in order.

In October, 1880, Mary Lincoln sailed from LeHavre on the *Amerique*. She very nearly did not make it home. She was standing at the top of a stairway when a wave rolled the ship. In her crippled condition she lost her footing and started to pitch forward. A woman next to her grabbed her by the bustle and was easily able to pull her back, since she weighed only about a hundred pounds. The incident slipped into history because Mrs. Lincoln's rescuer was one Sarah Bernhardt on her way to a triumphal acting tour of America. In her book *Memories of My Life*, Bernhardt recalled Mrs. Lincoln as a little woman "dressed in black with a sad, resigned face" who "thanked me in such a gentle, dreamy voice that my heart began to beat with emotion. 'You might have been killed, madame,' I said, 'down that horrible staircase!' 'Yes,' she answered with a sigh of regret, 'but it was not God's will.'" Bernhardt added that she had "just done this unhappy woman the only service that I ought not to have done her—I had saved her from death." After saving Mary Lincoln, Bernhardt completely upstaged her on the ship's arrival in New York. In an effort to get the actress' carriage through the fans crowding the gates to see her, a policeman asked a little lady in black to step aside. According to Lewis Baker who had come to meet his great-aunt at the gangplank, in unspoken acknowledgement that her own day in the limelight was over Mary Lincoln complied without a murmur.

Actually Mary Lincoln was a bit premature in thinking herself out of the public eye. With Lewis helping her, she returned to her room in the house on the hill in Springfield. In physical distress from the injury to her back and failing eyesight, in psychological distress from the disappointments of life, she allowed herself to become a recluse. Through that fall and winter, however, the rising star of her son, who so dreaded publicity, began to shine, albeit rather palely, as the political fate he could not quite escape caught up with him. The Lincolns were back in the news.

Whether out of loyalty to his old commander or out of a conviction that the pro-business policies of the Grant administration were good for America, Robert Lincoln remained a Stalwart, one of those Republicans who thought in '76 and again in '80 that Ulysses S. Grant should be given a third term. As such, he was a "Grant delegate" from Cook County to the convention in Chicago, where a slate consisting of James A. Garfield of Ohio and Chester A. Arthur of New York was chosen. The disappointment of the Stalwarts, who numbered among them many veterans of the Grand Army of the Republic, was strong enough that Garfield was advised to appoint a Stalwart to his cabinet. With this objective in view, President-elect Garfield created one of the stranger examples of political bedfellows by turning to Judge David Davis for confidential advice about the qualifications and availability of Robert Lincoln for the post of Secretary of War. Davis had by then quit the Supreme Court to return to politics and serve as the elected choice of the Democratic legislature of Illinois to the United States Senate. Nobody knew for sure whether Davis, one of the creators of Republican power as Lincoln's campaign manager, had changed party allegiance, but the Judge's relationship to Robert Lincoln as something of a surrogate father had been well and publicly established. Davis recommended Robert Lincoln highly, and his appointment was accordingly announced in March, 1881.

The newspapers could find little to say about the new Secretary. One of the most comprehensive reports appeared in the New York *Tribune*. Exactly equal in length to those about other appointees, it read in its entirety:

> "Robert T. Lincoln, son of the late President Abraham Lincoln, was born in Sangamon County, Ill., about forty years ago. He was graduated from the law school of Harvard University, and has since practised his profession at Chicago. Secretary Lincoln has often been urged to accept a nomination for the Legislature, but has always declined, saying that in his opinion a young lawyer should not enter politics until he had become well established in his profession.
>
> As a lawyer, Mr. Lincoln has been successful and has built up an extensive practice. He is a member of a firm which represents the interests in the West of many Eastern insurance companies which have loaned large sums of money in Illinois and other Western States. The management of this business has developed in Mr. Lincoln a superior executive ability, and a capacity for the management of large interests involving many intricate details. Illinois is included in the circuit of Justice Harlan; and, speaking of Mr. Lincoln some time ago, before his name was mentioned in connection with a Cabinet office, Justice Harlan said that, in his opinion, Mr. Lincoln was the brightest and ablest among the young lawyers of that circuit.
>
> Before the Chicago Convention Mr. Lincoln was an

ardent advocate of the nomination of General Grant, and he presided at the immense Grant meeting held in Chicago a few days before the nomination for the Presidency was made. Before that his only active efforts in politics had been as a member of citizen committees formed in Chicago to effect a reformation and purification in local political affairs. Intimate friends of Mr. Lincoln say that year after year he develops more strongly the traits which so distinguished his father, but they also declare that one may converse with him daily for years and not be made to feel that he remembers that he is the son of the Martyr President. In other words they declare that he is a man of great ability and force of character, but is at the same time modest and unassuming. The wife of Secretary Lincoln is the eldest daughter of ex-Secretary James Harlan of Iowa."

The Lincolns uprooted their family, which consisted of Mamie (Mary), Jack (Abraham) and Jessie and moved to Washington, where on July 2 Robert was involved again with the kind of tragic event that seemed to stalk the Lincolns. He had just arrived at the Washington railway station to join President Garfield for an official trip when he saw Charles J. Guiteau, a disgruntled Stalwart officer seeker, rush forward with a pistol and shoot the President. (Eerily, Robert Lincoln was also among the distinguished guests at the Buffalo Pan-American Exposition in 1901 and thus a close witness of Leon Czolgosz's fatal shooting of President McKinley.) Before that incident, however, Secretary of War Robert T. Lincoln had routed an official trip through Springfield where, using eleven-year-old Mamie as the dove, he apparently sought a rapprochement of sorts with his mother.

That presumably difficult interview after nearly five years of total separation and silence went unrecorded either by the press or the people involved. All that is known of Mrs. Lincoln's feelings is that she did receive him but Robert evidently still found his mother something of a "trouble." A letter that he wrote to their mutual friend, Mrs. Orne, suggests this: "She is undoubtedly far from well & has not been out of her room for more than six months and she thinks she is very ill. My own judgment is that some part of her trouble is imaginary." Unhappily this private opinion must have run through the gossip mills of Springfield, and in midsummer there appeared a strange newspaper story in the form of a letter to the editor of the Cincinnati *Commercial* that was printed in the New York *Times* and that took from Mary Lincoln the dignity she had earned in four years of exile. It read in part:

> "Mrs. Abraham Lincoln is not sick, in spite of paragraphs in a thousand newspapers of the country. She is peculiar, mentally a little 'off.' 'Hysterics' other old ladies call her complaint. But her pursuit of happiness is hardly more eccentric now than much of the time during her entire widowhood. How is she really? Well, she took a carriage ride of several miles the other day, returning to her home with a healthful glow upon her cheek. She wants to go again, and if this want doesn't wear out, it will be humored often. She said it was the best ride she'd had for a long time. And, sure enough, it was, for she had only just let herself out from continuous, self-inflicted confinement in an upper room during six months and more. Not even the kindest sisterly entreaty could persuade her feet to cross the chamber threshold till one morning early she descended the stairs, attired in pink silk and French laces and scolded her servant for not having breakfast ready. 'A pretty hotel,' she said scornfully, 'to keep guests waiting for meals until after train time.' Of course, the kitchen maid went nearly draft herself at the sight of this 'guest' and ran to apprise her mistress that Mrs. Lin-

coln had turned over a new leaf, and, sure enough, on returning to the kitchen, the maid found that this strange 'guest' had no thought of taking the 'train' on an empty stomach, but had turned the steak in the broiler and was removing the jackets from the boiled potatoes with all the house-wifely skill of her early days.

Mrs. Lincoln came to this city to reside soon after her return from Europe, in October last. She is most considerately cared for, and all her harmless weaknesses humored in the family of the Hon. N. Edwards, Mrs. Edwards being her sister. She arrived in November, and during the following holiday season she shut herself up in her room, mourning the extravagance of the times, and chiding those about her who displayed gifts of jewelry and the like. And there she stayed like a veritable silkworm in its self-woven cocoon, till the late morning adventure, as above narrated. What did she do there all that time? Principally, she overhauled her many trunks, complained that she was very sick, and ate full meals of substantial food three times a day. She reconciled ill-health and hearty eating by insisting to the few friends whom she admitted, that her malady was a very peculiar one, compelling her to consume large quantities of food. She would rise from a repast of roast beef, coffee, &c., and very dejectedly inform her attendant or visitor that in all human probability she should not see the light of another day; and often, in literal verification of her prophecy, she would close the window-shutters, increase the opaqueness of the curtains by pinning up shawls of quilts, and light a plain tallow candle. She rejects the use of gas. If asked to specify where she felt bad in body, she would reply, sometimes, 'I'm on fire, burning up; just feel of me and see how hot I am.' At the same time her temperature would appear perfectly normal for a lady above 60 years of age. At other times she would insist that she was 'being all hacked to pieces by knives; just feel that gash in my shoulder; don't think I can stand such wounding long, do you?' Yet tender and commiserating friends assured her that there was no trace of either blood or scar . . .

Her reputed illness has also brought her many letters of condolence from old friends of herself and husband, and some of congratulation on the appointment of her son to a position in the President's Cabinet . . . But she has not smiled over congratulations on Robert's honorable account. She sighs and broods upon his official holding as a new family risk. She often sits and repeats, 'Secretary of War? Secretary of War? Then he'll be shot for sure! That's always the way in war.' . . .

She has plenty of money, but it is in the hands of a banker here and is zealously guarded by family friends that she may not have it to lose or squander. Of course, the wicked, gossiping busybodies say that this friendly zeal amounts to the personal self-interest of residuary legatees. But that this lone woman of national interest has had more loose rein than under restraint in the use of her funds, her store-house of great trunks packed full would seem to attest to the satisfaction of the average man. There followed her hither from Europe a train of sixty trunks whose immensity and iron bindings sorely aggravated the men of baggage. Some of these, however, are filled with domestic debris and relics of White House life, and it is a part of the peculiar diagnosis of her case that she has lugged these things about the world with her as the weeds of distinguished widowhood, or amulets against harm . . . These trunks testify to Mrs. Lincoln's penchant for laying up treasures of wearing apparel against her imaginary day of want. It

was this trait which, five or six years ago, first convinced her best friends that she was the victim of serious mental wandering . . .

Mrs. Lincoln's look of health is better now than
then; in fact her general health is good for one of her
age, and she promises fairly to reach three score and
ten. But her mental strangeness will probably, also,
last as long as her body, though there is no indication
of its ever assuming a violent form, and the public
may safely leave her in the hands of her Springfield
friends whose love for her is older than that of the
Nation at Large . . ."

Having been subjected once more to such cruel and, indeed,
vicious comment, Mary Lincoln had little to lose and something
to gain by turning her illness into something of a *cause célèbre*.
Being left "safely" in the hands of Springfield friends who
thought her to be malingering seemed to hold little future for
her, and so that fall she went to New York to seek treatment
from Dr. Lewis Sayre, a childhood friend from Lexington who
had become one of the nation's leading orthopedic surgeons.
Just the month before her trip President Garfield died from the
shots Robert Lincoln witnessed. Although the cause and circumstances of Garfield's assassination were lacking in the emotional drama of Lincoln's, the consciousness of Congress had
evidently changed. It was immediately proposed that a pension
of $5000 a year be provided for Garfield's widow and five chil-
dren and that, accordingly, Mrs. Lincoln's pension be increased
by $2000 annually with a lump sum gift of $15,000—an amount
determined by the fact that it had been fifteen years since the
termination of Lincoln's pay. In Mrs. Lincoln's bitter experience there was much room for error and accident between proposal and disposal in this sort of Congressional action and she
wanted to be sure that the promise was fulfilled. Although her
estate had grown through the care she and Bunn had jointly

given it, her increased incapacity—she now had to be carried everywhere—and the cost of the medical treatments in New York renewed her financial anxieties. Dr. Sayre took up her cause in the press.

The same New York *Times* that had published reports of how healthy and wealthy she was in August ran an interview with Dr. Sayre on November 23, 1881, under the headlines: MRS. LINCOLN IN WANT: SICK AND UNABLE TO OBTAIN MUCH-NEEDED ATTENTIONS. Dr. Sayre provided something of a rebuke not only to the anonymous Springfield reporter but to Lizzie Edwards, who had shown impatience with her sister, and Robert Lincoln as well by confirming the seriousness of his patient's spinal injury and her need for baths, massages, electrical treatment and nursing care; Dr. Sayre also saw to it that the newspapers published reports of the eye doctors to whom he had referred Mrs. Lincoln, since they attributed her need to shun strong light to a physical condition caused by a combination of Bright's disease and developing cataracts. Then the doctor swung hard: "She is no more insane than you or I are, and if you could talk with her an hour you would agree with me. The poor woman has had trouble enough to drive many a strong man crazy, but she has borne up under the strain nobly, and these misrepresentations are unworthy the men who make them. I have known Mrs. Lincoln since she was a little girl, and I understand her situation thoroughly. If it were not for her illness, which may very possibly prove incurable, even with the best and most constant of attendance, I believe that she would get along on the paltry $3,000 which Congress has thrown to her, and the world would never know from her lips that the widow of the man who did more for his country than any other man in this century was poor and in want."

Mrs. Lincoln also enlisted Noyes Miner, a Baptist minister and brother of one of her old friends. He agreed to go down to Washington and buttonhole senators on her behalf. It is certainly a reflection on the lack of her reconciliation with her son that she instructed Miner by letter *not* to approach Secretary Lincoln. It may be unfair in the absence of concrete evidence to suggest that the two or three surprise visits that the Secretary *and* his wife, Mary Harlan Lincoln, paid to the former First Lady when they were in New York on official business were politically inspired. But with all the publicity Mary was getting her condition and whereabouts were so well-known that any attempt by Robert Lincoln or his wife to avoid her would have created an impression of inhuman indifference. In any case, the bill was passed and signed by President Chester Arthur early in the New Year and, like a fighter who has won what has to be a last victory, Mary Lincoln left the ring. She apparently felt in her bones that Dr. Sayre's dire prediction would come true, and in late March she went back to Springfield to die.

Her last months were a medley of creeping paralysis, burning boils and, quite probably, diabetic thirst. She spent most of her time in her darkened room where even her trunks were forgotten. She insisted on using only one side of the bed to keep the other open for Mr. Lincoln, with whom she knew that she would soon be joined as she had prayed to be for seventeen long years. Discussing her grief once in a letter, she wrote, *"Time* does not soften it, nor can I ever be reconciled to my loss, until the grave closes over the remembrance, and I am again reunited with *him.* " Feeling the grave closing at last, she did nothing to stop it, and on July 15, 1882, at 8:15 P.M., Mary Todd Lincoln died, aged sixty-four. Her family physician, Dr. T.W. Dresser, attributed the death to "paralysis" in the certificate he signed; other doctors since then have thought that the cause was more likely apoplexy or a diabetic coma. But the act of her dying had the character of a mercy—it was a release from what had become an intolerable life rather than a struggle against death.

Mary Lincoln's body was laid out in a coffin on the very spot in front of the Edwards' fireplace, where she and Abraham Lincoln had exchanged vows. In deference to her dislike of gas lighting, the illumination came from the same oil lamps on the mantle that had shone down on her wedding. Services in the First Presbyterian Church were graced by the presence of dignitaries, including Secretary of War Robert Lincoln and the governor of Illinois. Burial was in a vault at Oak Ridge Cemetery beside her husband and three of her sons.

A Captain of Industry as president of the Pullman Company, Robert Todd Lincoln was described by a contemporary observer as looking like "a man just out of the barber's chair." Courtesy of The Lincoln Museum, Fort Wayne IN (Ref. #114).

Shy and retiring but powerful in her influence over him, Robert's wife, Mary
Harlan Lincoln, had a falling out with her mother-in-law, Mary Todd Lincoln,
that led to disaster. Courtesy of The Lincoln Museum, Fort Wayne IN
(Ref. #119).

Mary "Mamie" Lincoln, Robert's oldest daughter, was the only grandchild with whom Mary Todd Lincoln had any contact before the family relationship was broken. Courtesy of The Lincoln Museum, Fort Wayne IN (Ref. #120).

The Lincoln tragedy continued into a third generation when Robert's son, Abraham Lincoln II, "Jack," died as a teenager, taking the Lincoln name to the grave with him. Courtesy of The Lincoln Museum, Fort Wayne IN (Ref. #125).

With his inheritance from his mother and his high salary as a Pullman executive, Robert Lincoln acquired this palatial home on Chicago's Lake Shore Drive. Courtesy of the Abraham Lincoln Presidential Library & Museum.

Afflicted with the Lincoln family "nerves," Robert Lincoln suffered something of a breakdown in old age and lived as a recluse, studying the stars and playing golf at his Vermont summer home. Courtesy of The Lincoln Museum, Fort Wayne IN (Ref. #3104).

CHAPTER XII:

"But he could run a railroad . . ."

I n the "MTL Insanity File," so carefully preserved by Robert Lincoln, there is a handwritten note that reads:

"Mrs. Lincoln's Estate
$72,000^{00} 4% U.S. bonds
550^{00} Currency
5,000^{00} Personal effects
Robert T. Lincoln signed bond in Sangamon County Ill. Probate Court Sept 28, 1882. Final payment was Nov 6, 1884, Robert received all plus 9 quarterly interest payments on bonds which was $6,480^{00} making a total of $84,035^{00} received."

The implications of this note must have haunted Robert Lincoln for the near half-century he lived after his mother's death as they haunt the reader today. Like her husband before her, Mary Lincoln, though surrounded by lawyers and demonstrably concerned about her financial situation, died intestate. Was this a deliberate act, a way of sending a message of forgiveness to her son without humbling herself in life? She had evidently scrapped the will that Judge Bradwell had drawn for her before Robert brought her to trial, and she had to have known that she was leaving everything to Robert by not making another will. The principal of the estate invested in bonds was increased by approximately the $15,000 outright gift from Congress over the amount restored to Mary Lincoln after her trials, and it added up to a tidy sum at a time when $5000 a year was considered a good income for a good lawyer.

Since Robert Lincoln was still in Washington when he came into his inheritance, it would be three years before he showed some signs of increased affluence by moving his family to an imposing residence at 60 Lake Shore Drive in Chicago. Whether his mother's gift made this possible is not recorded. Robert's way of handling his embarrassing relationship with his mother would today be called "stonewalling." For the rest of his long life he never voluntarily spoke of her. There is evidence that he even tried not to think about his mother's trials in a letter he wrote to his attorney, Leonard Swett, in May of 1884. Evidently Swett had asked to have his memory refreshed on some points with regard to the first trial in which Mrs. Lincoln was found insane, and Robert wrote: "It was not a verdict of seven doctors, but a verdict of six jurors, of whom one or two were doctors." Further along he said that *he* went to his mother's hotel with Isaac Arnold to get the bonds from her petticoat. Robert was making amazing mistakes for a man who had otherwise demonstrated an orderly and retentive mind. There were, for example, twelve jurors and only one of them was a doctor; and it was Swett who went with Arnold for the bonds, not Robert.

Whatever problems he might have had with his memory, stonewalling seemed to come naturally to Robert. Consider this interview in the New York *Tribune* of August 15, 1881:

"The Secretary of War, Robert Lincoln, spent yester-
day at Coney Island. In the evening on his return to the
Gilsey House he talked for a few moments with a
TRIBUNE reporter.

'There is really nothing for me to tell you about the
War Department,' he said. 'It goes on in the routine
way, about the only changes being those prescribed by
law. At present I do not know of any changes that are
likely to be made.'

'Do you expect new Indian troubles?'

'The Indians are causing a little trouble in the South-
west, but I have not received any late official information about what has happened. I do not think, however,
that there can be any serious disturbances.'

'Are you making any very extensive preparations for
the Yorktown celebration?'

'No. I am very sorry to say that I am not, simply
because I am powerless to do anything that costs much
money.' . . ."

This was the only story of more than one or two paragraphs
about Robert Lincoln that this writer could find in the New
York papers and national periodicals during his tenure in office;
his name is not even listed in the index of a major history of the
period. The reason for that is clear from a recent comment by
Amherst College's Henry Steele Commager, co-author of *The
Growth of the American Republic, 1865–1937*: "My impression is that
he was kind of a stuffed shirt. It's a good thing we weren't at war
when he was Secretary of War."

Kept on by President Arthur, also a Stalwart, after Garfield's
death, Lincoln served until 1886, when Democrat Grover Cleve-
land was elected to the White House for the first of his two split
terms. Because those years were free of incident and scandal
they must have been good years for Mary Harlan Lincoln, who
had returned in a kind of triumph to the Washington from

which her father had been banished in the wake of imputed corruption, though this can only be a surmise. Even more so than her husband Robert, Mary Harlan Lincoln kept her name out of the papers and the history books. She rates little more than a few lines acknowledging her existence in a full length biography of her father, James Harlan of Iowa, both Senator and Secretary of the Interior. Her husband does make husbandly references to her in some of his letters, usually describing the state of her health. Ironically the only glowing word-picture of her—small and pretty and gay—is embedded in the letters that Mary Todd Lincoln wrote to her from Europe in the early days of the young Lincolns' marriage.

In view of what happened Mary Harlan Lincoln does not appear to be such a doll-like creature by the time of Mary Todd Lincoln's trials. Even though she remains a shadowy figure lurking in the wings, her hand in shaping the drama on stage is quite visible. It must have been a hard hand. The only actual glimpse of her that we have comes from that anguished letter that Robert wrote about his mother to his aunt Lizzie Edwards on August 7, 1985, in which he said: "I could not take her into my house without a separation from my wife and children. I tried it after poor Tad's death, and had to break up housekeeping to end the trouble. In 1873 after my wife's return here, my mother became violently angry (I think you can imagine what her anger means) at my wife for some trifle and they have never met since." There are usually two sides to human standoffs like this, but Robert never acknowledged the possibility. Nowhere did he even hint at why his mother became angry, nor did he suggest in any way that Mary Harlan Lincoln might have had some faults. The odds against this being the whole truth are long. At any rate it is not farfetched, to say the least, to speculate about the part Mary Harlan Lincoln must have played in her mother-in-law's trials.

If Robert Lincoln did not obviously ride his father's coattails, as the *Tribune* claimed at the time of his cabinet appointment, and refused to mention his mother, as everybody who knew him said, he nevertheless devoted a great deal of time and energy to being a Lincoln. In part he wanted to preserve or enhance his father's reputation—and to a lesser extent the whole family's. Above all he did not want any revelations that might be embarrassing to himself. As inheritor and watchdog of his father's official papers he granted access to them only to John G. Nicolay and John Hay, President Lincoln's White House secretaries, and then edited every line of their ten-volume biography. To frustrate another biographer whose work he did not like, Robert gave the papers to the Library of Congress with the proviso that they not be made public until twenty-one years after his own death, which turned out to be 1947. He also prevailed upon Katherine Helm, daughter of his mother's half-sister Emilie Todd Helm, to delay publication until after his death of her book, which contained warm, intimate and admiring glimpses of Mrs. Lincoln—evidently painful to him. Generally Robert failed in his efforts to suppress either the fact or the fable of the growing Lincoln legend, as when he could not prevail upon Billy Herndon in the late '6o's to stop lecturing about Ann Rutledge and the "hell" Mary Lincoln supposedly created for her husband. But he kept trying. As late as 1891 his objections, relayed through the "old boy" network to which he then belonged, apparently influenced Scribner's not to publish a version of Herndon's Lincoln biography.

When Robert could not stop what he regarded as a slander, he was not above taking revenge on the author, as in the case of Ward Hill Lamon. An associate of Lincoln's on the legal circuit in Illinois and his "bodyguard" in Washington, Lamon brought out a behind-the-scenes biography in 1872. In order to fill in gaps in his own knowledge, Lamon had bought research from Herndon, including an imputation that Lincoln was illegitimate. Although this imputation could not be verified, Lamon published it. Robert Lincoln apparently felt it most personally. More than ten years later when he was Secretary of War, Robert read in a Washington newspaper that Lamon had applied for an appointment as postmaster of Denver, Colorado. He got the appointment quashed by telling Postmaster-General Walter Q. Gresham that it would be "personally offensive" to him. An exchange of bitter letters between Lamon and Robert followed. Lamon said that Robert's vindictiveness proved that he had inherited no character traits from the male side, and Robert accused Lamon of "an astonishing exhibition of malicious ingratitude on your part towards your dead benefactor."

In a sense Robert's concern about the Herndon/Lamon material was farsighted. Both men idolized Lincoln and both felt that they were enhancing his image by "humanizing" him. In Herndon's view, giving Lincoln a lost love and a shrew of a wife made sense of his otherwise inexplicable melancholy, and an illegitimate birth would only add to the difficulties he had had to surmount to achieve greatness. The public did seem to agree. People loved an up-from-nowhere Lincoln and the romantic Rutledge story; domestic discord was all too common to raise many doubts. Because it makes for a "sexier" treatment, popular biographers have tended to go with the Herndon/Lamon Lincoln; after all, they *did* know him, didn't they? Since Robert was so perceptive in this matter, the question arises as to why he would not also have foreseen that having his mother judged insane would lend credence to the "domestic hell" school of Lincoln scholars. To give just one instance of the trial's long-range effect: in his 1985 statement expressing doubts about Robert Lincoln's competence as Secretary of War, historian Henry Steele Commager added by way of explanation: "It's awfully hard to be the son of a great man and also of a half-crazy woman." If he failed in judgment in this particular, Robert later tried to make up for it by his stonewalling and by burning at least some of his mother's letters. The fact that he did not also destroy the "MTL Insanity File" is the most intriguing footnote to Robert Lincoln's careful life.

After his services in Washington Robert was unable to enjoy

his lucrative Chicago law practice and his new home for very long. In 1889 another Republican president, Benjamin Harrison, called upon him to serve as Minister to the Court of St. James. Between hobnobbing with high London society and dining out with Queen Victoria, the mission could have been a delightful interlude, especially for Mary Harlan Lincoln still seeking to rise above life's embarrassments, except for yet another visitation of Lincolnian tragedy. While studying French in Paris in preparation for entering Harvard, Abraham Lincoln II (Jack) contracted blood poisoning and died in March, 1890, taking the Lincoln name with him. Jack was buried in the Lincoln tomb at Springfield, and Robert carried on his diplomatic duties without much heart. An interview he granted in 1892 as a Minister had the same flavor as the one he gave as Secretary of War: "My personal relations with the British Government have been very pleasant. There is nothing connected with my official duties that I feel I can properly speak about except the forthcoming International Monetary Conference, in arranging for which it has fallen to me to have some share . . ."

Back in Chicago at the end of Harrison's term, Robert Lincoln at last realized his true destiny. He gave up both public service and the practice of law to become president of the Pullman Company and, as such, a true "Captain of Industry." Not long after his business career turned him into a millionaire he built Hildene, a summer mansion on several hundred acres of land at Manchester, Vermont. For a dozen years or so the son of a man born in a log cabin who rode the legal circuit on horseback would travel between his two palatial residences in one of his own Pullman cars with an entourage that consisted of three maids, a butler, valet, chef, chauffeur, groom, coachman and traveling secretary. With a small circle of equally rich or famous friends, he indulged in the businessman's recreations of golf and fishing at exclusive clubs. To friends he reported that the business life was "in every way pleasant," and it showed in his looks, according to journalist Ida M. Tarbell, who met Robert Lincoln for tea in the course of researching a popular biography of his father.

"To be drinking tea with the son of Abraham Lincoln was . . . unbelievable to me," she wrote. "I searched his face and manners for resemblances. There was nothing. He was all Todd, a big plump man perhaps fifty years old, perfectly groomed, with that freshness which makes men of his type look as if they were just out of the barber's chair, the admirable poise of the man who has seen the world's greatest and has come to be sure of himself; and this in spite of such buffeting as few men had had —the assassination of his father when he was twenty-four, the humiliation of Mary Lincoln's half-crazed public exhibition of herself and her needs, the death of his brother Tad, the heartbreaking necessity of having his mother committed for medical care, and more recently the loss of his only son. Robert Lincoln had had enough to crush him, but he was not crushed. At the moment he looked and felt, I think, that he had arrived where he belonged. The Republican party would have been happy, no doubt, to make him its leader if he had shown political genius recalling that of his father. They tried him out . . . but nothing happened. He was not political timber, but by this time big business wanted him. It was his field. He was now president of the Pullman Company."

It was, indeed, a big business that Robert Lincoln took over when the founder, George M. Pullman, died. Pullman's genius had been to hang onto monopolistic control of the sleeping cars he produced with the result that by Lincoln's time the company maintained and operated 7,500 cars on 137 railroads over 223,489 miles of track. The statistics of this operation were staggering and fascinating. Pullman employed 8,000 porters, mostly black, who used an inventory of 6,597,714 pieces of car linen worth $1,856,708 to change sheets and towels daily; 4000 more people worked in 225 yards at 158 different points across the nation to keep the cars squeaky clean. Small wonder that Robert Lincoln described business as a matter of "regularly renewing problems" which he considered "a positive pleasure to tackle." As one Lincoln student said of Robert, "He lived in the shadow of his father—but he could run a railroad."

In 1911 Robert Lincoln left the Pullman presidency to become chairman of the board of directors, giving the state of his health as a reason. The Lincolns also changed their winter residence to 3014 N Street, an eighteenth-century brick mansion in Washington's Georgetown section. One of Robert's pleasures there was making quiet visits to the magnificent memorial to his father. Robert commuted between Washington and Manchester in his private car and held his chairmanship until 1922, despite the fact that the Lincoln family "nerves" caught up with him in his early '70's and resulted in something of a breakdown. Increasingly, he led a reclusive life at Hildene, where he spent much of his time studying the stars from his private observatory. Still, distinguished visitors like Presidents Taft and Coolidge and Britain's Lloyd George sought him out, mostly for talk about his father. On July 26, 1926, a few days short of his eighty-third birthday, Robert Todd Lincoln died in his sleep of a cerebral hemorrhage.

Only after Robert's death did Mary Harlan Lincoln emerge from the shadows to play an open and obvious part in the Lincoln drama. But she did it without uttering a word. In 1922 there was a movement to move Abraham Lincoln's body from Springfield to Washington. Robert Lincoln vigorously opposed it and, in doing so, wrote to Nicholas Murray Butler, then president of Columbia University and a good friend, about the Lincoln tomb at Oak Ridge Cemetery: "Within it are entombed the bodies of my father and my mother and my only son, and it is arranged that my wife and myself shall be entombed there." Mary Harlan Lincoln had other ideas. Robert Lincoln's body was held in a vault at Dellwood Cemetery near Hildene for nearly two years until, on March 14, 1928, it was moved to a final resting place under a pink granite monument in Arlington National Cemetery in Washington. Two years later Jack Lincoln's body was removed from the tomb in Springfield and reburied beside that of his father. Robert Lincoln was forever separated from the family that nurtured him; Mary Harlan Lincoln had seen to it.

CHAPTER XIII:

The Re-Trials of Mrs. Lincoln

When you want to retry a case more than 100 years after the fact, where do you find witnesses? There are three main places to look—letters or other writings of the participants, published reports of observers at the scene, and the works of people who have made it their business down through the intervening years to restudy the case. Because of who Mary Todd Lincoln was there are many able witnesses to her trials and, as in the case of most trials, not all of them agree. Here are the ones I have found to be most important with an assessment of their testimony.

The "MTL Insanity File," collected and preserved by Robert Lincoln himself and located at the Louis A. Warren Lincoln Library and Museum in Fort Wayne, Indiana, is the newest and most direct source of information about Mrs. Lincoln's trials. I was guided there by Thomas F. Schwartz, curator of the Lincoln Collection, Illinois State Historical Library, Springfield, Illinois, repository of many ancillary letters and documents that have to do with the whole Lincoln legend. Not only were Mark E. Neely, Jr., director of the Fort Wayne Library and his colleagues very helpful in my study of the file, but Mr. Neely and his co-author, R. Gerald McMurtry, have summarized and interpreted the file in a book—*The Insanity File: The Case of Mary Todd Lincoln,* Southern Illinois University Press, 1986—that is itself one of the best witnesses available.

For better or worse very little happened to Mary Todd Lincoln in the years after she left the White House that did not get some mention in the press of the time. Fortunately for the researcher, Mrs. Lincoln lived in Chicago, a newspapering town if there ever was one, and the papers there often competed to cover her activities, especially during the trials. Indeed, as we have seen, they became participants in the action. Files of newspapers from major cities like Chicago and New York, usually on microfilm, can be found in major libraries. Few collections could be more comprehensive or under the care of more helpful people than that in the newspaper room of Sterling Library at Yale University in New Haven, Connecticut, where I found the material quoted in this book. Of great aid in summoning these vital witnesses was the journalistic practice in the 19th century of reprinting important items from out-of-town papers. The result was that anything about Mrs. Lincoln appearing in, say, a Springfield journal would eventually turn up in one of the Chicago or New York papers.

The third class of witnesses—the scholars and authors whose testimony is mostly to be found in books—are truly legion when it comes to anything having to do with the Lincolns. It has been said that Abraham Lincoln is the most written-about human being in American history and, possibly, in world history. To get background on the trials that his widow endured I read all of the standard Lincoln works and some not so standard but quite interesting ones such as *Recollections of Abraham Lincoln,* by Ward Hill Lamon, edited by Dorothy Lamon Teillard, Washington, 1911, and *Lincoln's Quest for Union,* by Charles B. Strozier, Basic Books, 1982. When it comes to Lincoln's reticent son Robert, biographers have not had much to work with, but in a spinoff from research on her many other Lincoln books, Ruth Painter Randall covers the major events of his life in *Lincoln's Sons,* Little Brown, 1955.

Other bits of essential background and relevant testimony can be found in a wide range of books such as *Lincoln's Herndon,* by David Donald, Knopf, 1948; *Sickles the Incredible,* by W.A. Swanberg, New York, 1956; *Tad Lincoln's Father,* by Julia Taft Bayne, Little Brown, 1931; *Ulysses S. Grant: Warrior & Statesman,* by U.S. Grant III, William Morrow, 1969; *Inside the White House* by William O. Stoddard, Charles L. Webster, 1890; *Lincoln's Manager David Davis,* by Willard L. King, Harvard University Press, 1960; *Diary of Gideon Welles,* Houghton Mifflin, 1911; *The Story of the Pullman Car,* by Joseph Husband, A.C. McClurg, 1917; *Portrait for Posterity,* by Benjamin P. Thomas, Rutgers University Press 1947/72; *The Physician and Sexuality In Victorian America,* by John S. Haller and Robin M. Haller, University of Illinois Press, 1974; *All In the Day's Work,* by Ida M. Tarbell, Macmillan, 1939. For a complete picture, more information has to be summoned from histories of the times, standard reference works and the like. The task of rounding up witnesses of this sort was facilitated by the reference staff of the Darien Library, which can conjure up books as if by magic from both distant places and distant times.

In the end, though, the case must rest on those people who either knew, or came to know, Mary Todd Lincoln well. In this connection it should be noted that few contemporaries wrote anything about her. For most, the Lincoln story ended abruptly with the assassination. Essentially the only books with more than superficial mention of Mary Lincoln were *Herndon's Lincoln,* in which she is depicted as a witch of a wife during the Springfield years and *Behind the Scenes: Thirty Years a Slave and Four Years in the White House,* the black seamstress' look at her employer. One of the first writers to become interested in Mary Lincoln *per se* was Honoré Willsie Morrow, who wrote *Mary Todd Lincoln* in 1928. One of her observations which has an indirect bearing on the case is worthy of quotation:

"By far the greatest problem was to find material on Mary Todd Lincoln . . . As I searched on and on it began to look as if there were a conspiracy of silence about Lincoln's wife. She had the reputation, I gathered, of having a bitter tongue. Did she say such dreadful things that people thought it best to leave her story untold? For a long time I thought that this was the reason for the mystery.

Then I observed an interesting fact. The wives of none of the great men of that period were written about. They were just wives and that was all, in the eyes of the biographers. William Seward was the Secretary of State, a very famous and influential man, with an extraordinarily colorful personality. Mrs. Seward, I gathered from a letter I found written by a friend of hers at the time of her death, was a remarkable human being who had had a profound influence on her husband's career. Seward's biographers utterly neglect her.

I learned from contemporary letters that Mrs. Welles, wife of Gideon Welles, the Secretary of the Navy, was a person of importance in Washington during the Civil War. But not Gideon nor any other writer I could find gives her the compliment of ten lines together. Mrs. Charles Eames, Charles Francis Adams notes in his diary, 'had the salon of Washington' of that day. Here he went when he wished to meet great men of the period in brilliant and informal discussion. William Russell, the famous British war correspondent, made the same statement about Mrs. Eames in his diary. Charles Sumner found her a brilliant intellectual companion and deferred to her opinions as did many other powerful men of that time. None of these men in their books give her more mention than they would to the keeper of an inn.

And so one might go on for pages. Viewed from this

angle, then, the silence about Mary Lincoln seems less a personal and more a general and customary conspiracy. It wasn't done. One didn't talk about their wives in writing men's histories."

But, of course, it was more than custom that led to a conspiracy of silence about Mary Lincoln. She had, in fact, been declared insane, and her story was too difficult to reconcile with the universal adulation of Lincoln. So even when the lives of women became a fit subject for books in the 20th century, few writers knew quite how to handle Mrs. Lincoln. Morrow herself—a Mary Todd Lincoln admirer—glossed over the trials; Irving Stone, making her the heroine of his very romantic novel, *Love Is Eternal,* dodged the issue entirely by running true to form and ending the Lincoln story at the assassination. Still, several books giving Mary Lincoln a life of her own began to accumulate and to cut closer to the realities. They must be heard even though none are based on Robert Lincoln's hidden file.

Among the very essential witnesses in book form not already named are these, listed in my own order of believability and importance: *Mary Todd Lincoln: Her Life and Letters,* by Justin G. & Linda Levitt Turner, Knopf, 1972; *Mary Lincoln: Biography of a Marriage,* by Ruth Painter Randall, Little Brown, 1953; *Mary, Wife of Lincoln,* by Katherine Helm, Harper, 1928; *Mrs. Abraham Lincoln: A Study of Her Personality and Her Influence on Lincoln,* by W.A. Evans, M.S., M.D., Knopf, 1932; *The President's Wife: Mary Todd Lincoln,* by Ishbell Ross, Putnam's, 1973; *The Trial of Mrs. Abraham Lincoln,* by Homer Croy, Duell, Sloan & Pearce, 1962; *The Trial of Mary Todd Lincoln,* by James A. Rhodes & Dean Jauchius, Bobbs-Merrill, 1959; *Mary Lincoln: Wife and Widow,* by Carl Sandburg & Paul Angle, Harcourt Brace, 1932; *Incidents in the Life of Mary Todd Lincoln,* by Carlos W. Goetz, Sioux City, 1928.

To what do these witnesses testify in regard to the trials of Mrs. Lincoln?

For the most part, they are as docile and damning as the parade of witnesses that attorneys Ayer and Swett marshalled on behalf of Robert Lincoln's petition to declare his mother insane in May of 1875. In general, but with varying degrees of reluctance and apology, they go along with the theme that the orchestrators of that trial had intended to sound. Nowhere is it more succinctly restated than in Ida Tarbell's lament for the plump president of the Pullman Company who, before attaining that eminence, had had to suffer "the humiliation of Mary Lincoln's half-crazed public exhibition of herself and her needs . . . the heartbreaking necessity of having his mother committed for medical care." Unlike Billy Herndon publicly—and Swett and Davis in their private correspondence—few latter-day writers strike a note critical of Mrs. Lincoln; it is one of pity, instead. Sure, Mary Lincoln had to be crazy with so many sane people saying so, goes the refrain, but who wouldn't be with what she went through? In putting her away and taking charge of her money, even at the high psychic cost of exposure through a public trial, Robert was only doing his sad, manly duty. Little attention, if any, was paid to the second trial in which the first verdict was completely set aside. It was too much of a relief to think of Mary Lincoln as crazy. Like Robert himself, Lincoln lovers could not apparently cope with Mary Lincoln's complicated and explosive personality—it did not fit into the Lincoln legend of superhuman goodness and greatness. Sandburg, for instance, ignoring the almost certain existence of migraine as well as the positive aspects of that ailment, saw a verdict of insanity as confirmation of the improbable assumption that she had had some kind of physical problem in her head, like a tumor, from childhood to the grave. Whatever, it was no longer necessary to take seriously the claims of an insane person, particularly a female one. For the sympathetic, the way to go was to follow the lead of her supposed defense attorney, Isaac N. Arnold, who might have done her more good by using his eloquence on a jury than in his book, *The Life of Abraham Lincoln,* where he wrote:

"There is nothing in American history so unmanly, so devoid of every chivalric impulse, as the treatment of this poor, broken-hearted woman, whose reason was shattered by the great tragedy of her life. One would have supposed it to be sufficient to secure the forbearance, the charitable construction, or the silence of the press, to remember that she was the widow of Abraham Lincoln. When the Duke of Burgundy was uttering his coarse and idle jests concerning Margaret of Anjou, the Earl of Oxford rebuked and silenced him by saying: 'My Lord, whatever may have been the defects of my mistress, she is in distress, and almost in desolation.' The abuse which a portion of the American press so pitilessly poured upon the head of Mary Lincoln recalls that splendid outburst of eloquence on the part of Burke when, speaking of the Queen of France, he said: 'Little did I dream that I should live to see such disasters fall upon her in a nation of gallant men; a nation of men of honor, cavaliers. I thought ten thousand swords must have leaped from their scabbards to avenge even a look that threatened her with insult. But the age of chivalry has gone.' "

Curiously, the only medical man to examine Mary Lincoln's case in retrospect and in depth was Dr. Evans. Working from what he understood of psychiatry in 1932, Dr. Evans concluded that Mrs. Lincoln was insane but then began backing and filling in a way that still left the issue wide open to doubt. For one thing, Dr. Evans' background made credible his blunt statement that "none of the physicians who testified when Mrs. Lincoln was on trial were specialists in mental disorders." Then he began to muddy the waters considerably when he asserted that "her conduct was determined by an insanity of her emotions rather than of her mind." Whatever manifestation of abnormality in Mrs. Lincoln he discussed was countered by a caveat. For example, in dealing with her extravagant mourning which once made Mr. Lincoln tease about putting her in an asylum at the time of Willie's death and which made Robert begin to question her sanity at the time of the assassination, Dr. Evans said: "These prolonged hysterical outbreaks were not manifestations of a diseased mentality . . . When she mourned as she did, she was influenced partly by the customs of her day and partly by her upbringing." This kind of waffling on Dr. Evans's part seems to have alerted Ruth Painter Randall, who in her 1953 biography was the first to come to her subject's defense and truly question what had been done to Mary Lincoln. Ms. Randall pointedly picked this portion of Dr. Evans' treatise to quote: "This complex of mania for money, extravagance, and miserliness—paradoxical as it appears to laymen—is well-known to psychiatrists. It is present in many people who are accepted as normal." Denied the knowledge of the insanity file but aware of such missing evidence as Mrs. Lincoln's letters to the Bradwells and letters that revealed, in Robert's words, "the distressing mental disorder of my mother," Ms. Randall ended up claiming that there were more mysteries than certainties in the whole affair.

Ms. Randall's suspicions may well have stirred up the interests and imaginations of the authors of the two books directly focused on the trials. In 1959, Rhodes and Jauchius took the position in *The Trial of Mary Todd Lincoln* that Mrs. Lincoln was the victim of a kangaroo court procedure inspired by the political motives of Davis, Swett, et. al., who were upset at the turn Lincoln Republicanism had taken, and in 1962 Croy also faulted the legal procedure in his *The Trial of Mrs. Abraham Lincoln.* Although possibly right in their conclusions both books stray so far from any factual foundations as to lose their effectiveness. The real witnesses to conjure with from the days before the new evidence was found are the Turners, whose 1972 book, *Mary Todd Lincoln: Her Life and Letters,* contains virtually every letter Mary Lincoln ever wrote that was known to be in existence up until that time. After poring over these for years, the Turners had to absorb a sense of Mrs. Lincoln's mind and spirit that few others could ever acquire. Here is their thoughtful, if cautious, testimony:

"A logical place to look for confirmation of their (the jury in the first trial) verdict would seem to be Mrs. Lincoln's own writings. Her letters tell us a great deal: that she was irrational on, and obsessed by, the subject of money, that she could not control her compulsion to buy, that she was abnormally acquisitive. We can see that she often felt depressed, fearful, and persecuted, that she could be hysterical, vindictive, self-pitying, and self-deluding. She was not above stretching or abandoning the truth to serve her own purposes, however obscure. Yet there is no letter that wanders off into total gibberish or wild fantasy: even her repeated, frantic communications attempted to deal with real problems. Most of her fears and animosities had roots in reality. For all her excessive grieving, there is nothing unduly morbid or macabre in her letters, nothing in her hand to prove that she thought of her dead as anything but dead. If the tragedies that befell her made her long for release, she never—until the night of her commitment—seriously threatened to take her own life. Although she nursed burning dislikes and predicted heavenly retribution for her enemies, she never even went so far as to wish them dead. She was not violent.

The most striking manifestations of her illness have come down to us almost exclusively through the statements of others; these persons may have exaggerated or misinterpreted her behavior, but they did not lie. Some of their most damning observations were recorded in private diaries as many as twelve years before the hearing, and were neither intended nor used as evidence against her. Perhaps it was too much to expect that doctors and lawyers in that era distinguish between areas and degrees of incompetence before branding a human being forever with the mark of lunatic—a fearsome stigma in 1875. It cannot be denied that Mary Lincoln was in some ways mentally disturbed even before her husband's death. Yet whatever else she has revealed of her mind and character in letters, she has, interestingly and ironically enough, refused to testify to her own madness."

And what of the witnesses who have seen the new evidence in the "MTL Insanity File"?

As of this writing, Neely, McMurtry and myself are the only ones speaking out. In keeping with the whole history of the Mary Lincoln question, we disagree. The authors of *Insanity File: The Case of Mary Todd Lincoln*, arrive at a very neat solution to the dilemmas still posed by incomplete information. It is this: "Mary Todd Lincoln was insane *in the spring of 1875* [my italics] by her own unconscious confession. On two occasions she admitted that her behavior was bizarre but explained it by her use of chloral hydrate and by physical illness. But Dr. Danforth testified under oath and after months of close personal medical examination that Mrs. Lincoln's behavior was not caused by physical illness, and medical science lets the historian know the harmless properties of chloral hydrate." Although this writer takes issue with their interpretation of the evidence in reaching this conclusion, he finds that the conclusion itself—that Mary Lincoln was insane only in the months surrounding the first trial—begs the whole question and lets everybody concerned off the hook—everybody but Mary Lincoln. It does explain why the authors experienced "fascination but not moral engagement." Moral engagement usually occurs when there is a conviction that some sort of evil or injustice has been done, and I think that this is clearly the case with respect to Mrs. Lincoln.

I have tried to tell this whole story in a way to make my conclusion self-evident. Nevertheless, in view of the weight of traditional thinking as well as the Neely/McMurtry thesis, a summary in the manner of a plea to the jury may be in order.

1) Whatever Mrs. Lincoln's psychological state may have been at any given time, her first trial was a gross miscarriage of justice. Neely and McMurtry are the first scholars to have dug into the legal background to make it clear that a public jury trial was the *only* way in the state of Illinois at that time to commit a non-consenting adult to an asylum and take control of his or her property. Granted, but *any* trial for *any* reason becomes a farce when the defendant is given only an hour's warning and assigned improper representation. Although it was evident even in the raw newspaper accounts of the trial, the letters in the insanity file further confirm the fact that the whole operation was a conspiracy, a frame-up, on the part of some of the sharpest legal minds in the country to make certain that they got the verdict that they wanted.

And *why* did they want it? The aroma of male chauvinism was very strong in that courtroom. Robert Lincoln and his advisers—Davis, Swett and, to a lesser extent, Stuart—had at last found a way to deal with an annoying "hysterical" female who, as Robert said, "never heeds my advice." All of Robert Lincoln's advisers were political animals, ever nervous that something Mary Lincoln might say or do would hurt their Lincoln-based careers. Although the Rhodes and Jauchius theory that Davis and Swett cynically and diabolically led Robert Lincoln on in order to wreck his political future as a Stalwart by making him look like a bad son is not believable in the light of the newly found letters and what actually happened to Robert, it nevertheless does reflect the detectable odor of politics that also pervaded the proceedings. For "respectable" men who like to run a tidy ship, Mary Lincoln was always a loose cannon on the decks.

2) If there had been a fair trial there is a strong probability that Robert Lincoln's petition would have been denied. Mrs. Lincoln

demonstrated her sanity at the time of the trial by her conduct, as noted by all the newspaper reporters. Even Leonard Swett, who had long been convinced of her insanity, had last minute doubts on the day of the trial. His self-justifying reason for going ahead, as expressed in a letter written to Judge Davis on May 24, 1875, days after the fact, is all but incredible. "From the beginning to the end of this ordeal, which was painful beyond parallel, she (Mary Lincoln) conducted herself like a lady in every regard," Swett reported. "She believed she was sane. She believed that I who ought to be her friend was conspiring with Robert and you, to lock her up and rob her of her money. Everything she did and said coincided with the condition of sanity, assuming these facts to have been true, *excepting there was a weakness in her, and a yielding to me which would not be found in a sane person.* [Italics mine.] In the court room . . . her conduct was as ladylike and as much above criticism as possible to be found in any person however well bred or cultivated."

No doubt Swett almost welcomed Mary Lincoln's suicide attempt after the trial as a sign that, all appearances to the contrary, he *had* been right in staging a legal farce that had to end in an insanity verdict. But, in fact, the suicide attempt was clearly *caused* by the trial; it now has to be viewed as a sign of how fully Mrs. Lincoln understood what had been done to her and what the unpleasant consequences would be. With all of her tribulations she had never tried such a thing under any other circumstances; nor, as the Turners noted, had she ever revealed the slightest tendency to self-destruction or physical violence in a lifetime of copious and unrestrained correspondence.

But was Mary Lincoln insane earlier that spring, as Neel and McMurtry conclude? They lean heavily on Dr. Danforth, but one must argue that they are wrong. According to the newspaper accounts of his trial testimony, Dr. Danforth visited Mrs. Lincoln only once that spring (although he had seen her regularly the previous fall), and he could not have made "close personal medical examination" during the time in question since

Dr. Isham, not Dr. Danforth, was then her attending physician. As Dr. Evans pointed out, none of the testifying physicians were experts in mental disease; only Doctors Patterson and McFarland, who were not in court, might have so qualified. With a famous patient putting his private-enterprise asylum on the map by her presence and paying handsomely for a suite of rooms and special attention, Dr. Patterson might have succumbed to some self-interest in supporting the jury's verdict; Dr. McFarland's greatest claim to fame was fighting a three-year battle to prevent Elizabeth Packard from escaping his control and thereby establishing a bias in favor of hanging onto female patients. As in the case of the legal background, Neely and McMurtry are to be credited with pioneering in establishing the prevailing prejudice against women among physicians at the time when Mrs. Lincoln was so unanimously diagnosed as insane, even though it tends to undermine their own conclusion. Since Mary Lincoln functioned adequately and rationally, however eccentrically, both before and after her trials, the preponderance of evidence is on the side of sanity. At the heart of the insanity file are the letters from the Edwardses, in which they, knowing her from childhood, declare her to be as competent as she ever was and often of even better disposition. The all-out defense she got from the Bradwells and the all-out love she got from Lewis Baker also speak volumes in Mary Lincoln's defense. Interestingly Dr. Evans once again undercuts his own case for Mrs. Lincoln's insanity by pointing out that she had the same degree of irrationality (or rationality?) at the second trial when she was declared "sane" as she had at the first. If she had had a real defense, it could certainly have raised the "reasonable doubt" that allows the accused to go free in most trials.

3) There can be no doubt, however, that Mary Lincoln's attitudes and behavior with respect to money tended to be extreme and upsetting to the people around her. Yet even in this, the record does not suggest any compelling reason for restraining her. The salient fact is that, while paying off her debts, going

abroad and indulging in shopping sprees, she never invaded her principal, and her charge that sane Robert would have shot it all on real estate speculation makes a good deal of sense, considering the troubled economic times that began with the 1873 Depression. After examining her ninety-plus letters from France about finances, the Turners wrote: "Even for a 'border-line' case, Mary Lincoln in her letters to Bunn, displayed an astonishing degree of perspicacity and control—the more so when it is realized that she was dealing exclusively with money, the one area in which she had been demonstrably irrational. When one considers further that it was chiefly because of her inability to handle her finances that she was sent to a mental institution, the Bunn correspondence becomes an even greater source of wonder. Or perhaps one should wonder at the confinement."

In this matter of money much of the case against Mrs. Lincoln rested on the clothes-sale in New York. The shock and aversion that Robert, and so many politicians and editorial writers, expressed about this was both insincere and silly. It is hardly necessary to argue further that Mary Lincoln was treated deplorably by a Congress and administration, most of whom really did owe their jobs directly to Lincoln or indirectly to his bringing the Republicans to power. Tweed's assertion that she was neglected because she had an abrasive personality is worse than irrelevant; it is an assertion that it is right and acceptable to deny *justice* to people on the grounds of personal dislike. The real basis for the hue and cry over Mary Lincoln's sale was that it cut to the quick of guilt and shame on the part of the people it exposed. As for it's being silly, how can the response to that sale be considered as anything more than a form of anti-feminist Victorian prudery in this day and age when the very rich routinely dispose of used goods in highly advertised tag sales and/or auctions at Parke-Bernet or Christie's? Mary Lincoln was not at all crazy in this; she was just ahead of her time—and not that far ahead either, as witness the Empress Eugénie.

Over and over again Robert Lincoln's apologists feel obliged to stress his supposed disinterest in his mother's money until it becomes a matter of protesting too much. Even if one takes at face value his own assertion that all he wanted to do was see to it that she did not spend it all and leave herself in "want," the step he took to wrest control of it from her hands and the delaying action that he fought to keep that control seem extreme. After all, she had not spent her principal in spite of her seemingly foolish shopping sprees which, as her sister Lizzie Edwards pointed out, were nothing new to her and were apparently her only remaining source of pleasure. While proclaiming no desire to inherit his mother's money, Robert often and explicity stated his fear that she would spend it and become a burden on him. In view of the fact that his mother had already set him up both in business and housekeeping, Robert's fear that she would become a burden is mean-spirited and unwarranted at the very least. Mary Lincoln's assumption that a very keen concern about what would happen to her money was one of Robert's motives in bringing her to trial may have been exaggerated by her other reactions to the event, but it was certainly not without foundation. In this connection there is a fascinating bit of what is sometimes called "internal evidence" as to why Robert Lincoln held onto the "MTL Insanity File." Many of his mother's letters to his wife during her first trip abroad are scissored into fragments that are retained only as evidence that various goods in the possession of the younger Lincolns were gifts that Mary Lincoln could not reclaim.

4) Aside from money there was a motive for Robert Lincoln's action that few people have been willing to discuss down the years and that Mary Lincoln herself probably did not want to face. Robert Lincoln wanted to be rid of his mother to be rid of an embarrassment and source of trouble to himself and his wife. Whether because, until a year or so ago, there were descendants who could sue or be hurt or whether because Lincoln buffs could not bear to think that the blood of the Martyr President might have created what his own mother

called "a monster of mankind," most people dealing with this subject have been delicate to a fault in assessing Robert's role. Robert was not a monster; he was very human, indeed, and this aspect of his motivation is now plain from the newly discovered correspondence. His struggle with the Edwardses to keep from freeing his mother is spelled out as a worry that she will get herself talked about, and over and over again he complains about the "trouble" she has made for him. In an exchange of letters with Mrs. Edwards while his mother was in Pau, Robert assures his aunt that he won't move against his mother, no matter what she does, if they can induce her to come back for the sake of her health. Then he admits that he made a mistake in bringing her to trial in the first place and offers this damning confession: "If I could have foreseen *my own experience* [italics mine] in the matter, no consideration would have induced me to go through with it . . . ." Nowhere, as far as this writer has been able to determine, does Robert Lincoln ever express an understanding, let alone a regret, for the terrible damage that the shame of being branded a lunatic inflicted upon his mother's psyche and reputation.

Filial ingratitude, especially on the part of spoiled children, is a recurring theme throughout the whole of human history, which is one reason that this story remains relevant. In this case the stature of the characters—the "Republican Queen" and the "Captain of Industry"—heightens the drama as in the biblical tales of sons dethroning their kingly fathers. In a variation on the familiar theme, Mrs. Lincoln was cruelly victimized, but what saves her story from being unrelieved tragedy is her own, lone fight to regain her freedom and dignity. She faced awesome odds. Against her was the will of her own son, the judgment of the courts, the diagnosis of the doctors, the doubts of her friends and relatives, the inferior position of all women in society, the misunderstanding of the general public, and yet she fought. The "weakness" that tough Leonard Swett found to be evidence of insanity turned out instead to be the wily strategy of the powerless against the oppressor. By never quitting, by never giving up on herself until she failed physically, Mary Todd Lincoln provided an enduring lesson and proved herself to be, in the opinion of this admitted advocate, a formidable First Lady, a fit consort for the Great Emancipator.

Index